The definitive A to Z listing of

Sheffield
Public
Houses

by
Michael Liversidge

A quick reference to just some of the articles that are included in this encyclopedia

Crime
Banner Cross	*Charlie Peace*
Catherine	*Drug substances*
East House	*Multiple Murders*
Firwood	*Surreal stabbings and shooting*
Lion	*Wedding day murders*
Springvale	*Last pint for the Ripper*
Staffordshire	*Both barrels*

Sheffield Flood
Cambridge	*Lucky escape*
Cleakum	*Not so lucky*
Farfield	*10ft waves at the door*
Hillsborough	*No doors or floorboards left*
Manchester H	*Facade ripped away*
Rose Inn	*Makeshift mortuary*
Rowell Bridge	*Totally swept away*

General Interest
Bridge	*Dr Bellamy finds figtree*
Fulwood Inn	*Million pounds + to refurbish*
Frog & Parrot	*Strongest ale in world*
Nottingham H	*Threads, film interiors*
Highcliffe	*Joe and Fred Davis*
John O'Gaunt	*Most Sheffield like pub?*

Music
Black Swan	*Joe Cocker, Fortunes, Jigsaw*
Blue Bell	*Tremeloes, Searchers, Price*
Broughton	*Engelbert Humperdink*
Highcliffe	*Big Yin, Barbara Dickson*
Hole in Wall	*Beautiful South*
Players Cafe	*Def Lepard*
Sportsman	*Jimi Hendrix*

Ghosts and Ghouls
Acorn	*Overnight stop*
Ball Inn	*Hung from rafters*
Norfolk Arms	*Don't move his picture*
Old No 12	*Police Siege*
Queens Head	*Mary Queen of Scots et al*
Staffordshire	*Return of slain landlord?*
Station	*Tipping the glasses*

Sport
Adelphi	*Cricket, Football, started here*
Albany	*George Harvey Flood, boxer*
Crown	*Owl's best centre forward?*
Enfield	*Once owned by the Steelers*
Kings Head	*World Champ endurance racer*
Masons Arms	*Darts World Champion*
Queens Ground	*20,000 crowds for athletics*
Wharncliffe	*Bare knuckle champion*

History
Alma	*Crimea battle*
Blucher	*OAP riding into history*
Crooked Billet	*A lethal 4 x 3*
Dog & Partridge	*Irish Imagination?*
Queens Ground	*The Stirrings*
Samuel Plimsoll	*Draw the line somewhere*
Shepley Spitfire	*Battle of Britain bravery*
Turks Head	*Spoils of war*

Introduction

Over a period of more than thirty years I have enjoyed my hobby, Sheffield Public Houses and their history, the local area, the breweries and the buildings . I have taken photographs, as well as drawing and painting some of the hostelries. Some have changed appearance dramatically, some several times (ie, the oft changed Talbot, alias The Old Toad, alias The Good Doctor on Hoyle Street, now just a big roundabout). Some pictures show buildings which have been demolished long ago or, because of the many brewery changes, they will be quite unrecognisable now.

News items in the form of newspaper clippings about certain pubs are used as and when thought necessary i.e. the East House Murders, the Marples bombing or the more up to date Pomona stabbings. Most opinions and views are my own and others, hearsay from locals of the particular hostelry being written about.

I found the research and the actual meeting of customers, landlords and landladies a very pleasant experience and at every turn they were consistently helpful and pleasant with anecdotes and recollections of their pub's history.

All in all a happy experience to research, write, photograph, sketch and layout for the printer.

I hope you get as much enjoyment from this book as I have from putting it together.

As Samuel Johnson once said:

Please do not dwell on that
which has been omitted,
but focus more on that
which has been included

ISBN 0 9534267 1 8

Printed and published by
Pickards Communication

Unit 11

Riverside Park

Sheaf Gardens

Sheffield S2 4BB

Telephone 0114 2757222 or 2757444

Abbey Hotel
944 Chesterfield Road, Sheffield 8

The Abbey was an old coach house situated on the Chesterfield - Sheffield run which was well used in the 18th and 19th centuries by steel traders, millers, farmers and general tradespeople switching from town to town to sell their wares.

The Abbey was only a medium sized building until it had considerable extension work done in the early twenties (possibly in 1922) which almost doubled the buildings size by adding the part you can see on the left hand side of the above photograph. The Abbey can boast one of only two bowling greens still attached to a public house, the other being the Wadsley Jack. It is also the oldest green, having been laid around the year 1885.

It probably gained its name from Beauchief Abbey, the remains of which are just a few hundred yards down Abbey Lane.

Aberdeen House
133 Upper Hanover Street,
2 Aberdeen Street, Sheffield 3

This house could probably have been named after the Scottish city, if the licensee of the time was from the granite city, but more probably named after the 4th Earl of Aberdeen, George Hamilton Gordon, (1784 -1860) who was foreign secretary to Wellington 1828-30, secretary for war under Peel 1841-46 and eventually Prime Minister himself 1852-55.

Acorn Inn
20 Burton Road, Sheffield

A beerhouse in 1905, later it became a boys' club.

Acorn Inn
516 Burncross Road, Chapeltown

The Acorn name/sign is most probably a use of a convenient visual symbol. Interpretations as to its meaning vary from the landlord's intention to grow, "giant oaks from little acorns grow", through some reference to Charles II alleged hiding place in the oak tree, or the very old custom of hanging a bush or branch outside a house that had brewed beer.

Acorn Inn
288-292 Shalesmoor, Sheffield 3

This public house, where lives were lost in the Great Sheffield Flood of 1864, is now a bathroom showroom. After about 135 years' trading as an Inn it was finally closed in 1960. It was used for a few years by a jazz club, Club 60, who rented the basement 2 or 3 times per week. The Acorn is supposed to have a resident ghost. A story in the local newspaper stated that for a dare (or a bet) one of the jazz club members would brave it out for a night on his own. It is said that the Sheffield Star photographer, sent to cover the story, tried to take a picture for his newspaper, but on each of his six attempts the flash failed to go off. The brave man was locked in at 11pm and was to stay for 10 hours, at half past 6 the next morning he said he could stand it no longer and rushed out.

Adam and Eve

17 Balaclava St, Sheffield

Balaclava Street is still standing but no detail can be found about this public house, only the occasional passing reference, in old local literature. Unknown if the Adam and Eve was a nickname or the correct title of the pub.

Adelaide Tavern

48 Mowbray St, Sheffield 3

Albert Piercey was landlord when it was a beerhouse in 1936.

Adelphi Hotel

13 Arundel Street, Sheffield 1

The Adelphi Hotel (a Wm. Stones - Cannon Ales pub) used to stand on the site which is now occupied by the Crucible Theatre, on the corner of Tudor Way and Sycamore Street. From an old dilapidated public house it was supposedly renovated to resemble the Adelphi Theatre in the Strand.

This is the place where Yorkshire County Cricket Club was formed on January 8th 1863, when nine acres of land was leased from the Duke of Norfolk and made into a cricket and bowling club, now Bramall Lane. Also Sheffield Wednesday Football Club was formed after meetings in the Adelphi in 1867. What an historic sporting pub this really was, unfortunately for Sheffield it was demolished, 102 years after Wednesday were formed, in May 1969. At least they left a plaque to commemorate its existence!

The Adelphi could have been another disaster like the Marples public house, in the history of Sheffield. During the Blitz a direct hit was made on the pub and an unexploded bomb complete with its parachute was found in one of the bedrooms by Vera Jenkins, the daughter of the then landlord. Upon finding the device, the army were informed and it was made a no go area for several days until it could be dealt with by the bomb disposal squad.

The name Adelphi is presumably borrowed from the London area of the same name or from the Greek word Adelphoi which means brothers.

Adelphi Hotel

15-17 Martin Street, Sheffield 6

Admiral Rodney

592 Loxley Road, Sheffield 6

Situated on Loxley Road, The Admiral Rodney, now, and for the last few years, has been noted for its fine carvery and meals, The lovely building you see pictured was built soon after the second world war. The old Admiral Rodney was kept by a lady named Mrs Trickett, who lived through into her nineties and did not like any sort of change to be made to her beloved Rodney.

The pub name is taken from George Brydges, Lord Rodney (1719-92) an Admiral (obviously) who achieved fame in the late 18th century by defeating the Spanish fleet at Cape St. Vincent in 1780 and victory over the French fleet in the West Indies in 1782 at the Battle of the Saintes, when he drove the French from the Atlantic. The Admiral had several ships named after him, although the last of these was broken up in 1948.

African Prince

Lambert Street, Sheffield

The African Prince was last referred to in the local directories of 1833.

Albany Hotel

38-40 Gloucester Street, Sheffield 10

An ancient Scottish ducal title, a poetic name for Britain similar to Albion. The Grand Old Duke of York, of nursery rhyme fame was actually Frederick, Duke of York and Albany, eldest brother of the Prince Regent. He died of dropsy, before he could claim accession to the throne of England.

Albany Hotel

Fargate, Surrey Street, Sheffield

This building was originally constructed for the Yorkshire Penny Bank in 1888-89. The bank itself occupied the left hand side of the building whilst the remainder around the corner into the newly built Surrey Street was the Albany Hotel. The hotel was officially opened on 2 October 1889 and was run by the Sheffield Cafe Society and based on temperance principles. The Albany consisted of 40 bedrooms and the whole of the top floor was the living quarters of the staff.

In the early part of the century the mother of George Harvey Flood, a well known Sheffield boxer, kept the license.

The hotel closed in 1958 when it was made into offices.

Albert

1-3 Division St - 2-4 Cambridge St., Sheff 1
(aka Union opened in 1797)

The Albert was situated opposite the City Hall on the Corner of Division Street and Cambridge Street and was named after the Prince Consort, Albert (whose full name was Francis Charles Augustus Albert Emanuel). He was the younger son of Ernest Duke of Saxe-Coburg-Gotha. He married Queen Victoria on February 10th 1840 and was given the title Prince Consort in 1857. He died of typhoid at Windsor Castle in 1861. Throughout England, inns, hotels and public houses were named and renamed after this well liked royal figure. Much grander places such as the Albert Hall which seats 10,000 people, and opposite this the Albert Memorial in Kensington Gardens, designed by Sir Gilbert Scott also show the great affection the country had for the Prince Consort.

Unfortunately the Albert public house we are referring to was by no means grand. In fact it was a rather dank and depressing place, which was demolished in the early 70s.

Albert Hotel

117 Penistone Rd, Sheffield 6

Closed c1913, situated on the corner of Albert Terrace Road, a Mrs Annie Sokell was the licensee in 1902. It had a lifespan of about 75 years from its doors first being opened to the drinking public.

Albert Inn

162 Darnall Road, Sheffield 9

Albert Inn

31 Sutherland St, Sheffield 4
(opened circa 1855-1996)

This public house was on its last legs in the mid 1990s with its trade fading, little in the steelworks industry remaining and with no housing locally it went the same way as the public house on the opposite side of Sutherland Street, the Plumpers, which was demolished a few years earlier through the same lack of custom.

It carries a little bit of Sheffield history with it in the fact that it was frequented by the rival gangs of the Sheffield gang wars, the Mooneys and the Garvins. On one occasion a man named Mr Foster, who had left the courthouse where a gang member called Handley had been convicted of assaulting him, called in at the Albert Inn. He ordered a drink and carried it into the snooker room, whereupon three men climbed out of a taxi and entered the Albert and called "Where's Foster?" On finding the hapless Foster they proceeded to hit him with a snooker cue and then kicked him about the head as he went to the floor. Three men were arrested the next day and charged with the assault. Nearby on Princess Street, the murder of a soldier on leave, an army private, named Plommer, more or less brought to an end the gang problems of Sheffield, as some gang members were caught and executed, some given prison sentences and Captain Sillitto and his aptly named Flying Squad came down strongly, to say the least, on the rest, forever ending the Sheffield Gang Wars problem.

Albert Inn

113 Broomhall St, Sheffield 3 (open c1834)

Long since closed.

Albion Hotel

2-4 Earsham St, Sheffield 4

This pub, originally called the Albion Hotel stands on the corner of Ellesmere Road and Spital Hill.

It was also called the Golden Perch for a couple of years but is now known as the Old Mill Tavern, a free house.

Its original name "Albion" probably comes from the latin albus 'white' with reference to the whiteness of the cliffs of the southern coast. The New Albion was the name given to an area of the American west coast by Sir Francis Drake, it is now California and the State of Oregon.

The Albion Hotel itself, was one of the few six day houses in Sheffield, it was always closed on Sunday (one of the others was the Lodge on Spital Hill, now a motorcycle dealers).

Upon its transformation from the Albion to the Golden Perch, it became somewhat of a flagship for the CAMRA organisation with a main customer base of students and real ale fans.

Later when its name changed again to the Old Mill Tavern it lost a lot of its student and CAMRA people and was mainly frequented by West Indians/Afro Caribbeans.

Albion Hotel

75 London Road, Sheffield 2

Albion

21-23 Adsetts St, Sheffield (circa 1860-1914)

Beer house with John Cocks as the landlord in 1902.

Albion Hotel

4 Mitchell Street, Sheffield 3 Brook Drive, (opened c 1835)

Albion

12 Sylvester Street, Sheffield (c1851-1926)

Albion

694 Attercliffe Road, Sheffield 9 (c1820 to 1942)

Some local books have stated that the Albion, which was on the corner of Brinsworth Road, and Attercliffe Road, ceased to trade as a public house in 1920, but this is not so. G. M. Cardwell, was licensee from 1921 until the late 30s and then Alfred Smith took the Albion into the war years. Its last mention in any local reference as a licensed premises was in 1942. Some years later the Matthews family used this address for their furniture business.

Albion

44 Johnson Street, Sheffield

Albion Tavern

46-48 Verdon Street, Sheffield 3 (c1855 to 1967)

The Albion was basically one terraced dwelling made into a beerhouse.

Albion Tavern

28 Lambert St, Sheffield

In a Sheffield street directory of 1902, numbers 26 and 34 Lambert Street were both beerhouses. Unfortunately no tavern names are given, just the owners, so we could assume the Albion was still a licensed premises in 1902, but in some local reference books we are informed that the Albion was demolished in 1896.

Alexandra
91 Dunlop Street, Carbrook, Sheffield 9

Alexandra
121 Eldon Street, 14 Milton Street, Sheffield

Alexandra
23 Dover Street, Sheffield (closed c1917)

Alexandra Hotel
549 Carlisle St East, Sheffield 9

The much loved Queen Alexandra also gave her name to the Alexandra Hotel on Carlisle Street East, which has now been demolished.

The Alexandra Hotel itself was a small public house built sometime in the 1860s and was situated on Carlisle Street East opposite the end of Newhall Road. Just after the turn of the century, The Alex, (pictured) was owned by a licensed victualler called Joshua Smith and sold Strout's Noted Ales. It was later to become a Whitbreads public house.

Along Carlisle Street east the Alex was one of 25 public houses in a mile stretch. After faithfully serving the steel workers, whose industry was built all around it, the Alexandra Hotel, finally closed its doors in the mid 1970s.

Alexandra Hotel
Exchange St, Sheffield 2

The Alexandra Hotel on the corner of Castle Gate and Exchange Street was named after King Edward VII's wife, the well liked, Alexandra who also gave her name to six more so named pubs in Sheffield. The 'Alex' as it is known, is a large public house and actually fits the name hotel, for it is one of the few places carrying that name on a pub sign that still lets rooms.

This pub is situated near the market trading area and a lot of its clientele frequent the 'Alex'.

Alexandra Hotel
42 Jericho Street, Sheffield 3

Alexandra Hotel
13 Furnival Road, Sheffield

Alhambra
1-17 Union Street, 1 Charles Street, Sheffield (aka Phoenix)

Destroyed by fire in 1882 and three years later rebuilt as the Phoenix. The old Empire Theatre was adjacent.

The name Alhambra comes from the palace of the Moorish kings which was in Granada, Spain. The Arabic word Alhambra, or more correctly al-hamra, means red (palace).

The Phoenix, a fabulous bird which every 100 years set fire to itself and emerges from the ashes to start life anew. At one time there used to be Phoenix-Men, who were employed by Phoenix Insurance Company, these were possibly the equivalent of today's firemen.

Alhambra Hotel
78 Meadow Street, 100 Hoyle St, Sheffield

All Nations
8 Water Lane, Sheffield

All Bar One

15 Leopold Street, Sheffield 1

One of the new city centre bars now occupying the old Abbey National building. A long bar, lined with shelves of wine, wooden floor, picture windows, canteen type tables and benches, games and newspapers available.
For the over 21s only.

Alma Hotel

23 Alma Street, Sheffield 3 (aka Fat Cat)

The name, the Alma, is from the Battle of the Alma River, a Crimean War engagement. In 1854 it became the scene of the first battle won by the Allies over the Russians. Many an Englishman took part in this famous victory and brought back memories from the Russian battlefields, to such an extent that a spate of public house had their names changed to Alma or related names. Also, many a soldier's daughter was christened Alma.

Alma Hotel

Trafalgar Street, Sheffield

Alma Cottage

56 Duke St, Sheffield

Laurance Naylor was landlord in 1902.

Amateurs Rest

17 Holly Street, Sheffield

Amberley Hotel

221 Attercliffe Common, Sheffield 9

The Amberley Hotel situated on the Corner of Attercliffe Common and Amberley Street. The Hotel itself was a large building, four floors, consisting of 28 to 32 rooms. All could be let, but by the mid 60s it had stopped letting rooms altogether.
The building consisted of a large concert room, where to hear the locals tell, good quality acts, (turns) were much in abundance two or three nights per week. It also had 2 smaller rooms, one directly on the corner, and the public bar whose entrance was on the Common, whilst entry into the concert room was gained from Amberley Street. The Amberley Hotel was a John Smiths House selling Magnet Ales. It also had livery stables attached to the premises at the turn of the century .
The Filesmiths Arms can by seen on the right, next door but one, with only Mrs Peacock's grocery shop separating them. This shop was once known as the Argentine Beef Company.
The Amberley Hotel was closed in the early to mid 1970s.

American Stores

36 West Bar Green, Sheffield (closed c1893)

Anchor

20 Pea Croft, Solly Street, Sheffield

This common visual symbol, was probably first used by landlords who had some connection with the sea or served as seamen themselves. Unfortunately, in Sheffield no coastline is within 70 miles, so it may just have been the navigation canal custom they were after.
There is supposedly a second reference that some landlords used, a theological virtue of hope, this comes from the bible, St Paul (Hebrews 6:19) referred to the "Anchor of the Soul, a hope...."

Anchor

223 Solly Street, Sheffield

Anchor

162 Darnall Road, Sheffield 9

Ancient Pine Apple

3 Radford Row, Sheffield (circa 1790-1895)

Seen in one entry in the Kelly Directory of 1839, with the address being Ratford Row and the landlord a Thomas Wilkinson.

Angel

West Bar Green, Sheffield

Angel Hotel

8 Angel St, Sheffield 1

The original Angel was built around 1650s, it was demolished and a new Angel, with the terracotta angel by Rossi adorning it frontage, rebuilt on the same site in 1816. It was finally closed after receiving a direct hit during the blitz of December 1940, when a good many people were injured.

In 1760 a man named Samuel Glanvill ran the first stage coach to London from Sheffield. The pick up point was from the Angel and it took approximately 30 hours to reach the capital.

The Angel, was also the venue for the official Sheffield celebration of the victory of the Battle of Waterloo in 1815.

Angel Inn

59 Sheffield Road, Woodhouse

Angel Inn

18-22 Button Ln, 218 Fitzwilliam St, Sheffield (aka Crown & Anchor)

Built in around 1825 and known as the Crown & Anchor until 1902, when for reasons unknown it was decided on a name change, to the Angel Inn.

John William Mottershaw, of Sheffield photography fame, along with his wife Mary, were the licensees of the Crown and Anchor in 1891. He also owned two chip shops, both, on Button Lane.

Mottershaw was landlord there for 10 years and his first daughter, Ivy, was born there. He had his own darkroom on the premises and his daughter, who showed a keen interest in photography throughout her life, would help him develop the glass negatives.

The Public House itself was a large premises, illustrated by the fact that when the circus came to Sheffield to perform at the Hippodrome or Empire Theatres up to 5 elephants could be tethered in the rear yard of the inn.

The Angel was demolished in 1956 and was sited just about where the traffic island is now situated behind Debenhams.

Angel Inn

151 Main Street, Grenoside

The Angel Inn has been a name often used, probably since the 12/13th century, signifying the religious beliefs of the people and the travellers, need to feel safety in these hostels. The religious name was safe to be used on public houses, but you couldn't go too far with the signs by depicting angels drinking or any indication that the holy establishment was condoning the low virtues of the drinker, or the church tended to come down on the offending hostelry, generally winning through and having the signs changed to give a more serene view of the place. Anyhow, this Angel in Grenoside, to my knowledge doesn't have too many customers who would worry about the depiction on the sign outside as long as the pub is serving good beer and a warm atmosphere, and that's just what's on offer.

Anglers Rest

93 Richmond Park Road, Sheffield 13

It is said that when the Anglers Rest in the centre of Sheffield was demolished they replaced it with this one on Richmond Park Road only to be told that it had been built on the wrong site. If it was a mistake the builders should be congratulated, because it has been a very well frequented pub for a lot of years, probably because it is set in a very populated area.

This Wards pub had a sign of two anglers which included two crossed fishing rods on top of the post, highly unusual.

Anglers Rest

46 New George Street, or 50 Boston Street, Sheffield (1841-c1901)

Anglers Rest

15 Snow Lane, Sheffield (c1830-1910)

Anvil Inn

106 Stannington Road, Sheffield 6

Directly opposite the pub, across Stannington Road, you can look down a lane and see Mousehole Forge, (which is pronounced Mousle, so I am reliably informed). It is an ancient water driven forge. Blacksmiths' anvils were produced at this forge, some examples of which won diplomas/certificates at the Crystal Palace Exhibition in 1861. Supposedly it was deemed to be logical that the pub should be named after this famous product.

Ted Catlin, ex Sheffield Wednesday captain, was at one time landlord of the Anvil.

Anvil

24 Waingate, Sheffield 1 (1828-1926)

This public house was demolished and replaced by a new clothing store (Fosters) in 1928.

Anvil

160-164 South Street, Moor, Sheffield

Anvil Makers Arms

119 Young Street, Sheffield (closed c 1917)

Arbourthorne

Errington Road, Manor, Sheffield

A large building with mock Tudor exterior. A lively, friendly pub. Large spacious public house, a so called estates pub.

Arena Square

Attercliffe Common, Sheffield 9

A large public house built by Whitbread in 1998 and the first new public house to be built on the Attercliffe Common, Attercliffe Road, main thoroughfare for, probably, 80 years. When it was being built the Whitbreads company along with the Sheffield Star ran a competition asking the Sheffield public to decide on the name of the pub. Not an awe inspiring choice.

Army Hotel/Inn

45 Hillfoot, 281 Penistone Road, Sheffield 6 (aka Clifton, Army Stores)

In the days when old horse trams were running, the terminus from Snig Hill to Hillfoot was located directly outside the Army Inn. Also being just across the river-bridge road from Neepsend railway station the Army Inn would have been a busy old place. The bridge, a wooden one, which led to the railway station was the first Hillfoot bridge and was washed away in the 1864 Sheffield Flood. It was replaced by the fine looking bridge that crosses the River Don, and connects Neepsend and Penistone Road, today. The Army Hotel or Clifton as it was finally known was demolished in the late 1960s.

Arrow Inn

location unknown

In some of the older books of Sheffield it is purported that Mrs Spence Broughton supposedly saw her husband's body being placed in a gibbet from the rear window of the Arrow. The Pheasant, Attercliffe Common, also claims this and they could well be one and the same pub.

Artillery Man

7 Bridge Street, Sheffield (opened c1827)

Arundel Castle

257 Arundel St, Sheffield (early 1800s - 1926)

Arundel Castle was the home of the Dukes of Norfolk who were the main Sheffield landowners.

Arundel Cottage

49 Arundel Lane, Sheffield (c1840-1918)

Arundel Inn

1 The Common, Ecclesfield, Sheffield

Run by the Pepper family from 1893 until 1955.

Ashberry Hotel

116 Addy Street, 1 Ashberry Rd, Sheffield 6

Athol Hotel

19 Charles St, Cross Burgess St, Pinstone Street, Sheffield 1

One of only 9 public houses which was granted a special license for supper meals. All these pubs were situated in the Pinstone Street area. Closed in the late 50s early 60s. It is now used as an amusement arcade.

Atlas

131 Carlisle Street, Sheffield (c1862-1922)

No known reason for the public house to be named so, but Atlas supporting the world on his shoulders presumably made it suitable for pub sign purposes. Atlas and Norfolk works, which was part of the Firth Brown company, also in Sheffield could be some connection to this.

Atlas Hotel

Bawtry Road, Brinsworth

The building now used for the Atlas Hotel was built originally as the local pit manager's house with accompanying stables which accommodated ponies and horses. At one time these stables were used as the local mortuary. This building has now been a pub for nearly 100 years.

Atlas Inn

278 Savile St, Sheffield 4 (c1860-1920)

Aunt Sally

Clarkehouse Road, Broomhill, Sheffield

Tom Cobleigh took a derelict building opposite the Hallamshire Hospital and at an extravagant cost of between £1.4 and £1.7 million renovated it into a smart, large, one roomed public house cum restaurant. The name Aunt Sally could be one of two possible references - that of the oldest form of skittles, nowadays confined mainly to the county of Oxfordshire or the Aunt Sally from the series of Books/TV series Worzel Gummage the character portrayed by Una Stubbs.

Australian Arms

49 West Bar, Sheffield (c1825-1893)

Bagshawe Arms

Hemsworth Road, Norton Avenue, Sheffield

One of Sheffield's oldest public houses. The building was formerly a farmhouse belonging to the Bagshawe family and was built by stone from the Mawfa Lane quarries. Some of the original farm buildings are still to be seen at the rear of the pub. In around 1830 the buildings were enlarged and one of them was used once a month by the local petty session court. There is a stone in the south end dated 1859 with the initials F W B - Francis Westby Bagshawe.

In the early 19th century a man named George Rogers was landlord, he was a printer by trade, who worked for the Weekly Independent. He was also a working farmer and was secretary of the farmers club. He earned himself the nickname of Lord George, obviously a very energetic man.

Bakers Arms

127 Clarence Street, Sheffield (opened circa 1823-now closed)

The pub sign used, dated from the 16th century and showed a hand holding a balance surrounded by corsheaves, with two anchors at the top. These signs tells of the close connection between the bakers' and brewers' trades, and in some cases both practices went on at the same premises.

Ball

20 Hawley Croft, Sheffield

Reputedly the Master Cutler of 1722, John Smith lived here many years before it became a public house. John Smith is an ancestor of Joseph Hunter, the historian.

One of its landlords in the late 18th century was a rate collector, named Thomas Bright, a man listed as one of the twelve 'gentlemen' in the town directory of 1787.

A gentleman and a rate collector?

Ball

203 Pond Street, Sheffield

Ball

8 Pea Croft, Solly Street, Sheffield (aka Ring O'Bells) (opened circa 1795)

Ball

72 Howard Street, Sheffield (opened c1845)

Ball

44 Broad Lane, Sheffield
or 44 Broad Street, in 1839 directory
(1825-1906)

Ball

50 Lambert Street, Sheffield

Some local books say this public house only had a lifespan of 29 years, from 1796 until 1825.

Ball

86 Carver Street, Sheffield (c1825-1905)
(aka Old Ball Inn)

At some time nicknamed The Charity Boy.

Ball

3 Norfolk Street, Sheffield (c1830-1900)

William Sayles was the first landlord of this public house.

Ball

2 Upper Osbourne Street, Sheffield

Following a radical meeting in Paradise Square in 1874, an unsatisfied and unruly crowd started to head from the square through the city, damaging property, breaking into public houses and purloining drink. This riotous behaviour lasted throughout the night and into the morning. It was in and around this Ball that the affray was finally quelled, and several of the hundreds who took part were arrested and sentenced to prison.

Ball

27 Spring Street, Sheffield 3
(aka Ball and Whitesmith in 1939)

Ball

17 Grindle Gate, Sheffield

Ball

31 Duke Street, Sheffield
(aka called Old Ball in 1861) (c1824-1900)

Ball

102 West Bar, Sheffield

Ball

52 Wicker, Sheffield (aka Golden Ball)
(open 1890)

Ball

Fitzalan Street, Sheffield

Ball

17 Scotland Street, Sheffield 3
(opened in the late 18th century)

Ball

60 Charles Street, Sheffield
(opened in first quarter of the 19th century)

Ball

28 Townhead Street, Sheffield

Ball

184 Young Street, Sheffield

Ball

34 Pye Bank, Sheffield (aka Red Lion)

Ball

95 Heeley Green Heeley, Sheffield

Ball

Burgess Street, Sheffield

Ball Inn

106 High Street, Ecclesfield

The City of Sheffield seemed to have the monopoly on this name. No other city or town in England had as many public houses called The Ball, plus the variances like Golden Ball, Blue Ball, Ball in Tree, etc. The significance of this, if any, is unknown, but it may be because of the ease at which a sign with a ball could be depicted. Some nowadays have football, cricket ball, orbs, etc.

Ball Inn

84 Green Lane, Sheffield 3
(first opened in 1830s)

As this encyclopaedia is going to print, plans are afoot to revive this old pub, a listed building, on the corner of Green Lane and Ball Street, within the complex of the new Cornish Works Redevelopment. If the first draft of the plan goes ahead the ground floor will be a public house and the upper floor a restaurant and micro brewery. Unfortunately another draft has been laid out as well which has both floors being turned into work studios with living accommodation. Let's hope the former plan wins through.

Ball Inn

26 Campo Lane, Sheffield
(aka Golden Ball)

The Ball sold Bentley's Rotherham Ales.

Ball Inn

70 Upwell Street, Sheffield 3
(open 1830 - still open)

Ball Inn

171 Crookes, Sheffield 10

One of Sheffield's bowling pubs. These pubs had their own crown bowling greens.

Ball Inn

46 Furnace Hill, Sheffield (aka Golden Ball)
(c1797-1920s)

Ball Inn

287 Darnall Road, Sheffield 9

Built around 1910, it is one of the tallest buildings in Darnall and at one time was used by the local firestation to train its men. The Ball Inn is reputed to have a ghost, that of a young woman who was a barmaid at the inn. It is said she hung herself from the attic rafters when she found out she was pregnant out of wedlock.

Ball Inn

230 Myrtle Road, Sheffield 2

Ball Inn

8 Pitsmoor Road, or Pye Bank, Sheffield 3

Ball Inn

43 Mansfield Road, Intake, Sheffield

Ball-in-Tree

Clarkehouse Road, Sheffield 11
(aka Balli'th'Tree, Ball)

This name is said to come from the fact that the pub was first called the Ball and when the sign or ball fell away or became detached it was picked up and tied or placed in the tree outside the pub. True or false, that's one version that has been put forward.

Balloon Tavern

21 Sycamore St, Sheffield (c1830-1900s)

Balloon Tavern

83 Trippet Lane, Sheffield

Baltic Hotel

420 Effingham Road, Sheffield 9
(opened in circa 1830)

Bankers Draft

1-3 Market Place, Castle Square, Sheffield 1

Transformed by Wetherspoons as a JJ Moons outlet from an old Midland Bank into the largest public house in Sheffield in 1996. The interior is made up of two floors all with tables for eating and ample standing room for the more athletic. It serves food throughout the day and is open all day, every day. The Bankers has no music and a 30% no smoking area and a smoke free area around the bar, unusual for a city centre pub.

Bank Inn

1 Penistone Road, Sheffield 6

Bank Street Hotel

24 Bank Street, Sheffield 1 (1850s-1900s)

Bank Tavern

4 Hartshead, Sheffield 1 (1840s)

Bank Tavern

65 Norfolk Street, Sheff (closed early 1900s)

Banner Cross Hotel

967 - 971 Ecclesall Road, Sheffield 11

The Banner Cross is a two roomed pub that has a wide range of clientele, and is a very comfortable house.

The Banner Cross is one of only two public houses with this name in England (the other being in Torquay) and is so named after a cross that was situated in this area.

This public house and the Prince of Wales situated further along Ecclesall Road, will probably have had, over the years, a few rogues but none more surely than one of their late 19th century customers, a certain Charles Peace. For here was a man who was a burglar, a bigamist, a fence (the modern terminology for buying and selling stolen goods), an adulterer and, because of his eye for the ladies, eventually a murderer.

Charles Peace lived two separate lives as a family man both in London and Sheffield. This was not enough for Charlie so he decided to make his life even more complex by forming a relationship with a Mrs Dyson who was living in the Darnall area. Her husband, suspecting something was amiss, even moved house to Banner Cross to escape Peace's attentions toward his wife. Peace, however, was not to be denied access to Mrs Dyson. In November of 1876, Mr Dyson walked in and found his wife and Charlie Peace in a compromising situation and proceeded to attack Peace. Charlie ran off but was pursued by Mr Dyson, whereupon Peace turned, revolver in hand and shot, fatally wounding, Dyson. The murder took place in the passage way that is at the side of the Banner Cross Hotel.

Peace was arrested and found guilty of murder and sentenced to death by hanging. Whilst being transported to be executed he made an attempt to escape by throwing himself through a train window

Charles Peace was finally hung in February 1879.

Barcentro

Cambridge Street, Sheffield 1

The Barcentro is new to the Sheffield pub/cafe/bar scene, being just a few years old. It has some reputation to live up to being situated in this the area of the famed Nells Bar, Barleycorn (next entry) and the Cambridge, all at one time thriving establishments on Cambridge Street or as it was previously known Coalpit Lane. The bar itself is comfortable with a dark wooden interior, sedately lit and it also boasts a terrace bar with heated dining area.

It is now itself in the midst of another lively modern area with Henrys Bar next door, the Casbah (Wapentake), Sportsman, Yorkshireman and the new Wetherspoons public house (as yet un-named) being built on the old Albert Inn site atop Cambridge Street.

Barleycorn

38 Coalpit Lane, 38 Cambridge Street, Sheffield 1 (opened late 18th century)

A name that refers to the cereal plant commonly used to make malt liquors and personified by John Barleycorn. Barleycorn is a jocular name for beer or ale or any malt liquor. He has been referred to by such famous writers as Walter Scott, Robert Burns, and Nathaniel Hawthorne. Also there is an old ballad about him in which he is described as of "noble blood, well beloved in England, a great supporter of the Crown, and a maintainer of both rich and poor".

Barleymow

99 Broomhall Street, Sheffield (opened in c1830)

Mow is a stack and a barley mow sign was meant to be a simple indication that beer was sold.

Barrack Tavern

High House Terrace, Philadelphia, Sheffield

This was the first Barrack Tavern built near to where the original Sheffield barracks were situated.

It was a haunt of the Cutlers Company of Sheffield who used to hold their Forfeit Feast at the Barrack when William Burrows was landlord in the early to mid 19th century.

Barrack Tavern

217 Penistone Road, Sheffield 6 (aka New Barrack Tavern)

This Tavern was built near to the site of the second barracks and was closed in the early 90s only to be reopened and renamed as the New Barrack Tavern. Now a stalwart of the Real Ale brigade and well worth a visit.

Barrel

64 Pinstone Street, Sheffield

The happenings at the Barrel would definitely make the present day practical joker think twice.

In 1789 whilst out for an evening's drinking in the town centre, two work colleagues, John Stevens and Thomas Lastley, button makers for John Hoole of Lady's Walk, met up with three friends, named Booth, Bingham and Wharton.

Wharton was carrying some groceries he had purchased earlier. For a joke the other four made off to the Barrel with the food. Once there they proceeded to cook a leg of mutton, expecting Wharton to join them in time to eat the meat. Upon finding his groceries gone Mr Wharton did not see the funny side of the situation and called for the local constable, who traced the four men and arrested them for highway robbery. Despite their obvious explanations and offer to refund the few pence the groceries cost, they were arrested and imprisoned. Tried at York, only Bingham was acquitted, the other three were sentenced to death. Booth's sentence was commuted to deportation to Australia, but Lastley and Stevens were hung. A pardon was given to the two men, but it arrived in York 48 hours too late.

Wharton was then treated by the local Sheffield people as an outcast and his house and his shop premises were ransacked. Supposedly he disguised himself as a woman and made good his escape, to Manchester, if the story is true. He was never to be seen in Sheffield again.

Barrel

9 Waingate, Sheffield (c 1830s-1898)

Barrel

Lane End, Chapeltown

This name commonly featured in pub signs, but now they have been replaced by the metal keg, not so common.

Barrel/Fagans

69 Broad Lane, Sheffield 1

The Barrel, on Broad Lane, was renamed Fagans, in 1985, after its landlord Joe Fagan, retired after 37 years continuous service. In 1948, Joe came straight from the Royal Air Force into the licensing trade and stayed through thick and thin, to see the job through till he pulled his final pint in September '85. Fagan's father Michael was also a Sheffield public house landlord of some note. Fagans won the CAMRA pub of the year in 1994 and is popular with the real ale crowd.

Barrel

31 Edward Street, Sheffield

Barrel

44 Pye Bank, Sheffield

Barrel

75 Pea Croft, Solly Street, Sheffield (c1825-early 1900s) (aka Old Barrel)

Barrel

40 Little Pond Street, Sheffield

Barrel

16 Charles Street, Sheffield 1

Barrel

36 Water Lane, Sheffield
(late 18th century - 1900)

Barrel

105 Pond Street, Sheffield

Barrel

36 Duke Street, Sheffield (1825-1903)

Barrel

134 Lord Street, Sheffield

Barrel

73-75 Solly Street, Sheffield

Barrel Inn

123 London Road, Sheffield 2

Situated in one of Sheffield most populated thoroughfares, this three, small roomed public house, opened in 1882 and is still going strong and is one of about 15 pubs on London Road. At one time in this area, known as Little Sheffield, there were about 35 to 50 public houses or beerhouses.

Bar Coast

Division Street, Sheffield 1,
The Old Fire Station

This conversion of the Sheffield Central Fire Station to a stainless steel clad, city centre bar is one of many in Sheffield that is taking old and listed buildings and turning them into café/bars/restaurants.

Barrow Boys

Under Canada House, Shude Hill, Sheffield

The Barrow Boys was conceived in the early eighties and whilst it was hidden away it was a little gem. As the name implies the barrow boys were a familiar sight in this part of town, situated near to all the markets and to the Dixon Lane area, also well known for its stall holders. The pub itself consisted of a large bar area and an offshot sizeable room where a game of pool or darts could be had, and an affordable priced meal enjoyed.

Barton Vaults

118 West Street, Sheffield

Basset

17 Cowper Avenue, Foxhill, Sheffield 5

The Basset along with the Beagle on Parson Cross were built in the 1950s. The name the basset hound is derived from the short legged dog that is/was used to unearth foxes, badgers, etc. History has it that a Sir Ralph Basset was a thirteenth century lord of the manor, in Lancashire, who kept a pack of such hounds for hunting which he had bred himself.

Basin Tavern

36 Blast Lane, Sheffield

Batemoor

1 White Thorns View, Sheffield 8

Bath

Whitehouse Road, Sheffield

Bath Hotel

139-143 Broomhall Street, Sheffield 3
(aka Bath Cottage at 125 in 1862)

During the late Edwardian era the landlord ran a charabanc travel business from this public house.

Bath Hotel

184 Burgoyne Road, Sheffield 6

Bath Hotel

66 Victoria Street, Sheffield 3

The Tetley owned Bath Hotel is situated just off the West Street/Glossop Road, and has earned the title of a Tetley Heritage Pub.

Dating from 1863, when the present lounge area was part of a shop. The owner at that time, a certain Charles Hoyland leased the building to a butcher, and insisted that the property should never operate as an inn, public house or beerhouse, or for that matter any other noxious activity. Just over 30 years later, in 1895 it had managed to acquire a license as a beerhouse despite the original requirements of the ground lease. By 1908 it was called the Bath Hotel and was doing a thriving business when Ind Coope purchased it just before the start of World War I, in 1914. At present the Bath Hotel is the only public house in South Yorkshire to be added to the National Inventory of Pub Interiors of Outstanding Heritage Interest, and has become a listed building under the auspices of the Department of Culture.

Bathfield Hotel

Weston Street, Sheffield 3

The Bathfield was opened in 1965. It used to get considerable numbers of students from the nearby University.

Bay Childers

4 Bridge Street, Sheffield

One train of thought about the name Bay Childer is that around 1740 a racehorse owner named Sir Hugh Childers had a horse called Flying Childers. This horse won many races, it is unknown whether it was a bay though. It has been said that the name could also come from the Flemish term for Bay, a sort of 'cloth'. Childers is an old English dialect word meaning "to bring forth", so could it be an old tailor/weavers term?

Bay Childers

48 High Street, Sheffield 1
(aka Horse & Cat, Bay Horse, Queen Victoria, Westminster)

Opened in 1761, and first called the Bay Childers, it went on to have many a different name, as can be seen from the also-known-as list above. It is said, it was situated on the south side of High Street, between Change Alley, Mulberry Street and George Street, which would now place it at the frontage of the National Westminster Bank and Timpsons.

In 1774 it was renamed the Horse & Cat. Some thirteen years later in a 1787 Sheffield directory, it was called the Bay Horse, and during this time ran a twice weekly carrier service from it doors to the city of Lincoln. The place was rebuilt in 1794 when a John Henson was landlord. He was followed by his son, Joseph, in whose ownership it had another name change, to the Queen Victoria, circa 1839. Many years later, probably in the 1900s it had its final renaming, to the Westminster. In the Sheffield blitz of 1940 the Westminster was bombed and decimated. It was demilished soon after the war.

Bay Horse

40 South Street, The Moor, Sheffield

A Bay is defined as a horse with colour ranging from light brown to a rich mahogany, but the horse always has black points ie mane and tail, which distinguish it from any variety of chestnuts. This particular Bay Horse was built in the early 1820s.

Bay Horse

227 Attercliffe Common, Sheffield 9

Bay Horse

143 Milton Street, Sheffield (c1823-1910)

Bay Horse

53 West Bar Green, Sheffield (1820s -1920s)

Bay Horse

46 Upper St Philips Road, Sheffield 3
(opened around 1840s)

The Weston Cinema was next door to the Bay horse.

Bay Horse

9 Willey Street, Sheffield

Bay Horse

1 Greystock Street, Sheffield 1

Bay Horse

Willoughby Colley, Wadsley, Sheffield

Bay Horse

463 Pitsmoor Road, Sheffield 3

Bay Tree

24 Snow Hill, Sheffield

Bazaar

114 - 116 South Road, Sheffield
(opened around 1828)

Beagle

Knutton Crescent, Sheffield 5

Beauchief Hotel

161 Abbeydale Road South, Sheffield 7

Bedford Hotel

71 Penistone Road, Sheffield

The pub closed in 1903 and later became a cafe around 1913.

Bee Hive

240 West Street, Sheffield 1
(aka B-Hive, Rockwells, Foundry & Firkin)

A man named Thomas Rose, a shoemaker by trade, was granted a license for a public house on West Street, and keeping bees in some adjoining gardens, Rose thought it would be a good idea to name it the Bee Hive.

In 1817 the Town Trustees granted the sum of £200 for a proposed turnpike from Glossop to Sheffield on the condition that the road enters the town of Sheffield through West Street. The Bee Hive was already standing at this time, and so dating it as having been a public house for nearly 200 years. Thomas Rose was still in residence at the Bee Hive in 1839.

In the mid 1990s around one million pounds was spent transforming the Bee Hive into the Foundry & Firkin, and incorporating the post office premises next door.

The public house with its bare wooden floorboards and no nonsense tables and chairs has a traditional alehouse feel about it. It brews its own beer and drinkers can enjoy a pre-arranged tour of the small brewery.

Bee Hive

7 Bowling Green Street, Sheffield

Bee Hive

13 Little Pond Street, Sheffield

Bee Hive Hotel

20 Upwell Lane, Sheffield 4
(closed in 1972)

Bee Hive Inn

115 Langsett Road, Sheffield 6

Bee Hive Inn

Dykes Hall Road, Sheffield 6

Bee Hive

Spring Street, Sheffield
(opened c1830)

Beeley Wood

500-502 Middlewood Road, Sheffield 6

Beeswing

34 Hartshead, Sheffield 1

Beeswing, in a public house/brewery context means the film which forms on port and some other wines, which are kept for many years. The actual film coating is said to look like that of a bee's wing. In the late 19th century it became the name of any genial drinker.

There was also a racehorse of this name who remained unbeaten between the years of 1835 and 1842, four times winning the Doncaster Gold Cup and the Ascot Gold Cup on one occasion. So this pub could have been named after either or both!

Bell Hotel

Fitzalan Square, Sheffield 1

The bell sign was said to speak all languages.

A distinctive, yet simple, shape made it a great favourite for sign makers throughout the centuries.

This Bell Hotel in Fitzalan Square became an amusement arcade for a few years but is now a sales outlet for cheap merchandise.

Pictured below is the Bell Hotel when it was still a thriving public house and was sandwiched between the Classic cinema and the old Sleep Shop.

Bell Hagg Inn

Manchester Road, Sheffield
(aka John Thomas)

Built in 1832 it was erected as a five storey house for a certain Doctor Hodgson, who had it built to antagonise the Vicar of Stannington after he turned down a generous donation, supposedly because Dr Hodgson had made a goodly proportion of his money from gambling. It was obviously a visual reminder to the Vicar.

For many years it was known locally as Hodgson's folly. A large imposing building standing seemingly on the edge of a precipice, it has a stunning view over the Rivelin Valley. It is the last building out of Sheffield on the Manchester Road.

In an old pub signs book it reads "the original form of the name was Belhaye, where the Old English word bel refers to a fire or beacon while the second element means enclosure

Bellefield

16 Bellefield Street, Sheffield 3

In 1903 this was a grocers shop and beer retailers and it was owned by a Tom Burgan.

Bellefield Inn

37 Bellefield Street, Sheffield 3

In 1903 it was a beerhouse run by William Dawson.

Bellefield Hotel

On the corner of 68-70 Bellefield Street and 90 Fawcett Street, Sheffield

Belle Vue

116 Fitzalan Street, Sheffield

Belle Vue Hotel

282 Whitehouse Lane, Sheffield 6

Belle Vue Hotel

229 Cricket Inn Road, Sheffield 2

Ben Lomond Tavern

23 Eyre Street, Sheffield (aka City Arms)

This tavern opened in the early part of the 19th century and it was still trading under the Ben Lomond name in 1888, it closed 20 years later in 1908

Berlin's

Arundel Gate, Sheffield 1

Bethel Arms

Backfield, Sheffield (opened in c1830s)

The Bethel Arms was sited on Backfields, which ran from Division Street to the Moor. Today, Yates Wine Lodge stands on the corner of this road.

Big Gun

17 The Wicker, Sheffield 3 (aka Great Gun) (opened in 1790s)

Big Tree

842 Chesterfield Road, Sheffield 8 (aka Masons Arms)

The Big Tree was originally named the Masons Arms and only became the Big Tree in around 1935. This was mainly due to the fact an oak tree of some proportion was growing in the forecourt, and most locals called it the 'tree' or the 'big tree' anyway. The original big tree, the tree, that is, was mortally injured when a touring circus tied their elephant to a large bough, the animal did not want to be so restrained and move off, branch and all, and split the tree in two. Another tree was planted in around 1936.

Many stories abound about who has sheltered by the tree, Wesley preached to the Woodseats villagers whilst standing in its shadow, Chantrey sat beneath the tree and did his wood carvings, possibly!

The more interesting story is in its masonic history, with a mosaic floor depicting the stonecutters trade. This, unfortunately, is now beneath the pubs carpets, but still on view is the masonic signs on the gable end which faces outwards to the main road.

The present tree is in fact a beech tree.

Bird in Hand

Church Street, Sheffield

Opened in around the mid 18th century, the Bird in Hand was sited on what was then called Church Lane. It was adjacent to the Cutlers Hall, where the cutlers would hold their meetings. In 1761, when William Parker was then the master cutler, the cutlers themselves, decided it would be better for their Worshipful Company meetings if alcohol was not served, so the license was stopped at the Cutlers Hall

Some of the more thirsty, knife and fork manufacturers decided they would do some of their business from the Bird in Hand, conveniently placed next door. The cutlers did business with chapmen (buyers and sellers of cutlery), they would barter for the keenest price, and then go and sell it, obviously at a profit, throughout England and sometimes even further afield.

Also, in the late 18th century, from outside the door of the Bird in Hand a cart owned by Swindons went to Tideswell every Tuesday.

Bird in Hand

49 Broughton Lane, Sheffield 9

The 'Bird' on Broughton Lane was a small, two roomed, old fashioned pub. It had a large gateway leading into a courtyard, probably at one time for horses to be stabled.

It was a well frequented place up to and including the 1960s, but from that point onwards, throughout the Attercliffe area, trade fell away and it was a case of how long pubs could survive. In the late 70s the 'Bird' closed and for a few years it was used as a typesetters (Forward Processing) and then it was purchased by the Carbrook Conservative Club. The CCC used to have premises on Attercliffe Common, but when this had a compulsory purchase order placed upon it they bought the old Bird in Hand and the Aston Villa's next door to form the New Carbrook Conservative Club.

Lee Froggatt, Allan Dent, Fred Needham and another lad whose name I forget used to play cards, in the Bird, seven nights a week for many years, and they invariably had seven pints every night. One of that group always missed his second round.

Bird in Hand

28 Spring Street, Bridge Street, Sheffield (aka Old Bird in Hand) (open in c1830s)

Traditional signage for these pubs was a mailed fist on which a falcon was perched, but more probably the name comes from an ancient English saying of 'A bird in the hand is worth two in the bush'.

25

Bird in Hand
624 Brightside Lane, Sheffield 9

Birley Hotel
66 Birley Moor Road, Sheffield 12

Birmingham Arms
20 Lambert Street, Sheffield

Birmingham Arms
40 Greystock Street, Sheffield

Birmingham Arms
93 Matilda Street, Sheffield 2

Black Boy
29 Bailey Lane, Sheffield
(aka Old Black Boy)

The more recent signage of Black Boy would have us see a Dickensian chimney sweep, but the original 17th and 18th Black Boy signs would have young negro page boys depicted on them. The more wealthy people who had personal servants, dressed them in brightly coloured clothing and around the city of London, where they were predominantly situated, they were known as Tigers, mainly because their uniforms generally had a striped design.

Black Bull
74 Hollis Croft, Sheffield

Many tavern owners were so disgusted with the Gin Act of 1736 that they added the name black to the inn's name and draped the outer signage in black velvet so as to indicate to the government their displeasure. As with most thing of this ilk the name has stayed on.

Black Bull
18 Church Street, Ecclesfield

Blackamoor Head
25 High Street, Sheffield (aka Grey Horse)

In 1675 the Girdler family owned the Blackamoor Head and it was sited in the High Street on the lower side of Aldine Court, now probably where the Blue Bell is to be found. In around 1788 it had a name change to the Grey Horse and it was thought to have been demolished in around 1917.

The word Blackamoor first appeared in England in the 16th century and simply meant 'a black Moor'

Black Eagle
80 Wellington Street, 73 Eldon Street, Sheffield (aka Eagle)

A Christian and heraldic symbol, the Eagle has been used as an inn sign since the fifteenth century. The Black Eagle was meant to be a harbinger of doom, not a good name for a tavern.

Black Horse
180 Upper Allen Street, Jericho Street, Jericho, Sheffield 3

This popular sign dates from at least the 14th century. By the 17th century it was the nickname of the 7th Dragoon Guards, who had black collars and cuffs on their jackets an rode mainly black horses. Some dragoons were stationed at the Sheffield Barracks.

This sign was also used by London Goldsmiths and is now a sign of the Lloyds Bank.

Black Horse
17 Edward Street, Sheffield (1790s-1906)

Black Horse
64 Howard Street, Sheffield (c 1800s-1902)

Black Horse/Darling
75 Talbot Street, Sheffield 2 (opened 1830s)

Black Lion

33 Snig Hill, Sheffield (aka Old Black Lion)

Signage wise there are two trains of thought on this one, an heraldic sign of Queen Philippa of Hainault, wife of Edward III, or more probably reference to Owen Glendower (Owain Glyndwr) a Welsh chieftain who fought against Henry at the battle of Shrewsbury in 1403 and who had a black lion on his coat of arms.

Black Lion

24 Bank Street, Sheffield

Black Rock

17-19 Castle Street, Sheffield (1797-1921)

The Royal Jubilee Friendly Society originated in 1809 in the Black Rock, but in 1822 it transferred to the George, in the Market Place. The Black Rock counteracted this by starting another society. This was called the Fitzwilliam Friendly Society and was started by John Fordham, the then landlord. This society was restricted to 100 original members and a limit of two new members per year.

These sick clubs and societies were a means for workers to make some, albeit, small provision for unemployment or just to cover the fear of injury at work, a common feature of these times.

Blacksmiths Arms

10 Sheldon Row, Sheffield

Blacksmiths Cottage

Button Lane, Sheffield

Opened as a beerhouse in around 1874 but by then the building was almost 150 years old, being built in 1705. Along with Button Lane and surrounding areas, long since demolished.

Blackstock

Blackstock Road, Sheffield 2

Black Swan

5 Black Swan Walk, Fargate, Sheffield 1

Black Swan Walk, which runs down the side the sports shop (the old Salisburys) atop Chapel Walk, used to house this hotel. It used to stand on what is now Barclays Bank.

Black Swan

39-41 Snig Hill, Sheffield 1 (aka Compleat Angler/Mucky Duck/Boardwalk)

A public house of many changes, the original Black Swan started serving the township of Sheffield in 1774. Fifty years later in the 1820s the Royal Jubilee Friendly Society, which is mentioned in the Black Rock caption above, moved from there to the Black Swan and was run for many years by the obviously trustworthy, landlord, John Crich.

It was rebuilt and in the new concert room area people like Joe Cocker started an illustrious career, singing for a few pound in the Swan, along with many of Sheffield's early 60s groups, O'Hara's Playboys (John O'Hara is still doing the local rounds), Wolves, Rainbow, Jigsaw and The Fortunes. Three of these acts reached number one in the British Charts.

The pub was then called the Compleat Angler, this was in reference to the famous fisherman author, Izaac Walton. It still seems somewhat of a mystery why this name was ever used for the Swan.

After this it was renamed the Mucky Duck, a name which most wags had called it all along. But, as usual, within a couple of years the name changed again. This time to the Boardwalk and significantly the room underneath was called, yes you've guessed, under the Boardwalk. Probably it will change back to the Black Swan, one day. Due to war damage the Black Swan continued for a time doing business as a one storey pub.

Black Swan

21 Burgess Street, Sheffield

A Roman satirist, Juvenal first referred to the black swan as an example of a rare bird. He had no knowledge that these birds did and do exist. Other references to Black Swan could have come from Australia since that is were they came from, but also Western Australia has the Black Swan as its emblem. Further reference may be from naval sources where an HMS Black Swan was active between 1939 and 1956.

Black Swan

1 Little Pond Street, Sheffield
(also said to be at 15 LPS and 60 LPS)

Blake Hotel

53 Blake Street, Sheffield 6
(aka Blake Street Hotel in or around 1902)

It is stated that the Blake Hotel and the street of the same name is called after Robert Blake who was born in 1599. He was a puritan and a republican who fought with distinction in the English Civil War as a general, and later went to sea and became an admiral. This is a pub that is situated at the top of one of, if not the steepest hill in Sheffield.

Bloomsbury Hotel

37 Albion St, Sheffield 6
(aka Bloomsbury Tavern) (opened c1840)

Blucher

672 Brightside Lane, Sheffield 9

This public house in the heart of Sheffield's steel making industry at the back of Attercliffe Common was built around the 1850s It is feasible that the landlord, the odd customer or some of the steelworkers could well have fought at Waterloo, some 35 years earlier.

Named after the man who was, without proper recognition, one of the biggest influences on English history. It may seem implausible now but Waterloo would most likely have been a French victory had not Field Marshall Gebhard Leberecht von Blücher, with his Prussian cavalry, come to the assistance of Wellington as the day and the battle seemed to be lost. A man who deserves much praise not only for making Waterloo a victory held dear in English hearts, but for the fact he was 72 years old at the time.

Blue Ball

320 Haggstones Road, Worrall

A sign used by various tradespeople including fortune tellers as an easy way of being identified. Now it seems to be more in line with sporting associations, blue ball-snooker, etc. In the West country it is of a more heraldic meaning relating to the Courteneys, the earls of Devon.

Blue Ball

Main Road, Wharncliffe

Blue Ball

91 Pond Street, Sheffield (aka Blue Bell)
(1830s-1910)

Blue Ball

44 Broad Street, Sheffield (c1820s-1907)

Blue Ball

Cattlefoulds or Castlefoulds, now Dixon Lane, Sheffield (opened in 1770s)

Blue Ball

Crookes, Sheffield 10

Blue Ball

52 Pye Bank, Sheffield

Blue Bell

13 Jehu Lane, or 4 Commercial Street, Sheff

Opened around 1825 this beerhouse was most likely situated where Jew Lane is now sited, between the amusement arcade and Corals bookmakers in Fitzalan Square. This very narrow little passage leads on to Commercial Street, probably giving rise to the use of both addresses in different street directories.

Blue Bell

31 High Street, Sheffield 1
(aka Cavells, Old Blue Bell)

Now, known as Cavells, it is an early opening and late closing pub, well used by business types for breakfast and by office workers at dinner-time and early evening.

Historically though it is another of the old town centre public houses whose history is almost indecipherable from that of many other beerhouses in the locale.

This particular Blue Bell seems to have been mixed up with the much older Blue Bell which was on the other side of High Street, and would have been sited now around where T J Hughes frontage stands. *(See the next entry).*

Blue Bell

High Street, Sheffield 1
(Norfolk Arms, Clarence House)

Supposedly started life as the Norfolk Arms and was situated three doors below Mulberry Street. Around 1740 it was kept by a man called Ben Steer and was later to become known as the Blue Bell. It changed hands down the years numerous times, but the Amory family seem to have kept it the for a good many years. Around 1830 it was rebuilt and locally written of as being the Clarence, formerly the Blue Bell, and was next to the old stone house. The Clarence which was said to have been sited at 56 High Street, Prior Court, was demolished to make way for John Walsh's.

Blue Bell

Silver Street Head, Sheffield

This pub closed around the turn of the century c1900.

Blue Bell

Main Street, Hackenthorpe

During the 1960s the Landlord, a man called Danny Wood, really used his concert room to further the cause of good music in the Sheffield area. The stars of the future who he had "doing a turn" were truly amazing for such a venue. He had the likes of Dave Berry, The Tremeloes, Alan Price, The Searchers and obviously Joe Cocker. All of these went on to greater things and all (I think) had Top five hits in the British Charts, The Crying Game, Silence is Golden, Simon Smith and his Amazing Dancing Bears, Needles and Pins, and Up Where We Belong respectively. Also in the 60s many a drinker made his way from Sheffield to the Blue Bell after closing time was called to get the extra half hour 'supping' time that Derbyshire licensing laws then allowed.

Blue Boar Hotel

22-26 West Bar, Sheffield 3

It is said that many blue boar signs were originally white boars whilst Richard III was king, but upon the Yorkists defeat at Bosworth in 1485 these were hastily painted blue, since the man who had the blue boar as his coat of arms was the Earl of Oxford who was a leading Lancastrian.

The Blue Boar Hotel itself was a large building reputedly opened in the 1770s. It was bought and occupied by Gordon Turner of GT News and used as offices and a warehouse in the mid to late 50s.

It was once kept by Sheffield boxer Gus Platts.

The law courts stand on this site today.

Blue Boar

16 Cross Burgess Street, Sheffield
(aka Cross Keys circa 1839)

Blue Boar

26 Bow Street, Sheffield

Blue Boy

41 Shepherd Street, Moorfields, Sheffield
(aka Original Blue Boy) (open c1829-1948)

Pub signage wise there are two versions on offer, the obvious one from the Gainsborough painting of the same name, the other more obscure but probably more noteworthy, John Coombs in 1499 established a school for orphans. All the pupil wore blue uniforms.

Blue Boy

9 Blue Boy Street, Allen Street, Sheffield

Blue Pig

22 Workhouse Lane, Sheffield (aka Oxford)

Board

6 Dixon Lane, Sheffield

One meaning of the word board is for the 'Council Meeting'.

Boatman

20 Ball Street, Sheffield

The Sheffield to Goole Canal is really the only place a boatman would probably have been found in Sheffield being as Sheffield is probably the most centrally sited large city in England.

Boatmans Mission

Near Corn Exchange, Sheffield

Bodega

High Street, Sheffield (1774-1940)

Opened in around 1682 and was said to have been sold soon after to a man named George Hutchinson for £500. At this time is was known as the George and Dragon, but was commonly known to most people as just the George. Some time later it was officially called this. Another transaction in 1782 meant it changed hands again for the princely sum of £1500, a vast amount in those days. It eventually changed to the Bodega around the end of the 19th century.

The name Bodega means below street level. This name was nearly correct, for in 1940, the Germans, during the blitz, flattened it to street level. It was sited around where T J Hughes now stands.

Bold Dragon

264 Langsett Road, Sheffield
(aka Bold Dragoon)

Possibly Bold Dragoon, as the Dragoons were garrisoned at the Hillsborough Barracks and a considerable amount of pubs in this area are/were named after the military.

Boomerang

Netherthorpe, Sheffield

Boot and Shoe

79 Campo Lane, Sheffield (1840s-1905)

Boot and Shoe

54 Pinstone Street, Sheffield
(aka Boot and Slipper in 1841)

Boston Castle

6 Castle Green, Sheffield (1790s-1898)

Boston Hotel

10 Lansdowne Road, Sheffield 2
(aka Derby) (demolished in 1960s)

The Boston was named from the Lincolnshire town, which was in turn named from St Botolph (Botolphs Stone).

Bottle & Barrel

Montgomery Road, Nether Edge, Sheffield
(opened 1998)

Bower Spring Tap

2 Bower Spring, Sheffield

Bowling Tavern

53 Montfort Street, Sheffield 3

Pubs with Bowling in their title generally had a green attached.

Bowling Green and Tea Gardens

Cherrytree Hill, Sheffield in 1833

In around 1650 Cherrytree House was built, and soon after was converted into the Bowling Green Inn. Supposedly at the rear of the Inn were large allotments and gardens and the area as well as the Inn became known as the Cherrytree Hill Bowling Club and Tea Gardens. It has now been turned into a privately owned dwelling.

Brackley Arms

14 Brackley Street, Sheffield 3

Bradway Hotel

Bradway Road, Sheffield
(aka Hogshead, Miner's Inn)

Now a Whitbread Beer Festival pub, this Bradway was built to quench the thirst of the Irish navvies who were employed cutting the railway tunnel from Totley to Dronfield. This tunnel runs almost beneath the pub. The Navvies were also called miners so the beerhouse was originally called the Miner's Inn. The present hotel was built in 1920 and it was called the Bradway Hotel not too many years ago

Bramwell Hotel

99 St Philips Road, Sheffield

Brave Old Oak

58 Charles Street, Sheffield

Possibly gained its name from the fact Charles II of England hid in a large oak to escape capture during the English Civil War.

Bressingham Arms

2 Bressingham St, Sheffield

Brewers Arms

36 Eyre Street, Sheffield

Brewers Inn

46 Blackmoor Street, Sheffield
(closed in 1926)

Brewery House

79 Button Lane, Sheffield (1770s-1910)

Bricklayers Arms

66-68 Hereford St, Sheffield 1
(aka The Mad House) (closed in 1960s)

Supposedly a rowdy and boisterous pub, a meeting place for ragmen and scrap metal dealers.

Bricklayers Arms

77 Wentworth St, Sheffield

Bricklayers Arms

8 Jehu Lane, Sheffield
(opened in the late 18th century)

Brickmakers Arms or Blademakers Arms

92 Eyre Lane, Sheffield

This pub is referred to on many different occasions and in many different local books by both names.

Brickmakers Arms

19-21 Newhall Road, Sheffield 9
(opened around 1860)

This was a John Smiths pub on the corner of Newhall Road and Alfred Road.

Bridge

2 Pond Street, Sheffield

Bridge Inn

219 Pond Street, Sheffield (1790s-1900)

Bridge Tavern/Inn

5 Bridge Street, Sheffield 1
(aka Brewery Tap, Fagans)

It was an Inn in 1940, and a tavern in the early part of the century. Its most noteworthy landlord was an Irishman named Michael Fagan who took over in the 30s and ran the Bridge, for over 20 years. He was so well thought of by the locals that they used to call the pub Fagans. His son Joe Fagan who ran the Barrel on Broad Street had the same accolade placed upon him when his beloved inn name was changed to, yes you've guessed it, Fagans.

The Bridge was the tap for the Nanson brewery for many years from the 1790s until taken over by Birks Brewery and then finally by the Duncan Gilmours brewers until both pub and brewery closed.

Bridge

7 Pinstone Street, Sheffield

Bridge Inn or Bridgehouses Inn

181 Nursery Street, or 1 Bridgehouses, Sheffield (opened in 1880s)

This inn used to stand near to the corner of Corporation Street and Nursery Street, adjacent to the old iron bridge which can still be seen from the present main road bridge. In 1843 the river Don frozen over for all of seven weeks and the Bridge Inn landlord had the presence of mind to have some outdoor sheep roastings and skating days.

Bridge Inn

509 London Road, Sheffield 2

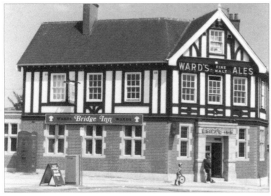

Built about 65 years ago the Bridge Inn was replacing a previous smaller pub that stood on the same site for about a century. It probably gets its name from the wrought iron bridge that spans London Road at one side of the pub. Supposedly much of its early trade came from passengers alighting at Heeley Road Station which was sited opposite. The station unfortunately, for the Bridge Inn, closed in around 1948.

Bridge Inn

2 Meadow Hall Road, Sheffield 9

The Bridge is the usual S H Wards fayre and has or had pictures adorning its walls of many of the famous bridges of the world. Also it has a small claim to fame, in that Dr David Bellamy visited to investigate the fact, for a TV company, that on the banks of the River Don it has a figtree which has grown and now overlooks the pub's backyard.

Bridge Inn

387 Attercliffe Road, Sheffield 9 (c1862)

Bridge Inn

45-47 Hereford Street, Sheffield 1

Bridgefield House

195 Fowler Street, Sheffield 3 (closed in the early 60s)

Brightmore Tavern

23 Brightmore Street, Sheffield

Brincliffe Oaks Hotel

9 Oak Hill Road, and Nether Edge Road, Sheffield 7

This public house was originally named Ye Olde Oak at Brincliffe and was built about 1619.
It had its own private bowling green adjacent to the public house.

Britannia

122-124 Portobello Street, Sheffield (aka Old Britannia, New Britannia)

Britannia was the Roman name for Britain. The first mention of the symbolic female figure occurs in the diaries of Samuel Pepys, 1665. The model for this inspiring figure was Frances Stewart a mistress of Charles II.

Britannia

24-26 Worksop Road, Sheffield 9

The Britannia Inn on Worksop Road, Attercliffe not only has a history entwined with the Sheffield tradition of steelmaking but also a mythical story of one of its many landlords burying a vast number of golden sovereigns, which have never been found.

My grandmother Doris Liversidge (née Hill) was in service at the pub in 1909-13 getting up at the crack of dawn and being sent to her shared bedroom at no later than 6pm. She, along with many more earnest searchers never found the sovereigns, but then again she told me she never had any time to look for them.

The historical side of the Britannia is that it housed Benjamin Huntsman, the man who fathered the steelmaking industry in Sheffield. The inventor of the process of making crucible steel. It is said that he lived for the latter years of his life at these premises. It is reputed by some, that the 24 inch high numbers/date 1772, on the side of the Britannia were made by Huntsman.

Huntsman himself was of Dutch origin and originally a clock maker based in Doncaster before moving to Handsworth near, Sheffield. He was not satisfied with the imported Swedish and German materials for his clocks and this led to his experimenting with steel. He found he could purify ordinary steel by melting it at high temperature in a sealed clay crucible with a flux, this composition he kept as his secret.

Huntsman is buried in Hill Top Cemetery, near the old chapel. His epitaph reads: Benjamin Huntsman of Attercliffe, Steel Refiner, Died June 20th 1776 aged 72 years.

Some people say it is the second oldest pub in Sheffield, others that it was not originally constructed as a public house, so, probably, no one really knows when it first became an inn. One story (unconfirmed) has it that it was converted from 2 dwelling houses to make a small school and later into a shop before being turned into the Britannia around the year 1840 when the area was called Goose Green.

British Lion

38 Thomas Street, Sheffield
(closed c1910)

Most pubs originally named Lion were during the Napoleonic wars transformed in to British Lion when a fervent patriotic renaming took place throughout Britain.

British Oak

227 Carbrook Street, Sheff 9
(open 1880s)

British Oak

28-30 Oak Street, Sheffield 8

British Queen

Penistone Road, Sheffield

Brittain Arms

120 Matilda Street, Sheffield 1
(c1820s-1960s)

Broadfield Hotel

482 Abbeydale Road, Sheffield 7

Brocco

167 Allen Street, Sheffield

Broomhall House

49 Broomhall Street, Sheffield

Broomhall Tavern

105-107 Broomhall Street,
2 Thomas Street, Sheffield 3
(opened c1830s closed 1964)

Broomhill Tavern

484 Glossop Road, Sheffield 10

Oldest pub in Broomhill built circa 1849, used to have Octopus on its Menu.

A Tetley owned pub, it is now most definitely a student haunt.

Broughton Inn

342 Attercliffe Common or
1 Broughton Lane, Sheffield 9

The Broughton Inn, and Broughton Lane at the corner of which the public house stood, and which is now the Sheffield Arena car park, both take their name from a Lincolnshire farmer turned highwayman, named Spence Broughton. Along with John Oxley they robbed the Royal Mail coach in February 1791, supposedly where Attercliffe Common is now situated. Both highwaymen were caught. Oxley escaped from Clerkenwell prison, but Broughton was tried, found guilty and sentenced to hang at York on 3rd April 1792. His body was brought back to Sheffield the very next day and put on display for all to see. His remains were encased in a gibbet which kept his decomposed body on show for many years (supposedly 27 years) until it eventually rotted away.

One gruesome story relates that 2 of his fingers were purloined from his body in the gibbet, ground down and used by Don Pottery of Swinton in a bone china jug, it was painted by Taylor Booth, and was originally sold for £4, a tidy sum in those days.

The public house itself was owned by Duncan Gilmour, it had a large concert room and a small offshot room. It was well frequented and many artists, including the young Gerry Dorsey, better known as Engelbert Humperdink, served their apprenticeship in the old Broughton concert room. The pub was demolished in the late 80s.

Brougham Tavern

Cattle Markets, Sheffield

A brougham is a one horse closed carriage which can have two or four wheels and seat two or four people. It was probably named in honour of Baron Brougham and Vaux 1778 -1868.

Brown Bear

109 Norfolk Street, Sheffield 1 (open 1820s)

Brown Cow

3 Radford Street, Sheffield
(aka Old Brown Cow)

Brown Cow

1 Mowbray Street, or 25 Bridgehouse,
Sheffield 3 (aka Morriseys Riverside)

Situated alongside the Borough Bridge which crosses the River Don on Corporation Street, this three roomed Victorian built pub, was at one stage in its history a residential hotel. The servants' quarters were situated in what is now one of the beer cellars. The Brown Cow has 10 large cellars which stretch out to the river. It was situated next door to the Corporation Street Swimming Baths.

Bought in 1995 by Brian Morrisey and went through the compulsory name change. The "Cow" is supposed to have the best range of Irish Whiskeys in Sheffield.

Brown Cow
1 Broad Lane, Sheffield

Brown Cow
1 Red Croft, Sheffield (was open c1770s)

Brown Cow
27 Trippet Lane, Sheffield
(aka Old Brown Cow)

Brown Cow
68 The Wicker, Sheffield 3

Now a fast food establishment.

Brunswick Hotel
13-15 Haymarket, Sheffield 1 (closed 1970s)
Possibly named after the Duke of Brunswick who lived in England for several years and was killed while fighting for the British at Waterloo.

Brunswick House
30 Tilford Road, Woodhouse

Brunswick Arms
46 Grimesthorpe Road, Sheffield 4
(1880s-1970s)

Brunswick House
50 Montford Street, Sheffield

Brunswick Inn
16 Ellin Street, Sheffield

Brunswick Hotel
54 Thomas Street, Sheffield 1
(closed 1964)

Brunswick House
98 Bramber St, Sheffield 3

Brushmakers Arms or Tavern
31 Pond Hill, Sheffield (1820s-1917)

Brushmakers Arms
Coalpit Lane, Sheffield
This pub was trading in 1830.

Buccaneer Bar
below Grand Hotel, Leopold Street, Sheffield

The word buccaneer is generally applied to seafaring men who plundered enemy ships for their valuables. The true meaning of Buccaneer is somewhat less swashbuckling, it was applied originally to men who hunted wild oxen, cooking its meat on a kind of grid-iron called a boucan.

This particular Buccaneer was situated under the Grand Hotel and to its credit brought something new to the Sheffield youth in the 60s. It was a downstairs bar, it had loud music, early video type juke box, was dimly lit, with seafaring paraphernalia all around and netting hanging just above head height, something slightly different.

It seems strange now to relate such minor changes but in the early sixties the Sheffield licensing industry took it for granted that trade would be automatic, no one seemed to work at enticing custom, especially the younger drinker.

Buckenham Hotel
62 Grimesthorpe Road, Pitsmoor, Sheffield
(1870s-1976)

Bulldog

387 Attercliffe Road, Washford Bridge,
Sheffield 9 (aka Bridge)

Roy Davey in his book "Pubs and People Around Sheffield" mentions that "the Bridge" was damaged by a bomb landing on or near Washford Bridge. This is confirmed by my father who told me that he used to have to clamber across the badly damaged Washford bridge to get to his place of work (Tempered Springs). The Bridge continued to trade as a one storey pub until it was demolished and upon this site a new pub was erected in the 1940s/1950s, and was called, The Bulldog allegedly because the new tenant bred bulldogs as a hobby.

Bull & Bitch

High Street, Sheffield

The location of this unusually named beerhouse is unknown but it was situated somewhere along the High Street around 1780.

Bull & Mouth

28-30 Waingate, Sheffield 3
(aka Bolougne Mouth, Tap and Spile, Tap and Barrel) (opened 1790s)

It is purported this name is derived from the Bolougne Mouth a name stemming from Henry VIIIs capture of Bolougne Harbour in 16th century. The present building was built in 1927. The old building was at the entrance to the Shambles, the old slaughterhouse on Castlegate. The pub itself is a basic affair, bare floorboards and brick walls in some areas. It is split into two spacious rooms, one at the moment where meals can be had in a smoke free environment and the other a bar area for the more discerning drinker. Owned by Pub Master.

Bull & Oak

76-78 The Wicker, Sheffield 3
(aka: Front Room Public House,
Assembly Rooms, Sembly Rooms,
Crown and Cushion and Sam Hills Parlour)

This Whitbreads public house which stood at 76-78 The Wicker was one of the oldest licensed houses in Sheffield, the original building being built in c1715. This area, now the Wicker, was open ground and by the side of the River Don willows grew in great profusion and were gathered by the local women who fashioned them into baskets. From this the name Wicker is supposedly derived. In 1795 a road was laid across this area and a hostelry called the Assembly House (Sembley House) was built. James Montgomery the editor of the Iris (one of Sheffield's earliest newspapers) along with many of his intellectual friends frequented this house which at the time was labelled a hotbed of sedition. The "Sembly House" building was replaced by the Bull & Oak pictured. This public house consisted of a large narrow room which incorporated the bar and a small games room off to the right as you entered. Unfortunately it was closed and demolished in early 1998.

Bull & Oak

26 Furnival Road, Sheffield
(aka New Bull & Oak) (opened in 1820s)

Bulls Head Hotel

18 Dun Street, Sheffield 3

This hotel, as history will have it, was one of, if not, the roughest place in the Sheffield township, and was nicknamed the Devil's Kitchen.
Dun Street which runs between Shalesmoor and Green Lane is no longer than 100 yards and at one time had no dwellings' only three public houses: the Bulls Head, the Queens and the Gardeners Rest.

Bulls Head Hotel

396 Fulwood Road, Ranmoor, Sheffield 10

Francis Methley was the owner for a period of time around the turn of the century, when the picture, below, was taken.

It is a public house that has not altered too drastically in exterior appearance over the years.

Bulls Head

2 Duke Street, Sheffield
(1820s-1902)

Bulls Head

2 Matilda Street and 31 South Street, Sheffield 2

Bulls Head

24 Cross Smithfield, Sheffield
(1790s-1920s)

Burgoyne Arms

246 Langsett Road, Sheffield 6

Could be named after John Burgoyne who led a poorly equipped army, untrained for frontier fighting, against the Americans in the War of Independence and who in 1777 at Saratoga was forced to surrender and give the Americans their first taste of victory.

It could be named, however, after Lady Burgoyne the last member of the Bamforth family, Lords of the manor of Owlerton and the widow of Sir Montague Roger Burgoyne, Bart.

At one time in its history it is said to have had a landlord who was some 29 stones in weight and seven feet eight inches tall, a man named Hales. Probably not too much trouble in his public house!

The Burgoyne had a spa well at the back of the premises.

Burlington Hotel

7 Burlington Street, Sheffield 6 (closed c 1957)

This pub and street was named after the Earl of Burlington, a minor title of the Dukes of Devonshire.

Burns Tavern

10 Townhead Street, Sheffield

Robert Burns is a name well known for poetry and humour. Sheffield being the type of city it was, in the 19th century, I think the Burns that this pub is named after is John Burns, a trade union official who led the national dock strike of 1889. He was a pioneer of the Labour Movement and represented Battersea for many years in Parliament.

Burns Hotel

2 Sheffield Road, Tinsley, Sheffield
(aka Burns Head)

Burns Head Tavern

10 Townhead Street, Sheffield
(aka Canterbury Inn) (1820s-1900s)

Burnt Tree Tavern

83 Hoyle Street, Sheffield

A large number of taverns were called Burnt Tree in the last century and some say the name seems to stem from an old folklore story about a tree that was struck by lightening and had a witch living in it and generally offering her services for a fee.

The truth is very similar in most ways to the story that is told above. A large tree was struck by lightening and was a giant charred mark on the landscape for many years. The public house built near the site was named after this lightening tree. No reference to the spirit though!

Burnt Tree Tavern

84-86 Allen Street, Sheffield

Burton Arms

434 Attercliffe Road, Sheffield (closed 1920s)

Bush Tavern

Little Sheffield

A pub sign of great antiquity, used by the Romans to indicate a wine shop in the form of a bunch of evergreens. Poles decorated with evergreens such as ivy were used as signs for early alehouses.

The only mention to be found of this tavern is from a passage in an old Sheffield almanac stating "A Commission of Lunacy sat at the house of William Watson, the sign of the Bush in Sheffield".

Butchers Arms

27 Townhead Street, Sheffield

Butchers Arms

158 Gibraltar Street, Sheffield

(landlord George Liversidge in 1862)

Butchers Arms

61 Bath Street, Sheffield

Butchers Arms

1 Langsett Road, Sheffield
(closed in late 1950s)

Byards Leap

43 Daresbury Drive, Sheffield

Fairly modern estates pub with two large rooms and excellent views over the city.

This unusually named pub, possibly the only one so called in England, comes from an ancient medieval romance. The hero, Rinaldo was riding his horse Bayardo and an old hag sprang on to the horse and it took three immense leaps by the horse to unseat her. The pub sign shows the hag on the horse's back.

Byron House Hotel

16 Nether Edge Road, Sheffield 7

Lord Byron, the Celebrated English Poet after whom the pub is named, was born in 1788 and lived only 36 years. He was married to Ann Isabella Milbanke and had one daughter by her, and another child by a Miss Clairmont. By the time he was 28 he had abandoned England and lived in Italy. Soon unsettled he moved on to Greece, a country for which he fought in 1823 when he became the Greek insurgents' commander in chief.

Cambridge Hotel

452 Penistone Road, Sheffield 6

The Cambridge Hotel was situated at the rear of the Hillsborough Barracks, opposite to where the MacDonalds Fast Food establishment stands today. The name of the public house, The Cambridge is not technically from the city of that name, but taken from one Adolphus Frederick, (1774 to 1850) Duke of Cambridge, who was the seventh son of the supposedly insane King George III.

The Cambridge Hotel along with the Garrison Arms which stood 2 doors away was flooded and damaged by the Great Sheffield Flood on Friday, 11th of March, 1864, when around 250 Sheffield inhabitants lost their lives.

The pub was a brick built, one room, John Smiths house and was demolished in the mid 1990s for road widening purposes. Sadly missed by many people.

Cambridge Hotel

73 Coalpit Lane, Sheffield
(aka Cambridge Arms, Yellow Lion)

Canine Inn

34 Lambert Street, Sheffield

Canning Tavern

15 Bower Street, Sheffield
(open 1820s)

Cannon Hall Hotel

Barnsley Road, Firvale, Sheffield 5

Cannon Hotel

30 Castle Street, Sheffield 3

Canteen (Barracks)

Langsett Road, Sheffield 6

Canterbury Hall

19 Pinfold Street, Sheffield
(1830s-1890s)

Canterbury Hotel

29 Egerton Street, Sheffield
(1830s-1900s)

Canterbury has been an important place since Roman times and became a place of pilgrimage after the murder of Thomas à Becket in December 1170. In fact the famous Geoffrey Chaucer's Canterbury Tales are short stories about these pilgrims.

Captive Queen
131 Guildford Avenue, Sheffield

The pub stands opposite the Manor House, where Mary Queen of Scots was once held prisoner.

Carbrook Hall
537 Attercliffe Common, Sheffield 9

The Carbrook Hall, was first mentioned in about 1170 when it was said to be the home of the Blunt family. Some four hundred years later, during the reign of Elizabeth I, we find it under the control of a Richard Fenton and then the Bright family, and by 1637 the Hall was owned by a John Bright, who fought, with some distinction alongside Oliver Cromwell, during the English Civil War, 1642-1649. Bright was appointed Governor of the Sheffield Castle, still standing at that time, after the Roundheads had won it from Royalist control in 1644. He left the army as a colonel in 1650, and was made a baronet by Charles II. He died in 1688.

From this point onwards the Hall passed down through the centuries until in the 19th century it became the Common Beer House and since then it has stayed a public house. The parlour is the centre of attraction, but I am led to believe the Black Oak room upstairs, which is not open for the public it the better of the two rooms. Treat yourself and go down Attercliffe and see the Jacobean fireplace, Elizabethan plastering and oak panelling, its well worth it. This Stones pub has a sign outside saying it is the most haunted pub in Sheffield. John Bright, in his puritan, roundhead garb, is said to haunt the Carbrook Hall. There are also several other ghostly figures, who are said to appear on occasions.

The Carbrook Hall has stood through many of England's, as well as, Sheffield's historic events. From green open countryside, through the civil war, the industrial revolution, having bodies swept past it during the Sheffield Flood, two World Wars - including the blitz, the depression and the Attercliffe Common slum clearances of the 60s, to, hopefully, the coming of a new age in the East End.

The word Carbrook is said to be a Saxon name meaning meadow stream.

Caravan Tavern
Little Sheffield

Cardigan Tavern
47 Ball Street, Sheffield 3

Probably named after Lord Cardigan, another of Sheffield pub connections to the Crimean War.

Carlisle Hotel
5 Carlisle Street East, Sheffield 4
(built around 1864)

Carlisle Tavern
67 Carlisle Street East, Sheffield 4
(1860s-1910)

Carlton
563 Attercliffe Road, Sheffield 9

Small, obviously, resilient pub, to have survived whilst most around it have floundered, due to less and less people dwelling in the area and with the local steel industry failing as well.

Carlton
17 Corporation St, Sheffield 1 (open c1830)

Carater's Rest
123 Matilda Street, Sheffield (opened 1820s)

Carousel

26 Burncross Road, Sheffield

Carwood Hotel

8 Carlisle Street East, Sheffield 4

Cask & Cutler

1 Henry Street, Sheffield (aka Wellington)

The Wellington, built in the 1850 was believed to have been the brewery tap for the Don Brewery. A. H. Smith & Co. owned the Don Brewery and for their 60 years partnership the Wellington thrived.

In 1916 Tennant Brothers, bought out Smiths, but as often happens in the brewing industry the all powerful bigger brewers gobble up everything and in 1962 Tennants was taken over by Whitbreads.

But the pub still goes on, and is a free house now, called the Cask and Cutler.

Castle House

1 Water Lane, Sheffield

This name, the Castle or Castle House, has been a pub name for centuries. It would be nice to connect it to the fact that An Englishman's Home is his Castle, a phrase that's been in use for over 300 years, but more likely it is because as in Sheffields' case there was a castle in very close proximity.

Castle Inn

46 Snig Hill, Sheffield 1

Castle Inn

111 Dykes Hall Road, Sheffield 6

Castle Inn

Castle Row, Twentywell Road, Sheffield

Originally two cottages built for the Irish Navvies who built the Bradway Tunnel, later made into one building.

Catherine Arms
29-31 Catherine Street, Sheffield 3

The Catherine Arms in the Burngreave/Pitsmoor area was one of only two Public Houses in the Sheffield area to double up as grocery shops. At one time you could walk through from the shop to the public bar.

It is unsure whether the name Catherine came from the street the pub was built on or being in close proximity to the Catholic Church of the same name, it could have been named more exotically after Saint Catherine of Alexandria who was martyred in the eleventh century.

This public house was stripped of its license in November 1995. It was axed following complaints about excessive noise and inquires revealing that its licensee was absent too often from the premises. This troubled public house linked several times with crack cocaine drug dealings had been under threat of closure since September. In the local newspaper the Sheffield Star, an Attercliffe police inspector said: "It was known to attract drug dealers, and it would be nice to think there may be a downturn in drug dealing in the area in light of the decision".

Cavendish
West Street, Sheffield

Opened in 1997 as a Scream theme bar like the Globe, Howard Street.
Cavendish is the family name of the dukes of Devonshire whose family seat is at Chatsworth.

Centre Spot
Frecheville, Sheffield

Ceylon Hotel
16 Wellington Street, Sheffield (1820s-1917)

Champs
Ecclesall Road, Sheffield

Chandlers Arms
Bull Stakes, Sheffield 1 (late 1700s)

Chandos
215-217 Rockingham Street, Sheffield 1

This public house was opened in around 1825 and took its name from Richard Grenville who it was said was created Duke of Buckingham and Chandos in 1822. His wife, Anne was the daughter of the 3rd Duke of Chandos.
Another reference is to one or other of the barons Chandos. The first such baron was ennobled in 1554.
There was also a Sir John Chandos, the most famous knight fighting for Edward III at the time of Crecy.

Chantrey Arms
11 Bramall Lane, Sheffield 2
(differing time of opening 1830, or 1880)

Chantrey Arms
733-735 Chesterfield Road, Sheffield 8

Chantrey, the man, has been called the "greatest sculptor that England has ever produced", praise indeed. Chantrey was born in Norton, then a small village just outside Sheffield, where as a young man he started his artistic career. He came to the 'big city' and rented a room at 24 Paradise Square, where his work flourished. He moved to London and spent most of the rest of his life there, but always requested upon his death to be returned to Norton Churchyard for burial. Many of Chantrey's works are on show in Sheffield Cathedral.

Charles Turnbull

Liberty Hill, Stannington, (aka Turnbull)

Mr Turnbull was formerly a director of the Tetley Walker brewery.

Charlie Parkers

Charles Street, Sheffield

Charlotte Tavern

17 Charlotte Street, Sheffield

Chequers

35 Fargate, Sheffield 1 (opened in 1830s)

An ancient tavern sign which was probably brought to Britain by the Romans. Historical evidence from Pompeii suggests that it was already in use there, perhaps referring to a game such as draughts played on the premises. This sign was later associated with a money table and indeed the 'exchequer' originally meant a kind of chessboard.
Also since 1921 Chequers has been the country seat of British Prime Ministers.

Chequers

64 Coalpit Lane, Cambridge Street, Sheffield (aka Old Cow) (opened in 1820s)

Chequers

68 Weigh Lane, Sheffield 2

Chequers

19 Rough Bank, Sheffield

Chequers

61 Wicker, Sheffield (1820s-1900s)

Chequers

2-4 Meadow Street, Sheffield

Cherry Tree

Carterknowle Road, Sheffield 11

The Cherry Tree Public House was built in 1961 on Cherry Tree Farm. The adjoining Knab Farm Residential estate was built about the same time.
It is reputed to have a very kindly, likeable ghost named Grace who sometimes appears standing behind the bar. (Wonder if she's got a spirit license?)

Chester Castle

62 Eldon Street, Sheffield

Clarence Hotel

109 Clarence Street, Sheffield

Most Clarence public houses are generally named after William IV, who before he became king was known as the Duke of Clarence. Or maybe, Duke of Clarence, Richard III's brother who was drowned in a vat of Malmsey (a sweet wine).

Clarence Hotel

133 Pond Street, Sheffield
(1820s-1900s)

Clarence Hotel

1 Paradise Square, Sheffield
(1820s-1920s)

Claymore

Arundel Gate, Sheffield 1 (aka Venue)

A commonly used pub name in Scotland, but not many other (if any) public houses in England have the name Claymore, which means great sword in Gaelic. Sheffield has some right to use the name though, because it did make these "Great Swords" at one time. In more modern times the term Claymore has been applied to the basket hilted swords worn by officers of the Highland regiments.

Cleakum Inn

Malin Bridge, Sheffield 6

The second pub to be swept away during the Sheffield Flood of 1864.
The name means to grab eagerly, probably a reference to the speed with which the beer was lifted off the bar.

Cleakham Inn

Cornish Place, Sheffield
(opened 1800s)

Cornish Place was supposedly sited off Cornish Street but this old inn's actual position is unknown and the only known fact was that the landlord was the owner of a bowling green, which was attached to the Cleakham. A Thomas Hobley or Thomas Copley was the landlord in 1839.

Clifton Beerhouse

79 Clifton Street, corner of Pickering Street, Sheffield
(opened in 1770s)

Clock

41 Porter Street, Sheffield
(1830s-1920s)

Clockmakers Arms

122 West Bar, Sheffield 3
(1830s-1890s)

Closed Shop

Commonside, Walkley, Sheffield 6

The name is a humourous reminder of the time the pub had to close because the license had not been renewed.

Clown and Monkey

Paradise Square, Sheffield

The exact location of the Clown & Monkey in Paradise Square is not now known, but in 1852 many an inhabitant of the Square knew exactly where this rowdy and raucous public house was sited. A reference in the Sheffield Independent stated that it was the "resort of thieves, dog fighters and the lowest possible company", it went on to say, "that after one quarrel about 150 people turned out into the square to watch a fight between two antagonists, all of this taking place in the middle of a market day".

Club Gardens Tavern

Club Gardens, Sheffield

Club Garden Inn

60 Lansdowne Road, Sheffield 11
(1830s-1967)

A very appropriate name as this public house was situated in or on, an area that once had over 160 club gardens.

Club Mill Inn

39 Smithfield, Sheffield
(aka Cornmill Inn, Old Clubmill Inn)

In the late 18th century a corn mill was built by the River Don at Neepsend. Near this site a public house was built and called the Corn Mill Inn, later to be changed to Club Mill Inn. Possibly from this Club Mill Lane was named, and still remains today which is more than can be said of the mill which failed and the inn which was closed in 1930.

Coach & Horses
756 Attercliffe Road, Sheffield (aka Barrel)

This was one of the oldest public houses in Attercliffe, it was opened as the Barrel around 1819 and changed its name to Coach and Horses in 1838, when coaches started to pass by. At this time there was a coach four times a week to Retford and Worksop, a daily service to Doncaster and an hourly service to Rotherham.
Now a small hotel.

Coach & Horses
16 Waingate, Sheffield 1 (1820s-1900s)

Coach & Horses
156 Gibraltar Street, Sheffield (1820s-1900s)

Coach & Horses
39 Water Lane, Sheffield (aka Coach)
(1830s-1890s)

Coach & Horses
147 Carlisle Street, Sheffield (1840s-1930s)

Coach & Horses
13 Station Road, Chapeltown

Coachmakers Arms
South Street, Sheffield

Coach and Six
Haymarket, Sheffield (opened 1790s)

Cobden View Hotel
40 Cobden View Road, Walkley, Sheff 10

Named after Richard Cobden, of Corn Laws repeal fame.

Cock Inn
5 Bridge Hill, Oughtibridge

Cock Inn
59 Hollis Croft, Sheffield

In around 1784 John Beardshaw started the 'Beardshaw Funding Society', at the Cock Inn and a few years later moved his funding society and himself to the Ball Inn on Hawley Croft. A Jonathan Beardshaw, possibly a son, then moved it to the Victoria on High Street and from this point onwards it was known as the Victoria Club Funding Society.
In the late 18th century this pub was used by Messrs Bardwell and Son for their auctions along with other public houses in the locale.

Cock

High Street, Sheffield (aka Star, Carlton)

The Cock is supposedly the oldest traceable public house of the old Sheffield township.

In around 1590 it was owned by a Richard Skinner and in 1593 he sold it to a William Shemeld (described as a Yeoman and Innholder) who kept it for about 10 years then sold it on to the Barlow family, who were chapmen (cutlery salesmen), and they kept it for four or five generations. It is said after a few more owners it closed as a public house in around 1750. Shortly after it was known as the Ceylon Café, then it became a private residence, from which time very little is known and even its siting was not certain.

This seems to make a nonsense of the fact that most references to the Star, and later the Carlton in 1901, both on the High Street were supposedly sited in or on the old Cock premises.

It is now said that it was directly facing Mulberry Street, just about where Cavells now stands.

Cock

26 The Wicker, Sheffield (opened 1820s)

The pub name cock is generally, but not definitely, connected to the fact that the premises used to have cock fighting in its yards or even in one of its rooms. The other explanation of the name cock could have arisen from the fact there used to be a drink called cock-ale, which was ale mixed with the jelly of minced meat of a boiled cock, lovely.

Cock

76 Broad Street, Sheffield (1830s-1910)

Cock

11 Paradise Square, Sheffield 1
(aka Old Cock, possibly Wig and Pen)
(1825-1900)

A lamentable drink problem was abundant in the early to mid 19th century around the Township of Sheffield, and the Cock along with other hostelries in the square was as culpable as any for supplying the alcohol. "Get drunk for a penny, dead drunk for tu'pence and have clean straw for nothing", this was the wording on the signage on one of the public houses in Paradise square.

The Cock is a symbol of St Peter.

Cock and Bottle

46 Hawley Croft, Sheffield
(aka Eagle Tavern)

Cocked Hat Inn

73-75 Worksop Road, Sheffield 9

It used to stand in the dark shadow that Brown Baileys Steel works cast, and definitely benefited from the shiftworkers who worked there, as they filtered into the 'Hat' when their shifts came to an end.

Times move on and this refurbished Marston's public house has moved on well. It has justifiably won quite a few honours and in 1987 claimed CAMRA's pub of the year award and has also claimed many a monthly good beer awards. It serves good value meals and is situated very near to the Don Valley Stadium, and when events do take place the Cocked Hat is generally full to capacity.

Colliers Arms

37 Duke Street, Sheffield
(aka Park Tavern) (1830s-1900s)

Columbia Tavern

10 Forkham Street, Sheffield

Commercial Hotel

34 Button Lane, Sheffield
(1790s-1908)

Commercial Hotel

4-6 Bank Street, Sheffield

Commercial Hotel

104 Old Haymarket, Sheffield

Commercial Inn/Hotel

3 Sheffield Road, Sheffield 9

The Commercial Inn is situated on the corner of Weedon Street and Sheffield Road. Built on land known as Woodcrofts in 1870 the Inn was originally a dwelling house and brewery sited in the township of Tinsley, Borough of Rotherham, but later pulled into Sheffield's ever widening boundaries. The Inn was for many years the haunt of the transport workers, whose terminal for the tramcars was sited next door until it was closed in the mid 50s. The pub itself consists of three rooms two small ones on the ground floor and a slightly larger one upstairs. The latter room being used mostly for darts and the occasional function. One landlord, Reg Williams, came from the Royal Marines in 1952/3 and served the locals through good and bad times for 38 consecutive years until 1990, when he retired. The custom now seems sparse at all the old Attercliffe pubs, but the Commercial still somehow manages to keep its business ticking over nicely. With the upgrading of the East End the pub may well survive into the Millennium. It did close for a period of time but has since, thankfully, reopened.

Commercial Tap

3 Commercial Street, Sheffield

Commercial Hotel

107-109 Station Road, Chapeltown

The Hotel opened around 1890 and was originally a Strout's Brewery house. Strout's, a well known thriving brewery at the turn of the century, was bought out by Tennants Brother who themselves fell takeover prey to the Whitbreads conglomerate.

Compass

38 Orchard Street, Sheffield

Usually a reference to the compass or compasses which appear in the arms of the masons, joiners or carpenters. Also it may be interpreted as the compass used by mariners to guide their ships.

Consort

215 Eyre Street, Sheffield (1800s-1900s)

Coopers Hotel

Brightside Lane, Sheffield 9

The Coopers Company dates from the 16 century. The ancient craft of making barrels, casks and tubs from staves and hoops now hardly survives in the brewing industry.

Corner Pin

84 Blonk Street, Sheffield

The general reference to this pub name is from the game of skittles, the 'corner pin' is the outside pin and the most difficult to knock down. Sometimes it is so named because of its position on the corner of a street, road, etc.

Corner Pin

80 Allen Street, Sheffield (1830s-1900s)

Corner Pin

23 Burlington Street, Sheffield (opened in the first quarter of 19th century)

Corner Pin

235 Carlisle Street East, Sheffield 4

The Corner Pin has stood the test of time, over 160 years to be precise. It was first licensed to sell beer in 1840 and is still doing so today. It was one of 26 public houses, serving the steel industry, along a three-quarter mile stretch of Carlisle Street, which started at the corner of Spital Hill and Carlisle Street, where the Midland Hotel stood and ended at the Alexandra Hotel at Newhall Road. This particular Corner Pin is said to have a ghost who likes to turn the lights on in the middle of the night and footfalls can sometimes be heard.

Corner Pin

14 The Wicker, Sheffield

Cornish Inn

46 Cornish Street, Sheffield
(opened in early 19th century)

Corporation Inn

37 Corporation Street, Sheffield 3
(aka Swarf 'Ole)

Corporation Arms

27 West Bar Green, Sheffield 3

Cossack

45 Howard Street, Sheffield 1
(aka But'n Ben)

Close to the Sheffield Hallam University this newish looking prefabricated building actually dates back nearly 200 years to the late 18th century. The Cossack, during the 1960s and 1970s, was the forerunner of the gay bars of today. Unknown if the pub is named after the southern Russian skilled warriors of this name or the Derby Winner of 1847. But being as the Cossacks fought on the Nazi's side during WWII, only 50 years ago, we will invariably be told it is from the Derby Winner theory.
In its recent history the Cossack was called the But'n Ben, this refers to the opposite ends of a house or passage or sometimes a small country cottage.

Cow and Calf Inn

88 Skew Hill Lane, Grenoside

Large and imposing converted farmhouse, which was originally built in 1798, and converted to a public house in 1978 with one bar and four separate drinking areas including a no smoking room. The earliest reference to the original site is in 1161 when it was known as the Cross House.

Crabtree

121 Scotland Street, Sheffield

Crabtree Vaults

74 Langsett Road, Sheffield
(aka Old Crabtree Vaults)

This building is now used to house a dental surgery. It is situated across from the bottom of Burgoyne Road.

Cremorne Hotel

185 London Road, Sheffield 2

Another Sheffield pub that was named after a Derby winner, this one from the year 1872.

Cricket Ball

2 Savile Street east, 38 Sutherland Street, Sheffield 4 (aka Victoria Arches, Cricket Inn)

This public house changed its name from the Victoria Arches to the Cricket Ball or Cricket Inn, in the First World War, 1914-1918. It probably changed names because it had been known locally for many years as the cricket ball because of the local vicinity of the Gentlemen's Cricket Ground which was a forerunner of Bramall Lane. This cricket ground was part of a common known as Local Fields.

Cricket Inn

317 Cricket Inn Road, Sheffield 2

This mock Tudor, Stones public house consisted of 2 large rooms and was built in around 1936 to serve the local estate, and at one time was a thriving local. It was noted for a collection of model ships it had on display. It fell into some disrepair in the 80s and was never brought back up to standard and was finally demolished in the mid 1990s. The name the Cricketers probably comes from a cricket ground which was adjacent to this location, it was first used in 1826 and a team of Yorkshire cricketers (before the Yorkshire County Cricket Club was founded) played a Norfolk X1 in 1833. The ground was then transformed into the Hyde Park Greyhound Stadium and eventually after the demolition of the dog track, used as a recreation area for the Hyde Park flats.

Cricket Inn

Penny Lane, Totley, Sheffield

Set snugly in the original Totley Bents on the south west boundary of Sheffield the Cricket Inn is an old farmhouse, first licensed to sell alcohol in 1889, this mostly to bolster the Irish Navvies who built the nearby famous Totley railway tunnel.

The present Barn Room was once used as a mortuary when a typhoid outbreak hit the Irishmen and they were laid out in this room.

Cricketers Arms

106 Bramall Lane, Sheffield 2

Cricketers Inn

37 Sheldon Street, Sheffield

Crimea Tavern

63 Earl Street, Sheffield (1830s-1900s)

Cromwell View

80 Spital Street, 19 Verdon Street, Sheff 3

Oliver Cromwell was well supported in Sheffield and its outlying areas during the English Civil War, and this could be the reason for such a pub name.

Crooked Billet

62 Scotland Street, Sheffield

This is often associated, as you would imagine, in Sheffield with the steel industry. But more likely it is a reference to the billet (also called a ragged staff) being used in its older sense of a thick piece of wood used as a head cracking weapon. It was said to have been in common use amongst the protagonists at Towton, near York in 1461, the fiercest battle in the War of the Roses, at which over 28,000 lives were lost, more than 20,000 of them Lancastrians.

Cross Daggers

**Cross Daggers Yard,
26 Fruit Market, High Street, Sheffield**

The Cross Daggers in different reference books has been sited on Commercial Street, Change Alley and Cross Daggers Yard, and it is said when the Kings Head, Change Alley was extended, at the turn of the 19th century, it was built on the Cross Daggers site. A passage from Fruit Market to Norfolk Street was called Cross Daggers yard on an old Ordnance Survey map of 1853.

In the late 18th century, Anne Asline was owner, Robert Sandy came next in 1791, and in 1828 it was kept by Richard Greenwood. By 1847 it may have been used as a warehouse.

The cross daggers is a reference to the badge of the Hallamshire Cutlers Company.

Cross Daggers

Fleece Yard, Wharf St, Waingate, Sheffield

This Cross Daggers was bought along with the Golden Fleece by a man named Francis Colley in c1850. He then promptly closed them down with the "expressed intention of stopping a nuisance".

No other reference can be found to this Cross Daggers so it may well be the one addressed previously, because this also ceased trading about the same time.

Cross Daggers

52 West Bar Green, Sheffield (1790s-1920s)

Cross Daggers

14 Market Square, Woodhouse, Sheffield

The Cross Daggers public house, the stocks and the base of the market cross are the only remnants of this medieval site. The old buildings, farms and old workers cottages have all been demolished to site the housing estate that is now part of the new Woodhouse.

Cross Guns

122 Sharrow Lane, Sheffield 11

Cross Guns

115 Franklin Street, Sheffield
(aka Great Guns)

Cross Inn

Low Bradfield, near Sheffield

An old cross was found in a field many years ago. Part of this cross, with its carved celtic knotwork, is now to be found in High Bradfield Church. The Cross Inn is said to be built on or near the site of the find.

The Cross Inn is now a private dwelling.

Cross Keys

400 Handsworth Road, Sheffield 13

The pub itself is said to date back to the 13th century when one William de Lovetot had it built along with the Church. The pub building was the church house and used by the chaplains. It was reputedly used as a schoolroom for about 200 years and then sold for £43 before becoming a public house in the mid 19th century. It has a dubious distinction of being one of the few pubs in England situated in a cemetery, the old nearby St Mary's Church graveyard, to be exact.

The tap room which is the oldest part of the building has one timber that is reputedly dated from the 13th century. The present building is probably dated from around the 17th century.

The "Keys" is supposedly haunted by the ghost of the Grey Lady who reputedly lingers in and along a series of tunnels that runs from the pub across the road and into what used to be an old farm or Handsworth Hall. These tunnels were probably built for the quick exit of any Catholic priests, during England's change to protestantism.

Mary Queen of Scots reputedly stayed here for some while, but there is no real evidence to validate this, although rumour does have it that a tunnel did connect to the Manor Lodge, a mile away.

Cross Keys
9 Bower Street, Sheffield

Cross Keys
91 Pea Croft, Sheffield
(aka Filesmiths Arms)

Cross Scythes (old)
Baslow Road, Totley

Well over 300 years old, this inn was first opened by a farmer and scythe maker called Samuel Hopkinson, and was so named because scythes were manufactured in this area.

The Cross Scythes served as a temporary church for over 8 years until a church was built in the area.

Cross Scythes Inn
145-147 Derbyshire Lane, Sheffield 8

The old building was demolished in 1939 when it was replaced by the present building, photographed.

Crossfield Tavern
201 Mortomley Lane, Chapeltown, Sheffield

Crosspool Tavern
468 Manchester Road, Sheffield 10

Toby Restaurants owns the Crosspool Tavern and as recently as 1996 spent over £200,000 on refurbishment. As with all alterations the locals fear that their pub will lose its "feel" - not so with this transformation. It has kept its olde worlde feel with its oak panelling, fire places, brass fitting and pictures. Also in the restaurant section it has a no smoking policy which has won a Roy Castle Clean Air Award.

Crown
52 Harvest Lane, Sheffield

The pub name/title, Crown has possibly been in existence for well over 600 years. It was easy to depict and a short succinct name, its only drawback over the period of time was when old Oliver Cromwell came on the scene with his roundhead new model army. Nearly all these signs then disappeared, as did most things to do with the monarchy. They came back in abundance after the Restoration.

Crown
21 Pinstone Street, Sheffield
(1790s-1890s)

Crown
Attercliffe Common, Sheffield
(aka Old Crown)

Crown

15 Duke Street, Sheffield (aka Old Crown)
(1820s 1900s)

Crown

31 Grindlegate, Sheffield

Crown

High Street, Sheffield (1700s-1770s)

This public house was probably situated close to where
Bradford and Bingley are now, atop York Street.

An 'Inn of High Repute', was how it was described in
1710, at that time the Sheffield Town Trustees and the
River Don Navigation Proprietors used the Crown as a
meeting place and would have been entertained by the
then landlord and Master Cutler of Sheffield, John
Morton. Morton is reputed to have had the Archbishop of
York stay at his premises and also supplied the Duke of
Norfolk with crockery, pewter, plates and table linen when
he gave a series of dinners for the leading Sheffield
inhabitants. When Morton died, in 1744, his wife retired
and put the Crown up for sale. She put an advertisement
in the Leeds Mercury, and it stated "to let, that very good
accustomed Inn known by the sign of the 'Crown' near to
the church gates and with stabling for 24 horses." It shows
that the Crown must have been a very sizeable and
desirable property.

Crown

2 Walkley Bank Road, Sheffield 6

Crown

52 Silver Street Head, Sheffield

Crown

28 The Wicker, Sheffield 3

Crown

33 Holly Street, Sheffield

Crown

43 Summerfield Street, Sheffield

Crown Inn

116 Neepsend Lane, Sheffield 3

The Crown was what is termed as the tap for the Stones
brewery on Rutland Road, Neepsend Lane for many
years. The 'Tap' being the on site beer facility, but as in
most cases it was also open to the public for selling the
breweries wares.

The Crown as a public house closed in 1992 and became
the hospitality area for the Cannon Brewery itself,
generally used for guests or customers on guided tours of
this famous beer making facility.

The brewery was started by a farmer named William
Stones, in partnership with Joseph Watts. They originally
started with a small brewery on the corner of Acorn Street
and Shalesmoor, and it's at this premises that the
partnership came to an end when Stones bought Watts out
in 1856.

Stones then bought the premises at Rutland Road in 1860,
and this stayed as the Cannon Brewery for 138 years,
supplying Sheffield and a much wider area. In 1950s
Stones bought the assets and 100 pubs of Mappins
Masboro Old Brewery in Rotherham and long established
beer bottlers, Wards of Swinton. Stones also took joint
control of the Sheffield Free Brewery with Tennant
Brothers

Crown Inn

21 Meadowhall Road, Sheffield 9

Former Sheffield Wednesday player David 'Bronco' Layne has been the landlord of the Crown for many years. Layne, unfortunately for the Owls, was caught up in the sixties bribes scandal which ended the career of not only David but also England internationals Peter Swan and, then Everton player, Tony Kay. All three were tremendous players and Layne himself scored 53 goals in just over 70 appearances for Wednesday. No better centre forward has played for the Owls since his untimely departure.

Crown Inn

54 Campo Lane, Lee Croft, Sheffield 1

Over the door of this pub were the date, 1726 and initials I T B. It was the residence of Isaac Barnes, one of the oldest cutlery manufacturers in Sheffield.

Crown

6 West Bar Green, Sheffield 3

Crown Inn

88 Blackburn Road, Sheffield

Situated on Blackburn Road, around the back of Meadowhall, between what is left of the steelworks and the M1 motorway. A Tetleys pub, the Crown, up until '79 was a little 3 roomed normal backstreet pub, well liked by locals but with a little bit of a downbeat feel about it. But then the tap room and lounge were made into one smart and sizeable open plan area with a central bar. The back garden was turned into an aviary and pets' corner, containing many exotic species of bird including peacocks, Japanese quails, lovebirds, finches and rabbits.

Crown Inn

Hillfoot Road, Totley

Transformed from three cottages into a public house in about 1727 it was on land owned by Lord Middleton who was then Lord of the Manor of Totley. In the late 18th century a lady called Dorothy Dalton ran the Crown for many years before her son, Thomas took over the tenancy from her. Thomas Dalton, as in most cases at this time, also carried on his tradesman's work as a firebrick maker. In 1936 the final meeting, at the Crown, of the Barlow hunt took place.

Crown Inn

53 Bessemer Road, Sheffield 9

Crown Inn

23 Blue Boy Street, Sheffield 3 (1830s-1938)

Crown

Lee Croft, Sheffield 3 (opened 1726)

Crown Inn

2 Albert Road, Heeley, Sheffield 8

Built in the mid to late 19th century the Crown was nicknamed the palace of varieties. This name is supposedly taken from the fact that on any given night you could enter and find a Duke to a pauper sat side by side, probably a slight exaggeration. Some would say there has not been much change then, except the well frequented off sales has disappeared.

Crown Inn
87/89 Forncett Street, Sheffield (open c1865)

In 1916 during the world's first ever air raid on civilian populous, the Zeppelin L22 flew over Sheffield after crossing the North Sea and dropped 36 bombs on the city. The bomb that caused most damage landed not 50 yards from the Crown in Cossey Street and this high explosive device killed 13 people including some children.

The Crown itself is set in, or rather hidden away in, the heart of Sheffield's steel industry, just off Carlisle Street east. Well worth seeking out though.

At one time it had a drinks dispenser over the bar which was an old cart wheel with all the bottles attached, around the metal edge.

Crown Inn
41 Carlisle Road, Sheffield

Crown Inn
109 Corby Street, Sheffield (1860s-1920s)

Crown & Anchor
Fitzwilliam Street, Sheffield

The man stood at the entrance to the Crown and Anchor is the landlord J Arthur Pashley.

Crown & Anchor
18 Stanley Street, Sheffield (opened 1830s)

This is the emblem of the Lord High Admiral, but also the arm badge of the Royal Naval Petty Officer. The Crown and Anchor in the Strand, London was where the tune of American anthem 'The Star Spangled Banner' was written in the 1790s.

Crown & Cushions
1 Chapel Road, Burncross

Crown & Cushion
21 Old Street, Park, Sheffield (opened 1820s)

In the 1830s this public house was run/owned by a Mr Abraham Amory, whose family were owners of the Blue Bell on High Street for many years.

Generally the image of a crown resting on a cushion is showing the Crown Jewels being carried for the Coronation or some other such events.

Crown & Cushion
23 Broad Lane, Sheffield (opened in 1841)

Crown & Cushion
Sycamore Street, Tudor Street, Sheffield (opened in 1780s)

The Crown & Cushion was run by one Benjamin Crofts in 1789, and it was he who started the Revolution Sick Society. Its members paid £0-1s-4d a month into a kitty, of which £0-1s-2d was put away for cover/insurance in case the participant was to become ill or infirm and could then be drawn, the other tu'pence was for beer.

Mr Crofts must have been seen as a trustworthy man for a Society to have originated at his establishment, but in the late 18th century many banks had failed in Sheffield and people would put more faith in someone who they knew. The money was kept in a strongbox at the inn and considered by all to be safer than the banks.

Crown and Cross Daggers
35 West Bar Green, Sheffield 3

Crown and Glove

96 Uppergate, Stannington, Sheffield 6

"A particularly pleasant pub with a sense of well being" - this was how it was described by the Royal Institute of British Architects upon a visit whilst compiling a series of reports on pubs in the Sheffield area. Most of the locals, of which there are plenty, wouldn't quarrel with that appraisal of this 18th century coaching house. Atop one of Sheffield's seven hills it has excellent views of Sheffield and the Rivelin Valley. It is told by Keith Ravenhall, landlord for about 20 years, that the "top house" as it is known locally is the highest point for 2000 miles until you reach the Urals in the USSR (or whichever soviet satellite they are now in). This could well be true, as the village of Stannington does seem to get higher winds and more snow than almost any other area of Sheffield.

The Crown & Glove has 2/3 rooms, one a cosy well lit room, where it's more the order of the day to play dominoes or crib than the other pastimes that seem to have sprung up in pubs these days (no video games, pool, dartboard or one armed bandits here). Quizzes seem the only modern idiom the pub has taken to, with two or three a week. On the walls in this room they have a range of photographs, sketches, watercolours and a centrepiece giant oil painting by Joe Scarborough, all of the public house itself.

The other room is more sedate in its lighting and it has a room off at a slightly higher level (in times gone by used as the scullery). In this area they serve meals at dinner time. (all reasonably priced and very tasty). These rooms have a vast range of brasses, and in the hallway is a photograph from the turn of the century of a bus station which used to be situated in front of the Crown & Glove. It is said it was made into a public house by converting a number of cottages, and around this time a man named Belgrave Goodison was the landlord. It was then further modernised about 1962 transforming it into the comfortable public house it is today.

The name is a reference to the gauntlet thrown down on Coronation day daring anyone to dispute the right of succession.

Crown and Thistle

Fargate, Sheffield

Crow's Nest Hotel

High Pavement, St Johns Rd, Hyde Park, Sheffield

Usually the sign depicts a naval type of crow's nest, the look out position on the mast head of a ship.

Crystal Palace

56 Town Head Street, Sheffield (1790s-1890s)

Being as this public house was built before the Crystal Palace of Great Exhibition fame, it probably had an original name. Unfortunately, this is unknown.

The mainly glass building commissioned by Prince Albert, the original Crystal Palace, was designed by Joseph Paxton, but it was destroyed by fire in 1936. Its foundations are still visible to this day.

Cup

52 Button Lane, Sheffield

Cup

19 Paternoster Row, Sheffield

Cup

112 Sorby Street, Sheffield (1860s-1930s)

Cup

7 Market Street, Sheffield (aka Old Cup, Market Tav) (1820s-1900s)

Cup

120 Duke Street, Sheffield

Cup

11-15 or 17 Dun Street, Sheffield 3 (aka Gardeners Rest)

Cuthbert Arms

296 Langsett Rd, Sheffield 6

Cuthbert Arms
Cuthbert Road, Sheffield 6

Cuthbert Bank Hotel
164 Langsett Rd, Sheffield 6

Cutlers Arms
66 Edward Street, Sheffield

This region, Sheffield, is well known for its manufacture of knives and other cutting instruments, hence the name.

Cutlers Arms
88 Fargate, Sheffield

The landlord in 1839 was a John Daft.

Cutlers Arms
38 Fargate, Sheffield

Cutlers Inn
86 Fargate, Sheffield

Cutlers Inn
Hillfoot, Sheffield

In 1841 Thomas Shirton was landlord of this Inn but unfortunately the actual location is unknown.

Cutlers Hall
Church Street or Church Lane, Sheffield

The Cutlers Hall was housed in several premises before settling in its present day site. It was based in the Cutlers Inn at 86 Fargate and originally had a license to sell alcohol from around the 1750s when William Truelove was its first tenant. After a while the Cutlers found it inconvenient to have the building used as a public house so they gave the then incumbent tenant John Thompson notice to quit. If a drink or further discussion was needed after their meetings they would take it into the snug parlour of the nearby Bird in Hand, on Church Street.

Cutlers Arms
7 New Church Street, Sheffield

In 1839 the Cutlers Arms was sited at Number 3 New Church Street and Joseph Green was the landlord.

Cutlers Arms
74 Worksop Road, Sheffield 9

'Early 19th century property, it comprised of a Public House, yard, garden, stable, workshop, orchard and a skittle alley'. This is how it was described when it was put up for sale.

Cutlers Arms
Leighton Road, Sheffield

Cyclops
101 Carlisle Street, Sheffield (1860s-1920s)

The origin of the word cyclops is from Greek mythology.

Daniels Rest

29 Cliffe Street, Sheffield 11

Danville Hotel

1 Danville Street, Sheffield 4 (1880s-1920s)

David and Goliath

111 Devonshire Street, Sheffield 3
(opened around 1840)

Deep End

Langsett Road, Sheffield 6

The Old Hillsborough & Walkley Baths was converted into the aptly named Deep End in '98. It did seem around this time every building in Sheffield of any architectural interest seemed to be being turned into a Restaurant or Bar of some kind, but at least the Deep End tried to keep the feel of the old baths, which had been closed for some years. The swimming pool area is now a seated area with tables and chairs and sometimes doubles up as a dancefloor. The old original changing cubicles have been refurbished without much alteration to provide comfy seating booths. It has a 590 capacity, a vast number. At the moment, 1999, the Deep End has jam nights, soul nights, live bands, retro eighties, comedy nights, ladies nights, karaoke. Basically, if you like your pubs to be lively this is for you.

Deerstalker

Deer Park Road, Stannington, Sheffield 6

Supposedly named in reference to the deers which roamed this area. The area itself was at one time called Deerlands.

Dempsey's

1 Hereford Street, Sheffield 2

A small wine bar standing in the shadow of the Manpower Services Commission building, at the Moorfoot, from whom it gets a fair amount of its custom.

Denison Arms

33 Watery Street, 64 Malinda Street, Sheff
(aka possibly, Old House at Home)

Derby Hotel

53 Egerton Street, Sheffield

Derby Hotel

25 Lawson Street, Sheffield 3

Devonshire Arms

Division Street, Sheffield

Devonshire Arms

57 Eldon Street, Sheffield
(closed around 1917)

Devonshire Arms

Herries Road, Sheffield 5

This Devonshire Arms is synonymous with the same named pub which stood on the Moor. This Devonshire was sited on the Moorhead at 23 South Street, and was blitzed in 1940. It was rebuilt, in a fashion. The site was cleared and a prefab (prefabricated building) was built and was kept going by its fervent customers for a good few years. When the Sheffield city centre renovations took place, the public house took its license and opened a small premises on Herries Road. In the last 40 years it has been refurbished and refitted and is now a fine pub in its own right.

Devonshire Arms

11 High Street, Dore

This large, stone walled, 2 roomed public house was built in the year 1771. One room is now a restaurant and the other a large, panelled wall snooker room.
Supposedly the land on which the Devonshire now stands was a public water trough. One of the many variations on the name Dore is Duir, a welsh word meaning pure water.

Devonshire Arms

118 Ecclesall Road, Sheffield 11

The Devonshire Arms was one of four public houses in Sheffield having this name. This one, a Wards Brewery pub, is on Ecclesall Road facing the Brewery itself. The building was erected in c1840, and has the Duke of Devonshire's coat of arms etched into the impressive bay windows, and with the greenish tiles on the outside and its brass hand rails up to the doorway, it was an imposing sight. It was a quiet little pub with a wide range of customers, young (mainly students with the university being fairly close by) and old. But in the 1980s, the brewery built on a conservatory and made it more of a restaurant, still pleasant but has now a little less of its old quaintness.

Dickens

35 Carver Street, Sheffield 1

The Dickens is a large open plan bar with elevated areas and cubicles. Supposedly built as a school in 1812, the year Charles Dickens was born, the building was used as a warehouse for many years until renovation to its present status. Downstairs from the Dickens is the Le Metro.
It is fitting that the name Dickens is used for a public bar, as Dickens often used the alehouse in his stories. Throughout England, inns are named after places or characters in his book, e.g. Oliver Twist, Old Curiosity Shop, Copperfields, Bleak House.

Dog and Gun

108 Carver Street, Sheffield
(opened in late 18th century)

Dog and Gun

122 Trafalgar Street, Sheffield
(1820s-1900s)

Dog and Gun

18 Headford Street, Sheffield 3
(1830s-1960s)

Dog & Gun

102 Button Lane, Sheffield (1820s-1910s)

Dog & Gun

Nethershire, Shiregreen, Sheffield 5

In the 1833 Whites local directory this address was stated to be a beerhouse.

Dog and Partridge

56 Trippet Lane, Sheffield 1

This "very" Irish traditional pub set on Trippet Lane near the city centre, supposedly housed the former terrorist Eamonn De Valera, who was sprung from Lincoln prison by Michael Collins, during the Irish war for independence. De Valera was later to become three times prime minister and later the president of Eire. A romantic story but, probably untrue.

The pub itself is over 200 years old and with its Gaelic writings on the walls and elsewhere it is very much the original Irish themed pub in Sheffield.

Dog and Partridge

52 Coalpit Lane, Sheffield (aka Nell's Bar)

Dog and Partridge

112 West Bar, Sheffield 3

Dog and Partridge

575 Attercliffe Road, Sheffield 9

In 1860 John Backhouse was landlord of the 'Dog' and he along with a Mr Parker ran a foundry and in early 1860 patented a Spring Piston Plunger, which was widely advertised. This sideline subsidised his business. One hundred and forty years later the pub seems to be subsidised by its stripping, male and female activities.

Dolphin

34 Adsett Street, Sheffield
(opened mid 19th century)

Where the name comes from is obvious, but the reason for it being displayed on a pub sign is not so straightforward. Since 1648 the Royal Navy has used the word Dolphin for one ship or another. The dolphin also features in many a coat of arms, the Fishmongers Company and the Watermen and Lightermen Company. In France the son of the king was known as le Dauphin, this word is derived from dolphin. Or possibly it was named after a famous 19th century swimming club headquarters in Norwich.

Dolphin

37 Division Street, Sheffield (1840s-1900)

Domino

Egerton Street, Sheffield

The Domino opened in 1970 and as we go to print is supposedly being turned into student accommodation. It is/was situated on the corner of Egerton Street and Headford Street in the Broomhall area of Sheffield.

Possibly the pub name is a reference to the table game of dominoes or a kind of cloak, originally worn by priests.

Don Brewery

Penistone Road, Sheffield 6

Don Inn

67 Penistone Road, Sheffield 6
(opened around 1830 closed in 1960s)

Dore Junction

Abbeydale Road South, Sheffield

Dore Moor

Hathersage Road, Dore, Sheffield

Douglas Inn

209-211 Douglas Road, Sheffield 3

The Douglas was set atop the Parkwood Springs where the Sheffield Ski Village now stands. An area of Sheffield that hardly any public transport could reach because of a very low bridge at the bottom of the hill. The Douglas was one of only two public houses in Sheffield that sold groceries, which must have been a real boon to the locals, it was a long walk down the hill, even longer coming up it.

A William Proctor was landlord in the late fifties and early sixties, when a Children's Foundation film was made in this area, starring a certain Judy Geeson (the younger reader will not remember her) and the man who wrote the famous play the 'Ghost Train', Arnold Ridley. It was called 'Flight of the Pigeon'. So if you can find a copy of this film you may see the Douglas in all its glory.

Dove & Rainbow

25 Hartshead, Sheffield 1
(aka Butt'n'Ben, Tut'n'Shive)

This building is a new one, the old structure was on Watsons Walk along with other public houses the Shades Vaults and the Vine Vaults. In December 1783 a fire broke out and the landlord's wife a Mrs Oates and a young apprentice, who was lodging there, were trapped inside and burnt to death. A new building was built and stood for a great many years, until it was demolished to widen the road. The present building was erected in around 1957.

It was reputed to have been a regular haunt of the army recruiting groups that used to frequent Sheffield centre, in the late 18th and 19th centuries, looking for fit young Yorkshiremen to bolster the services.

The present day public house has a caravan perched at one end to accommodate the DJ and standing at the side of the newish Bankers Draft it seems a little run down. Whilst it is appreciated this may be the idea, let's hope the next alteration, which is sure to come, will make it more upbeat.

Generally, such named pubs are from the religious wording Rainbow and Dove.

Dove & Rainbow

172 Portobello, Sheffield

Dragon Inn

135 Infirmary Road, Sheffield 6

Druid Tavern

37 Bailey Street, Sheffield (1820s-1900s)

Duke Inn

7 Duke Street, Sheffield (1820s-1900s)

Duke of Clarence

7 Radford Row, Sheffield (1790s-1900s)

Duke of York
135 Main Road, Darnall, Sheffield 9

There have been many dukes of York since the title was created by Edmund in 1385. Richard Duke of Yorks' claim to the throne started the War of the Roses. The well known children's song about the grand old Duke of York refers in fact to Frederick Augustus the second son of George III. A slight misrepresentation is made in this song; the old Duke of York, was in fact only 31, he had 30,000 men not 10,000, and the area in Flanders where he commanded the English army was flat as a pancake, no hills in sight - a fine song though!

Dunlop Inn
Dunlop Street, Sheffield 9

Durham Ox
15 Cricket Inn Road, Sheffield 2

This and other public houses so named were to commemorate a superior type of Ox bred by one Charles Collings a well known cattle breeder from Ketton near Darlington. By the time the ox was six years old it weighed in at nearly two tons. Collings made more money by touring the great beast around the country than using it for the Sunday joint.

Durham Ox
51 or 53 Exchange Street, Sheffield

Dusty Miller
24 Nursery Street, Sheffield

This public house was sited near to Sheffield Castle nurseries.

Dusty Miller
69 Carlisle Street, Sheffield (1850s-1930s)

Eagle & Child
28 Smithfield, Sheffield (1800s-1920s)

This is a reference to the arms of the earls of Derby, the Stanleys. A Sir Thomas Latham, one of the family ancestors in the 14th century, had an illegitimate son. He placed the baby under a tree in which an eagle nested. He then deceptively took his wife for a walk in this area and let her find the young child. Sir Thomas persuaded her they should adopt the child. In spite of the successful deception, he still left all his wealth and riches to his daughter Isobel, who married Sir John Stanley. In this way the Stanleys inherited both the estates and the heraldic 'eagle and child' sign.

Eagle Tavern
10 Orchard Street/Harvest Lane, Sheffield (closed in 1912)

Eagle Tavern
46 Hawley Croft, Sheffield (aka Cock & Bottle) (1820s-1890s)

Eagle Tavern
75 Queens Street, Sheffield

Eagle Tavern
111 Duke Street, Sheffield

Eagle Tavern
26 Shepherd Street, Sheffield

Eagle Vaults
41 West Bar, Sheffield 3 (closed c1900)

Earl of Arundel and Surrey
528 Queens Road, Sheffield 2

This is the only remaining pound house in Sheffield and as such the landlord is required by an Act of Parliament to look after stray animals brought to the door. The wordage or instruction that the law lays down is as follows: "keep a stable and provender for any stray animals which the police or any other authority cares to bring at any time day or night".

Earl Francis Hotel

64 Manor Oaks Road, Sheffield

Earl George

61 the Pavement, Sheffield

Earl Grey

97 Ecclesall Road, Sheffield 11

Charles Grey, 2nd Earl Grey 1764-1845 was British Prime Minister 1830-34, and it was he who put through the Wilberforce Act to abolish the African slave trade.

Earl Grey

226 Moorfields, Sheffield

Earl Grey Compass

928 Orchard Street, Sheffield

Earl Grey Tavern

1 Silver Street Head, Sheffield

Earl Marshal

291 East Bank Road, Sheffield 2

Opened around 1984 when it was transformed from the old Midhill Working Men's club which went into liquidation. It had a lovely American Colonial Bar built into the main room.

It is named after the area's long association with the Dukes of Norfolk. The Earl Marshal stage manages state ceremonies and makes all arrangements for them. He is also governor of the College of Arms. Since 1672 the office has been held by the Dukes of Norfolk.

East House

18 Spital Hill, Sheffield 4 (aka Morriseys East House)

A small one-room/bar pub with a pleasant Irish feel to it, especially over the past few years since Brian Morrisey took it over.

Its history though is not so pleasant. Having had a license for over a hundred years it is unfortunate that the East House will probably fade into Sheffield's history with only one story being remembered. A Somalian named Mohamed Ishmail calmly walked into the 'House' drew a revolver and discharged all six rounds into the customers as they sat around enjoying New Year's Day 1960. Three died almost instantly and two more were seriously injured, one, Don McFarland was crippled for life. The Somali was caught hiding in the toilets and upon his arrest, stated that he wanted to kill himself but his religious beliefs forbade him from doing so. He thought being that we, the British, would hang him for the crime of murder, therefore fulfiling his desire to die. Unfortunately, we the British, deported him back to Somalia after six months. A pub talk by local historian Douglas Lamb stated that Ishmail had ran amok when he returned home and was gunned down. Hopefully true, but no definite evidence of this incident has come to light.

East Parade Hotel
2 Campo Lane, Sheffield

Ebenezer
42 Russell Street, Sheffield (closed in 1900s)

Could possibly be named after Ebenezer Elliott the Sheffield based poet. Born in 1781 he was known as the Corn Law Rhymer and was a much loved character in Sheffield. After his death in 1849 a statue, paid for by local subscription, was erected in Market Place in 1854. This was later moved to Weston Park where it can still be seen to this day.

Ecclesall Tavern
273/275 Hanover Street, Sheffield 3

Economical Hotel
132 Eldon Street, Sheffield

This name may well be a nickname for another public house as only one small reference was found about this hostelry.

Effingham Arms
19-21 Sussex Street, Sheffield

Egerton Hotel
138 Fitzwilliam Street, Sheffield

Elephant Inn
2/4 Norfolk Street, Sheffield 1
(aka Elephant Vaults)

This public house stood where the charity shop now stands in Fitzalan Square opposite the Odeon/Mecca Bingo.
The term elephant's trunk is cockney rhyming slang for drunk, this term is often reduced to he's "elephants".

Elephant and Castle
117 Arundel Street, Sheffield

It could have acquired its name from the Cutlers Company coat of arms which incorporates the Elephant and Castle and seems likely in Sheffield. It has also been said that the name is a corruption of Eleanor of Castille, who was the first wife of King Edward I. That should have pleased her majesty!

Elephant and Castle
beside Lady's Bridge, Sheffield

Ellesmere Hotel
55 Ellesmere Road, Sheffield 4

Ellis Street Tavern
21 Ellis Street, Sheffield

Elm Tree
980 City Road, Sheffield 12

The name is because at one time a large elm tree was to be found around this area.

Empire Bar
25-33 Charter Square, Sheffield

Empire "on which the sun never sets" - somehow I don't think this bar was named with the old colonial catch phrase in mind, more the Empire film magazine, whose typeface it uses above its frontage. Still it has put some of the old life back into an area where the Angel, Button Lane, used to stand and it does have a continental feel with its outdoor seating and electric heaters - rather a nice place.

Enfield Arms
95 Broughton Lane, Sheffield 9

Possibly after the rifle, Lee Enfield, which was used by the British Army.
At one time owned by Sheffield Steelers ice hockey team.

Engineers

2 Fife Street, Sheffield
(aka Dallas Bar, Barrow House)

The Engineer is now known as the Barrow House. One would assume the name change is because it is on the corner of Barrow Street. The reason for changing the name seems obscure, but then again a good third of the pubs in the Sheffield area have had a name change of some sort, and more often than not turned back to the original name.

In between its time as the Engineers and the Barrow House, the pub was known for a short period of time as The Dallas Bar, a fun pub. I called in once or twice whilst it was a fun pub, the brewery should be prosecuted for misrepresentation.

One of the pub's windows still has Berrys Lion Ale engraved upon it, a long since departed drink.

Engineers

116 Carlisle Street east, Sheffield

Engineers Arms

45 Sussex Street, Sheffield
(aka Providence Inn)

Eversley House

117 Upperthorpe Road, Sheffield 6
(aka Office)

Evening Gun

8 Scotland Street, Sheffield
(aka Cannon) (opened in the 18th century)

One of the stories put forward for the name of this pub is that the local nightwatch when doing their nightly round would fire off a pistol at exactly 10pm to let the land owners of the area know all was well.

Everest

Ballifield Drive, Sheffield 13

This pub was built to commemorate the conquest of Everest in 1953. The name Everest is derived from the surveyor general of India, Sir George Everest 1790-1866 - as well as the world highest mountain.

Excelsior

1 Carbrook St, Attercliffe Common, Sheff 9

The Original Excelsior Inn was one of Wards Brewery's smallest houses, but a development in the late 70s/early 80s doubled it in size to a nice cosy pub. The original inn was 2 dwelling places knocked into one set in the middle of Carbrook Terrace. To keep some of the old Excelsior origins, the old date stone was built into the new extended building.

The older pub had 3 very small rooms, one of which you had to go through the bar to get into. After its refurbishment it became a 2 roomed establishment and Wards made the Excelsior into a very nice comfortable little pub, with its brasses and its tasteful pictures. It was a place for young and old to visit. With a pool table and darts in one room and a organ and singalong microphone in the other.

Unfortunately the "Excel" as it was known was demolished in June 1993 to make way for the Sheffield Corridor widening in the East End of Sheffield. The Excelsior was situated on the corner of Carbrook Street and Attercliffe Common, a lovely pub, sadly missed.

Exchange Hotel

53 Eldon Street, Sheffield

Exchange

13 or 14 Corn Exchange Buildings or
40 Exchange Street, Sheffield
(aka Maunche Hotel)

Exchange

89 Thomas Street, Sheffield

Fair Trades

118 Carlisle Street East, Sheffield
(aka Free Trades) (1860s-1920s)

Fair Trades Hotel

137 Scotland Street, Sheffield 1

Falcon

13 Flat Street, Sheffield

Falconry was a royal sport for centuries. Falcons appear in
the Coat of Arms of Elizabeth I and William Shakespeare,
amongst many others.

Falcon

18 Leicester Street, Sheffield

Falcon

Pea Croft now Solly Street, Sheffield

Falstaff

56-58 The Wicker, Sheffield 3

This Shakespearian character who appeared in three of the
Bard's plays was a fat, boastful liar fond of practical jokes
and often projected himself as a loveable old rogue.

Farfield Inn

376 Neepsend Lane, Hillfoot Bridge, Sheff 3
(aka Owl, Muff Inn)

During the night of the Sheffield Flood a wall of water
over ten foot high swept past the Farfield and was still
doing vast damage to property and person seven miles
down from where Dale Dyke Dam burst its banks.

Far Lees

300 Leighton Road, Sheffield

Farmyard Vaults

102 Scotland Street, Sheffield

Farries Arms

145 Gibraltar Street, Sheffield

Fat Cat
23 Alma Street, Sheffield 3 (aka Alma)

The Fat Cat was originally called the Alma. Sheffield's first Real Ale freehouse, the 'Cat' is owned by Dave Wickett and now has its own brewery on the Kelham Island premises brewing among other beers the horribly named First Worts. This name refers to the beer before yeast is added.

No juke box, no TV and no fruit machines here, people come for the vast range of beers and they invariably make return visits.

Feathers
48 High Street Lane corner, Sheffield
(aka Old Feathers Inn, 46 Bard Street,)

Fellbrigg
331 Arbourthorne Road, Sheffield

Fiery Fred
Clipstone Gardens, Sheffield 9
(aka Greenland)

Name after Fred Trueman the Yorkshire cricketer who took 307 test wickets for England. The pub was officially opened by him in 1982, the pub sign shows Fred bowling at his fiery best.

Fighting Cock
Monteney Crescent, Sheffield 5

This name is reference to the specially bred birds who were brought up to fight to the death for the enjoyment of the customers who crowded around gambling on the outcome. Oliver Cromwell outlawed this barbaric sport, but it still lingered on for more than 200 years until sterner measures were taken (how do you take sterner measures than old Oliver Cromwell did?).

File Smiths' Arms
229 Attercliffe Common, Sheffield 9

The File Smiths Arms was situated between the Amberley Hotel on the opposite side of Tuxford Road and Frank Cutts Turf accountants, lovely pub.
A Mr Goodchild was the landlord in the 50s.

Filesmiths' Arms
61 Charles Street, Sheffield 1

Filesmiths' Arms
1 Lord Street, Sheffield

Filesmiths' Arms
40 Trinity Street, Sheffield

Filesmiths' Arms
128 Scotland Street, Sheffield

Filesmiths' Arms
66 Orchard Street, Sheffield

Firth Park Hotel

127 Page Hall Road, Sheffield 4

Firwood Cottage

279 Whitehouse Lane, Sheffield 6

Not a pub with much claim to fame, but it did have its headline in the Sheffield Star, in 98, when a wake/funeral went awry. Two members of the same family (possibly brother and sister) didn't see eye to eye over certain family arrangement, and a fracas developed. One man who was stabbed, took the knife of his attacker and stabbed him and at this stage the story disturbing as it is gets surreal. Another man (who has never been identified) walked up to them and with a small calibre revolver shot them both. No lives were lost but surely not what the dearly departed had in mind.

Fisherman's Inn

115 Carlisle Street, Sheffield

Fisherman's Rest

93 Tinsley Park Road, Sheffield 9
(closed in 1970s-80s)

Fisherman's Tavern

100 Backfields, Sheffield

Fitzalan Inn

38 Montford Road,
123 to 127 Fitzalan Street, Sheffield 3

Commonly referred to as the Top Fitzalan, so as to distinguish it from the Fitzalan Tavern.

Fitzalan Tavern

58 Fitzalan Street, Sheffield 3

Fitzalan Vaults

Haymarket, Sheffield 1 (1780-1930s)

Fitzwilliam Hotel

14 Milford Street, Sheffield (closed in the 60s)

Fitzwilliam Hotel

70 Fitzwilliam Street, Sheffield

Fitzwilliam Hotel

55 Broomhall Street, Sheffield

Five Alls

168 Infirmary Road, S 6 (aka Old Five Alls)

Usually this signage means "I rule All, King, I pray for All, parson, I plead for All, lawyer, I fight for All, soldier, I work for All, labourer-workman.

Five Arches Hotel

Herries Road, Sheffield 5

Fleur de Lys (Lis)

Attercliffe Road, Sheffield 9

It is said that at the back of Don Terrace, a row of houses that ran at the side of the River Don at Washford Bridge, was a small house called 'Sugar House'. This dwelling had been especially built for a widow called Mrs Roades in around 1671 for her to spend her retirement years in. One hundred and twenty years later it was an inn, and in 1879 a well known drawing by William Topham depicts it as an inn called the Fleur-De-Lis. It was reputedly closed in around 1890-1900.

Fleur de Lys

Totley Hall Lane, Totley Rise, Sheffield

Literally this means lily-flower, but a heraldic lily is meant rather than a real one. When Edward III assumed the title King of France we the English incorporated the Fleur De Lys into our coat of arms where it has since remained. It has also been incorporated into the Boy Scouts emblem.

There has been an inn on this site for hundreds of years, but the present building is not the original.

Fleur de Lys

7 Angel Street, Sheffield 1
(aka Three Fleur de Lys)

Fleur de Lis

66 Fargate, Sheffield 1

The public house offered sixpenny meals for servicemen in World War II. Unfortunately, or fortunately it was being run on temperance principles (moderation and all that). It was later occupied by Dean and Dawson, a railway ticket office and travel agent and later the Western Jean Company.

Florist Inn

185 Walkley Road, Sheffield 6

Florist Inn

119 Broad Lane, Sheffield

Flouch Inn

Oughtibridge, Sheffield 6 (aka New Inn)

In 1827 this inn was supposedly opened as the New Inn and sometime later changed its name to the Flouch. Too many tales have now been told of the origin of the name the flouch, and unfortunately it is now pure guesswork as to the correct version. An early landlord had a slouch lip, a physical defect, and so called his pub the Flouch. Another has it that the incumbent landlord wanted it to be called the Plough and jotted the name down, the signwriter misread it, the P as F and the G as a C. All a little unbelievable.

Flying Dutchman

33 Silver Street Head, Sheffield

Possibly two versions for the pub name. One is the obvious, the ghostly ship which was supposed to haunt the Cape of Good Hope, luring unsuspecting ships to their destruction. The second, now not so well known, is that in 1849 a Derby winner was called the Flying Dutchman, the landlord, as they did regularly, may have changed the pub name if he won a bob or two on the nag.

Forest

48 Rutland Road, Sheffield 3

In 1990 The Forest was relicensed to sell wines and spirits as well as beer, this made it the last beer only pub in South Yorkshire. It was previously only licensed to sell beer, cider and porter.

Foresters Arms

127 Penistone Road, Sheffield 6

Foresters Arms

91 Headford Street, Sheffield

Foresters Arms

45 Eyre Street, Sheffield

Foresters

14 Union Buildings, Bridge Street, Sheffield

Foresters Inn

73-75 Division Street, Sheffield (aka Yorick)

The old pub had uncomfortable old railway like seating. The Foresters reference is to the Ancient Order of Foresters, a large friendly society with lodges called courts, popular in America and Britain.

Forge Inn

95 Newhall Road, Sheffield 9

Forge Tavern

Millsands, Sheffield

Such names as these are generally found around the area where there was a smithy or a foundry.

Fortunes of War

108 Scotland Street, Sheffield 3

The pub name is generally associated with a merchant ship which in times of war armed itself and would attack enemy shipping, anything gained by such a raid was termed as the 'Fortunes of War'.

Forty Foot

Wordsworth Avenue, Sheffield 5

Forty Foot was the name given to the stretch of water along the River Witham where many a fishing competition was held. Stones Brewery, owners of the Forty Foot pub, often held their own Angling Championship there. Built around 1960 as a Parson Cross estate pub it used to have a keep net as its pub sign.

Forum

Sandstone Road, Wincobank, Sheffield 9

Forum Cafe

127-129 Devonshire Street, Sheffield

Started life as a café in the Forum complex in the Devonshire quarter. It has a bohemian feel with its stylish iron framed furniture and all its contemporary art on the wall.

Foundry Arms

111 Barrow Road, Sheffield 9

Foundry Arms

101 Green Lane, Sheffield

Fountain

19 Pinfold Street, Sheffield

This sign can be heraldic referring to the crest of the Plumbers Company and also the badge of the Master Mariners, or it can refer to a nearby spring or well. As you can imagine before piped water such natural sources of water were very important places

Fountain

West Bar, Sheffield

Fountain Bar

Leopold Street, Sheffield 1 (aka Houlihans)

Supposedly, the first place to charge £1 per pint in Sheffield in September 1987 (a sorry day).

Fowler Street Hotel
37 Haywood Street, Sheffield

Fox Inn
250 Foxhill Road, Sheffield 6

Fox & Duck
50 Broad Lane, Sheffield
(aka Old Fox & Duck)

Fox & Duck
174 Pye Bank, or 174 Pitsmoor Road, Sheff

Fox & Duck
Sheffield Road, Sheffield 9

Fox & Duck
227 Fulwood Road, Sheffield 10

This public house now owned by the Sheffield Student Union was once known for housing The Gentlepersons Sports Club in around 1836 and included in its rank the likes of Amy Johnson who studied at Sheffield University. It was established by businessmen, and expanded enough to have its own sportsground and to send teams to play cricket and polo against opposition throughout the British Empire. The Sports Club was 102 years old and still thriving when disaster struck, off Cape Horn. A ship carrying members of the club was sunk and many lives were lost. The club never regained its popularity and slipped into oblivion. The Fox and Duck now has on show various remnants of this Gentlepersons Club.
Worth a visit.

Fox & Grapes
519 Meadow Hall Road, Sheffield 9

The pub title is probably an allusion to Aesop's well known fable of the fox who would dearly love to reach and eat them, but alas they are beyond his reach. He therefore declared that it was of no importance and that they were probably sour anyway.
It was this fable that gave rise to the term "sour grapes".

Fox House Inn
Hathersage Road, Dore

Another public house to undergo a recent transformation is the Foxhouse. In early 1998 it had quite a substantial amount spent on it by its owners Bass. It will be the latest addition to the Vintage Inns concept, a new name for the Fork and Pitcher Inns, which include the Admiral Rodney in Loxley Valley and the Dore More Inn. Supposedly it will be traditional high quality pub serving British food and cask ales, real fires and traditional materials. What does that mean?

Fox House Hotel

1 Ardmore St, & 11 Shirland Lane, Sheff 9

A Whitbreads, Castle Eden house situated on the corner of Ardmore Street and Shirland Lane, it consisted of 3 sizeable rooms, it used to be a very lively pub in the 60s 70s and 80s, music, groups and local games leagues being the order of the day.

It was purported that Spence Broughton's wife looked out on to his gibbeted body from an upstairs room of this hostel in the late 18th century. All this seems rather unlikely, not only geographically, but we don't know if the Fox House or an earlier building of that name was even built then. There was, however, a letter signed by Ms Broughton which was kept on one of the walls, stating her kind treatment by the landlord. It was reported stolen some years ago in the mid 60s. Could it have been the genuine article?

The Fox House closed in the late 1990s.

Foxwood Inn

57 Mansfield Road, Sheffield

Franklin Hotel

118 Franklin Street, Sharrow Lane, Sheffield 11 (closed around 1970)

Fraternity House

Norfolk Street, Old Bank, Sheffield 1 (aka Old Monk)

This old TSB building with its amazingly high roof and wooden floors and tables serves food all day and is another of the new Café Bars that have sprung up in the larger old buildings of Sheffield. This one does have a nice feel to it though, especially in summer when the rear doors are opened on to Tudor Square. Next door to the Brown Bear.

Frecheville Hotel

1 Birley Moor Crescent, Sheffield 12

Freedom Hotel

26 Walkley Road, Sheffield 6
(aka Freedom View, Freedom)

Freedom House

369-371 South Road, Sheffield 6

The Freedom House is somewhat of a throwback in time - it serves good beer and does it in comfortable surroundings. The Pub consist of a two pleasant rooms, a comfortable lounge and a smaller bar area with a pool table and walls inundated with mirrors (it does give it a feel of being bigger than it really is). The Freedom House has a good mix of customers. The sign outside of a man putting a fish back into the water is obviously depicting freedom.

Freemasons Arms

8 Hartshead, Sheffield (1790s-1893)

The original Freemasons were stone masons in medieval times who operated a closed shop union. They used secret signs in an effort to exclude what would now be termed as "cowboy" builders.

Freemasons Arms

383 Walkley Lane, Sheffield 6 (aka Masons Arms)

The landlord, landlady, her sister and a boarder were all drowned at this pub in 1864 as the Sheffield Flood water swept through Hillsborough totally destroying the Masons. The bridge it stands on is called Hill Bridge. Graham Pugh, one of the few players ever to play at Wembley in a FA Cup Final for Sheffield Wednesday is the landlord at this pub.

Free Trades Inn

66 Allen Street, Sheffield

Free trade should be free of all restrictions, so said John Bright, MP for Manchester and Richard Cobden, MP for Stockport. There must have been some difficulty in depicting on the pub sign such an abstract concept.

French Horn

34 Pea Croft, Sheffield

French Horn

5 Shude Hill, Sheffield (late 18th C-1900s)

Friendship Inn

4 Tinsley Park Rd, 1 March St, Sheffield 9

Frog and Parrott

94 Division Street, Sheffield 1 (aka Prince of Wales)

The Frog and Parrot on the corner of Division Street , was opened in mid 1982 and through its landlord Roger Nowill, who came 9 months later, gained a reputation for selling strong beer. His own brew, Roger and Out, is believed to be the strongest traditional draught beer in the world, and got extensive media attention, as well as appearing in the Guinness Book of Records, when it was first brewed. To be fair the landlord, does inform the customers to drink the heavy stuff in moderation. In fact it was only sold in third pint glasses and supposedly no one was allowed more than three. Sadly, Roger has now departed the Frog.

The Frog and Parrot was built on a site occupied by the old Prince of Wales hotel.

Fullerton Arms Hotel

301 Sheffield Road, Templeborough, Sheffield (aka Yorkshireman)

Full Moon

25 Silver Street, Sheffield (late 18th Cent)

Fulton

2 Fulton Road & 1 Walkley Street, Sheffield 6 (aka Prospect House)

Fulwood Inn

Tapton Park Road, Sheffield

Moordale, a derelict mansion formerly owned and built by James Nicholson, a Sheffield steel merchant, has been turned into the Fulwood Inn at a cost of over £1 million by Mansfield Brewery. After a long running three year planning saga when opposition to the public house came from the Sheffield City Council, environmentalists and some local residents, Mansfield finally won through in 1999. Gerald and Linda Jones are the first licensees of the Fulwood.

The building was once the home of the National Coal Board and then computer company EDP.

Furnival

Verdon Street, Sheffield 3

This fairly recent, (late 1960s), purpose built public house was situated in the Pitsmoor local council housing estate, maisonettes, flats etc. on Verdon Street, in a small necessity type shopping precinct. It had a shorter lifespan than most Sheffield public houses, a paltry 30 years.

The building is still standing but now it belongs to the church and is used as community rooms/centre. The pub become the second Sheffield Inner City Ecumenical Mission purchase with an alcoholic flavour, in 1997 they bought an off-license in Grimesthorpe.

The Tetleys house itself was made up of two sizeable rooms, the public bar, where table games, darts, pool and the noisier clients resided, the second room, the lounge, was the complete opposite, sedate and comfortable.

The name of the pub and the street both appear in Ralph Gosling's Map of Sheffield which was drawn up in 1736 in deference to the Noble families of this area, one section read "Furnival of Sheffield, Hallamshire, Worksop and Verdon"

Gaiety Bar

100 West Bar, Sheffield (aka Gaiety Palace)

Gardeners Rest

Cobden View, Sheffield

Gardeners Rest

105 Neepsend Lane, Sheffield

One train of thought as to why the pub is so called is that it reflects the rural theme and that it comes from Neepsend's origin as the market garden for ancient Sheffield. Rumour has it that before all the industrialisation of this area there were some 900 - 1000 acres of gardens and allotments. Quite feasible, just look at the local road names: Nursery Street, Farfield Road, Harvest Lane, Parkwood. Perhaps it was literally the Gardeners Rest.

The Rest is opposite the former Stones Brewery which is on the corner of Rutland Road.

Gardeners Rest

21 Ellis Street, Sheffield (aka Ellis St Tav.)

Gardeners Rest

55 Townhead Street, Sheffield

Garrison Arms

456 Penistone Road, Sheffield 6

Garrick Tavern or Hotel

6 Sycamore Street, Sheffield (1830s-1910s)

Probably named after David Garrick 1717-1779, who was a famous English actor and theatrical manager. He had a manner of speaking and behaving which made the declamatory actors of his time appear foolish. He was one of Dr Johnson's close friends.

Gas Tank Inn

8 Sussex Street, Sheffield

Gas Tank Tavern

259 Arundel Street, Sheffield

Gatefield Tavern
165 Infirmary Road, Sheff 6 (closed 1980s)

This tavern was built into the ground floor of the Kelvin Flats, a vast structure, that housed thousands of Sheffield's residents. The pub itself was a well frequented house during its short lifespan as one of the many Infirmary Road pubs.

Gate
10 Hollis Croft, Sheffield 3 (aka Old Gate)

Any proximity to a church gate, toll gate, or town gate was usually enough to bring about a pub being so named.

Gate
76-78 Attercliffe Common, Sheffield 9 (aka Old Gate Inn)

Gate Inn
78 Penistone Road North, Sheffield 6

General Gordon Inn
49 Cross Bedford Street, Sheffield

Named after the soldier and administrator, Charles Gordon, who was sometimes known as "Chinese Gordon", for the fact that he commanded the Chinese army that suppressed the Taiping Rebellion in 1860. He was Governor of Egyptian Sudan in 1884 when he was ordered to evacuate Khartoum. He disobeyed the order and held out for 10 months until he was killed 2 days before relief came. This delay in sending aid to help Gordon so antagonised the British public that it brought the government of the day crashing down.

George
95 Worksop Road, Sheffield 9

The name George, you would think, should be connected with the Kings of England, of which there have been six. More likely the George public houses with no roman numeral may well have been from the patron saint of England, St George.

George
24 Savile Street, Sheffield

George Inn
Hill Top Stannington, Sheffield 6

The George Inn, was a beer selling establishment as early as the mid 19th century and was said to have ceased trading in 1940, but some of the locals remember it still being open for trade in the early 1950s.

It is now the George House Farm, and used for private dwelling.

George Hotel

52 Boston Street, also New George Street, Sheffield

Some 20 customers left the George, on 25th August 1907, in a charabanc bound for a day trip to Derbyshire. After an enjoyable outing the party was on its way back into Sheffield when the charabanc overtook a horse drawn carriage and skidded into a telegraph pole. Three of the passengers were killed outright and another died some days later in hospital. Twelve other people sustained serious injuries. This was Sheffield's first major traffic accident.

George

56 West Bar, Sheffield 3

George IV

216 Infirmary Road, Sheffield 6

The king who reigned from 1820-1830 and more commonly this individual is better known as the prince regent. (At one time the pub was owned by Sheffield and District Public House Trust Co. Limited)

George Inn

11 Market Street, Woodhouse, Sheffield

George & Dragon Inn

High Street, or 70 Market Place, Hartshead Passage, Sheffield (aka George, Bodega)

This public house is mentioned as being in the ownership of a James Hoole, a pewterer in 1682. In that same year it was sold to a man named George Hutchison for £500. In 1769 a Mr Thomas Watson owned the inn and it was known by the sign of "The George in Sheffield". The inn stayed in the Watson family's ownership until 1782 when it was sold to a Samuel Peech for £1,500. The business must have been thriving to pay, what was then, a vast sum of money. In 1787 the inn was described in a local paper when put up for sale, again, as "George in Market Place where 2 hackney coaches are kept and stabling for 40 horses".

George & Dragon

93-95 Broad Lane, Sheffield

George & Dragon

39-41 Bank Street, Sheffield

George & Dragon

17 Queens St, Sheffield

George & Dragon

Church St, Ecclesfield, Sheffield

George & Dragon

94-96 West Bar, Sheffield

George Street Tavern

1 Cross Gilpin Street, Sheffield

Gladstones

4 St James St, Sheffield 1
(aka Ferret and Trouserleg)

Named after William Ewart Gladstone (1809-98) who was the main figure of the Liberal Party 1868-94. He was Prime Minister on four occasions and was a noted orator, and supposedly had a phenomenal grasp of financial matters.

This Scottish and Newcastle public house is now called the Ferret and Trouserleg. It is set in an old, listed, former church building, close to Sheffield Cathedral and the city centre. The clientele ranges from the office workers who seem to be regular dinner time drinkers to the younger people doing the town circuit.

Globe Inn (Scream bar)

54 Howard Street, Sheffield 1

This Bass/Stones owned public house has four small rooms which branch out from the bar and corridor area, which in itself is as big as some of the rooms. Being in the shadow of the Hallam University a large number of the customers are students, but it does have a hard core of regulars. It has pool table, quiz and fruit machines.

The Inn, during the mid 90s was turned into a Scream themed pub, (using the instantly recognisable visual image of the famous painting by Edvard Munch) make of that what you will.

This pub name is generally linked to the Globe Theatre, of Shakespearian association.

Globe

105 Porter Street, Sheffield

Globe

52 Broad Street, Sheffield

Globe

Burgess Street, Sheffield

Golden Ball

27 Spring Street, Sheffield

Golden Ball

69 Campo Lane, Sheffield

Built in around 1825, it was demolished and rebuilt in or about 1900, and finally re-sited on its present location in 1968. In the later years of the first building, in the 1890s the wonderfully named Antipas Stevens was the landlord.

Golden Ball

72 Howard Street, Sheffield

Golden Ball

16 Pond Street, Sheffield

Golden Ball

203 Pond Street, Sheffield (1820s-1900s)

Golden Ball

76 Burgess Street, Sheffield

Golden Ball

63 Duke Street, Sheffield

Golden Ball

838 Attercliffe Road and Old Hall Road, Sheff 9 (aka Turnpike, New Inn - possibly)

Two versions of the history of this public house:
Firstly; it was built in 1828 and was originally called the New Inn and was owned and run by a Shovel and Spade maker called John Davis. He was followed by George Watson, then George Dawson who stayed for 30 years and was understood to be the local registrar of births and deaths. He was succeeded by a John King.

Secondly; Built in 1838 as a tavern, and originally called the Golden Ball it stood on the corner of Old Hall Road and Attercliffe Road.

A Mrs Margaret Arnold who was born at the Golden Ball in 1920, told how her mother had started work at the pub during the first world war. It was then owned by the Cannon Brewery and the licensee was a man named Tom W Elliott, his name can just be seen above the door on the older photograph. The Elliott's lived at Fulwood and let Mrs Arnold's father, William Henry Arnold, look after the Golden Ball and occasionally called in to oversee proceedings. The Arnold's later moved on to the Meadow at Darnall.

The Golden Ball closed its doors for the last time in 1984. In 1985 Brian and Carrie Neely took the shutters down from the windows and doors and renamed it the Turnpike, the name came from the fact that the junction where it stands was once named Turnpike Road. It was also the city's first tram terminus. But the emblem on the sign outside did not represent any of these associations, it was just a pike (Brian said they did it because Sheffield is fishing mad). More likely because they couldn't figure out how to illustrate a Turnpike.
The Golden Ball or Turnpike was badly damaged by fire in January 1989 and was demolished sometime later to make way for the Sheffield Stadium.

Golden Ball

39 Forge Lane, or Shude Lane, Sheffield (aka Ball) (opened circa 1796)

Golden Cock

82 Broad Street, Sheffield

This used to be sign used by many tradesmen. It is now the trade mark of the Courage brewery.

Golden Cross

High Street, Sheffield (1770s) (exact location unknown)

Golden Fleece

12 Wharf Street, Sheffield (New Haymarket 1841)

Four possibilities:
Firstly; Jason and the Golden Fleece. The fleece of a ram was hung on a tree at Colchis and to gain the throne Jason, along with the members of his ship, the Argo, had to return it. This he did with some magical help from Medea.
Secondly; The name may also refer to the fact that gold prospectors used to stretch a sheepskin across small streams and collect particles of gold as they were being washed downstream.
Thirdly; The Knights of the Golden Fleece is a chivalric Order founded in 1492 for the protection of the church. The Order's badge is a ram with a red band around its middle.
Fourthly: It was situated in Fleece Yard.

Golden Lion

5 Forge Lane, Sheffield

A popular sign referring heraldically to Henry I, or to the Dukes of Northumberland, the Percy's.

Golden Lion

2 Shude Hill, Sheffield

Golden Lion

69 Alderson Road, Sheffield 2

Golden Plover

Occupation Lane, Hackenthorpe

Gooseberry

Peacroft, Sheffield

Gossips

Arundel Gate, Sheffield

Gower Arms

47 Gower Street, Sheffield 4

Graduate

6 Montgomery Road, Sheffield 6

Granby's Head

1 or 35 Hartshead, Sheffield 1

Grand Hotel

Leopold Street, Sheffield

Demolished in the early 1970s.

Grand Theatre

Spring Street, Coulson Street, Sheffield
(aka Squints, Bijou, The Star Music Hall)

This type of Public House cum Theatre was very popular at the turn of the century, especially for some reason in the West Bar area of Sheffield. The Grand, had a large stage, gallery and auditorium and could accommodate hundreds of people. Unfortunately when movies (moving pictures) came along this type of Music Hall theatre/pub was doomed, The Grand was demolished in 1920

Granville Inn

89 Granville Street, Sheffield 2

Named after the First Earl of Granville who married Harriet Cavendish, sister of the 6th Duke of Devonshire.

Grapes

95-97 Pond Street, Sheffield

Grapes

Langsett Road, Sheffield

Grapes

80 Trippet Lane, Sheffield

Used to be the venue of the Transatlantic Brides and Parents Association.

Grapes

15 Lock Street, Sheffield

Grapes

Queens Street, Infirmary Road, Sheffield 1

Grapes

5 South Street, Sheffield

Grapes Hotel

Moorhead, Sheffield 1

Grapes Inn

51 Gower Street, Sheffield 4
(aka Rovers Rest, Rovers Return)

Grapes Inn

99 Carlisle Street, Sheffield

Grapes Inn

74 Furnace Hill, Sheffield

Grapes Tavern

11 or 13 New Church Street, Sheffield

Great Britain

28 John Street, Sheffield 2

Feasibly named after our great nation, but more probably after Isambard Kingdom Brunel's famous ship, The Great Britain. The ship was launched in 1843. It foundered some years later on the Falkland Islands and was towed back to Bristol, where it was restored in 1970 with money raised by public subscription.

Great Gun

115 Franklin Street, Sheffield

Great Gun

39 Greystock Street, Sheffield
(closed in circa 1932)

Great Gun

186 Savile Street, Sheffield

Great Tankard

62 West Bar Green, Sheffield

Greaves Hotel

23 Orchard St/Harvest Lane
or 23 Apple St, Sheffield

Green Dragon

44 Fargate, Sheffield 1 (Closed 1925)

Winchester House, which accommodated the Provincial Insurance Company, was rebuilt in the early 1960s and this was preceded by the Green Dragon which occupied the second floor. To get to this hotel you had to enter through a narrow door which was between two small shops. The Green Dragon lost its license in 1925.

Green Dragon

67 South Street, Park, Sheffield

Green Dragon

469-471 Attercliffe Road, Sheffield 9
(aka Old Green Dragon)

The Old Green Dragon was situated across from the junction of Attercliffe Road and Effingham Road on the corner of Baldwin Street.
Could also be from the coat of arms of the earls of Pembroke.

Green Inn

Slitting Mill Road, Sheffield 9

Green Man

9 New Church Street, Sheffield

Generally the sign of the Green Man represents the spirit of fertility, the rejuvenating power of nature. A popular medieval image which appeared in many church carvings. It was also associated with Robin Hood and his men who were supposedly garbed in Green Cloth. This may have some truth to it, but Kendal green cloth, made for foresters, woodmen, and the like was only made from the 16th century onwards, a little after Robin was supposedly around. Some Green Man signs show a wild man in the forest, some show a woodcutter. Probably the new millennium ones somewhere will show an alien!

Green Man

23 Broad Street, Sheffield

Green Seedling

57 Bailey Street, Sheffield

Grennel Mower

264 Low Edges Road, Greenhill, Sheffield 8

Grey Horse Inn

25 High Street, Aldine Court, Sheffield 1 (aka Blackamore Head)

The Girdler family owned the Blackamoor Head in 1675. It changed name to the Grey Horse Inn in 1787. Once a famous coaching house in Aldine Court off High Street, it is famous for the fact that King John stayed one night, on his way to York. Unlikely, as King John (who was the less famous brother of Richard the Lionheart) was around in 12th century and there is no evidence that the Grey Horse was even built by then.

Its other tenuous claim to Royal fame, was when it was kept by a John Trippet, alehouse keeper and churchwarden who supposedly supplied ale for the rejoicing when George I was crowned King of England in 1714. Closed circa 1917 and long since demolished.

Grey Horse Inn

Blast Lane, Sheffield

Grey Horse Inn

57 Chester Street, Sheffield 1

Technically speaking there is no such thing as a grey horse, they just have a mixture of black and white hairs. They always foal black, then gradually become iron grey, then turn white in old age.

Grey Horse Inn

25 Stoke Street, Sheffield 9

Grey Horse Inn

15 Crown Alley, Sheffield

Greyhound

66 Holly Street, Sheffield

Greyhound

77 Pond Street, Sheffield

Greyhound Inn

822 Attercliffe Road, Sheffield 9

The Greyhound Inn was built in the year 1884 and is quite typical of the type of public house that sprang up and thrived during the great steel producing days of this era. Sheffield at this time in the late 19th century was the greatest steel producing place on earth. Originally a coaching inn that provided welcome respite for travellers coming into Sheffield.

In the early 20th century 1906 to be precise, a Mr Ernest Marcroft was the landlord and he took over from his father-in-law a Mr Isaac Parker who saw in the new century as landlord.

It is now one of the few Attercliffe Road pubs to have survived the industrial decline and in fact with the Stadium being built nearby has seen an increase in its recent trade. This Gilmour Windsor, later Stones public house has seen and withstood the varied changes that all go to make Attercliffe what it is today.

Greyhound

217 Gibraltar Street, Sheffield 3

An inconceivable thought now, but 200 years ago the Greyhound, Gibraltar Street, was the last building of the town of Sheffield in that direction. In 1812, three years before the Battle of Waterloo, the Greyhound housed the only constable in Sheffield, a man called Hinchcliffe and it was he who owned a bowling green, which was on the site where the Ebenezer Chapel was built. From this came the street name, Bowling Green Street, which still stands close by the long closed pub today.

The Greyhound itself is still standing, and with a rather grand lintel of a Greyhound over the corner door, go take a look for yourselves. It stands on the corner of Copper Street and Gibraltar Street.

The name Greyhound could obviously be from the dog of that name, but also famous mail-coaches which were so named or heraldic references to the Dukes of Newcastle.

Greyhound Inn

122 High Street, Ecclesfield

The Greyhound was originally a farm about 300 years ago. The structure you see today has a considerable amount of the original stonework in it. An extension in 1909 had to use stone of similar character so as to blend in with the original structure.

Greyhound Tavern

3 Pinfold Street, Sheffield

Greyhound Tavern

38 Hermitage Street, Sheffield

Griffin Inn

5 Spital Street, Sheffield 3
(closed in the 1960s)

Griffin, a fabulous monster, the offspring of a Lion and an Eagle. This sign is represented on many coat of arms.

Griffin Inn

8 Town End Road, Ecclesfield

Grinders Rest

43 Charles Lane, Sheffield

Grouse Inn

Penney Lane, Totley Bents, Totley

Grouse and Trout

Upper Hallam, Redmires, Sheffield

The three dams at Redmires were constructed between 1836 and 1854, the Grouse and Trout overlooked the middle dam and like a lot of other farms in the area took out a license and started to cater for the large influx of workers who were now present. Supposedly the navvies had a nickname for the Grouse and Trout, it was called the "Eyes and Ears". Figure that one out!

Also in the close proximity was a racecourse, which later became an army camp during the First World War.

It ceased trading as a public house in around 1913 when the landlord, a Mr Wilson of Beauchief Hall had the license withdrawn, supposedly, to stop the townspeople ruining the grouse moors.

The premises changed into a tea and refreshment outpost for the many walkers and ramblers who frequented this pleasant area. It was demolished soon after the Second World War.

Grove

49 Grove Street, Sheffield

Probably in reference to the proximity of a grove.

Guards Rest

2 Marshall Street and 8 Fowler St, Sheffield
(aka Old Albion)

Guards Rest

41 Sorby Street, Sheffield 4

The building is still standing but the public house has long since been closed. The Guards Rest had a local nickname of the Widow's Hut.

No real indication, even on the old pub signage, as to which regiment of the guards it would allow to rest there, Grenadiers, Coldstream, Scots, Welsh or Irish, probably all.

Hadfield Hotel

26/28 Barber Road, Sheffield 10

Hague Tree

Snow Lane, Sheffield

It is unknown if there is any connection between the two public houses, Hague Tree or Haigh Tree Inn.

Haigh Tree Inn

1 Bernard Street, Sheffield 2
(aka Old Haigh Tree)

Half Moon

71 Mather Road, Sheffield 9

Set in the Littledale estate just off Prince of Wales Road, Darnall.

Halfpenny

Set into the Kelvin Flats, Sheffield

In around August 1992 it was closed with the epitaph that; gun thugs helped to close this small pub.

Halfway House

80 Britannia Road, Sheffield 9

Public houses so named are generally on country roads and indicate convenient stopping places for travellers. At one time this would have been such a house.

Halfway House

195 Attercliffe Road, Sheffield 9

Hallamshire Hotel

182 West Street, Sheffield 1

A pub built in the Edwardian era circa 1901-1910 showing on its tiled exterior an affiliation with Greaves and Company.

Hallamshire Hotel

155-157 Lydgate Lane, Crookes, Sheffield 10

Hallamshire Hotel

123 Martin St, Sheffield or 2 Bond Street and 156 Wentworth Street, Sheffield 6

Hallamshire House

49-51 Commonside Walkley, Sheffield

This nineteenth century coaching house stood facing the old manor-type Spring Farm that was bounded by the farm workers tied cottages. There is not much in evidence today to suggest that this area was rich farmland.

Hallcar

2 Carwood Terrace, Sheffield 4 (aka Grove)

Hammer & Pincers

Ringinglow Road, Hill Top, Sheffield 11

Record shows that the Hammer and Pincers on Ringinglow Road, was a public house as long ago as 1760, so men who fought at Culloden 1745, could have drunk the first few pints of ale at this establishment. It is said to have been constructed in the 17th century by the Osborn family.

The Hammer served travellers on the packhorse route over the moors and also doubled as a smithy, with the landlord wearing both hats. The smithy remained in use up until the end of the first world war c1918.

It is said that bear baiting went on at the Hammer and Pincers, being staged about once a year. It drew large crowds and was eagerly awaited by locals and the gambling fraternity alike.

It was reputedly stopped when a landlord was worried by a bear. (Perhaps the bear asked for his pint topped up).

Hammond

143 Upper St Philips Road, Sheffield 6
(closed around 1950)

Hampden View Hotel

231-233 Langsett Rd, Sheffield (closed 1960s)

Hand In Hand

Bridgehouses, Sheffield
(aka t'owd shake hands)

The sign above the door was of two hands clasped together.

Hanover House

132/134 Upper Hanover Street, Sheffield 3

This was a beer-off converted, in around 1935, into a public house.

The Royal House of Hanover succeeded to the English throne in 1714. The Hanoverian monarchs were George I, II, III, IV, William IV and Queen Victoria although when Victoria came to the throne in 1837 the thrones of England and Hanover were separated.

Hanrahans

375-385 Glossop Road, Sheffield

Formerly a large block of houses converted in to an American style bar, it was opened in 1984. Hanrahans to its credit was one of the few pubs/bars not to keep changing its decor, it stayed much the same for its first 15 years. It may not have been everybody's idea of a good pub, but it seemed to have stood the test of time with the Sheffield drinker and seem to be as popular as when it first opened.

In mid 1999 it had an auction to sell off everything in the pub (for charity, it has to be said) tables, chairs, glasses, pots etc. As this book goes to press it is in the transitional phase and no one yet knows what it will turn out like. As usual large sums of money will be spent on the alterations.

Hare & Hounds

51 Trinity Street, Sheffield

Hare & Hounds

128 Clarence Street, Sheffield

Hare & Hounds
72 Duke Street, Sheffield

Hare & Hounds
27-29 Nursery Street, Sheffield 3

Most pubs so named are traditionally associated with the pack of beagles who hunt the hare

Hare & Hounds
7 Church Lane, Dore

Hare & Hounds
6 Church Street, Oughtibridge

Hare & Hounds
Church Street, Stannington
(aka Well Green House, Blue Boar)

The present, modern, building replaced the original Hare and Hounds, though not on the same location, which was destroyed by fire about 40 years ago.
The original (pictured below) stood on Gray's Hill, the locals' name for Uppergate Road.

It was first recorded in around 1790 as the Well Green House and was later known under the sign of the Blue Boar. It is first mentioned as the Hare and Hounds around 1837 in local reference.
The John Smiths Magnet Brewery purchased the pub on October 1st 1900.

Harley Hotel
Glossop Road, Sheffield

The present day Harley Hotel is now open to the public, and is situated on the stretch of Glossop Road between the University students union building and the junction with West Street.

Harlequin

26 Johnson Street, Sheffield 3
(aka Harlequin and Clown)

Set just off the Wicker it was originally called the Harlequin and Clown. The Harlequin is the only Sheffield pub so named, It seems reasonable to think it was named after the pantomime character in spangled dress, but unfortunately, no one knows why it came to be so called, maybe it was because there was a theatre or music hall in the close proximity.

The pub is tucked away among the back streets, but still gets plenty of custom from the light engineering and other small businesses that have cropped up around the Wicker area. It is one of the few, if not the last to have windows around the bar area. Also in the dram shop stands the original pot bellied stove, believed to be well over 100 years old, sometimes fired up just to roast chestnuts or potatoes.

The Harlequin, which is a Wards brewery pub, has 3 rooms, one is directly as you come off the street, the others are reached by going through the bar corridor. The room at the back is generally used for a quiet drink on games nights for dominoes cards etc, there is also a pool room with not much room for anything else. And a little room at the side of the bar where the more discerning drinkers sit. Upstairs is a medium sized room generally used for small functions, meetings, darts nights etc. It is one of the three river pubs in Sheffield.

Harold Hotel

32 Hardy Street, Sheffield

Harp Tavern

33 Walker Street, Sheffield

Normally the harp sign is symbolic of Ireland. It was first adopted by Henry VIII as the Irish Badge, while James I was the first king to include it in the royal arms.

Harp Tavern

109 St Philips Road, Sheffield

George Harvey Flood, a well known Sheffield boxer, held the license for the Harp for a time

Harwood House

103/105 Hill Street, Sheffield 2

Harrow

80 Broad Street and Harvest Lane, Sheffield
(opened in mid 18th century)
(aka Ye Olde Harrow)

Havana Hotel

57 Meadow Street, Sheffield 3

Hawk and Dove

Thorpe Green, Waterthorpe

Hawthorne

23 Park Hill Lane, Sheffield

Haw Thorne Tree

Snow Hill, Park, Sheffield

Haychatter Inn

Bradfield Dale, Bradfield
(aka Reservoir Inn)

The Reservoir Inn was built soon after the Sheffield flood in 1864 and served the people working on restoring the dam. It is said that for some time the Reservoir Inn had a stained glass light hung outside, this was taken into the lounge area, and is still on show to this day.

Welcoming open fired, comfortable public house set in idyllic countryside surroundings. A little off the beaten track but worth the effort to seek it out.

Named after the whinchat, a bird which makes its nest principally from dried grass.

Haylock

104 Allen Street, Sheffield
(aka Havelock Inn)

Hay's Spirit Vaults

97 Norfolk Street, Sheffield

Originally the public house was built in 1797 and served the Sheffield township for many years. We now know this building as the Ruskin Gallery, (Hays gallery) which has a frequently changing format and is one of Sheffield council's better investments in the last few years.

Heeley and Sheffield House

781 Gleadless Road, Sheffield 12

Hen & Chickens

3 Castle Green, Sheffield 3
(aka Old Hen and Chickens)

The Hen and Chickens is just off Castle Street opposite the Brightside and Carbrook Co-operative store.

In the same year as Victoria was crowned Queen of England, 1837, a slightly lesser event took place in the Hen and Chickens. A gentleman by the name of Henry White was purchasing a drink at the bar of the 'Chickens' when it was noticed something was awry with his shilling. He was accosted and it was found he was carrying a large amount of counterfeit shillings. His alibi was that he was a undercover agent for the English Mint, this obviously did not prove to be true and White was sentenced to transportation for 15 years hard labour. Whilst all this seems to be a heavy price for a little monetary deception, it has to be said he was lucky to escape with his life as counterfeiters, in this era, were generally hung for treason.

Hen & Chickens

18 Bow Street, Sheffield

In the 17th century this term was used to describe the Pleiads, the group of stars in the constellation Taurus. In the 18th century it was used to name a compound daisy, such as London Pride. In the 19th century it was used as a terminology for a children's game. Supposedly, in slang 'chickens' were small pewter pots, 'hens' were the larger pots. It is probably from this pewter pot theory that the pub names arise.

Henrys Bar

28 Cambridge Street, Sheffield 1

Probably the first of the new Café/Bars in Sheffield.

Hereford Arms

17 Hereford Street, Sheffield 1

Hermitage

11 London Road, Sheffield 2
(aka Harvey's Tavern, Harvey's Bar, R & R)

This pub was the Wards brewery's first managed house in Sheffield. Situated close to the Sheffield United Football Club from where a good amount of custom comes on a Saturday, when the Blades play at home. One of the first, if not the first, double deck pub layout, with an upstairs open plan area overlooking London Road.

Inside there is a plaque commemorating the fact that the original Hermitage was bombed on December 12th 1940 when some customers were injured during the German blitzing of Sheffield.

Highcliffe Hotel

Greystones Road, Sheffield 11

Perched near the top of Greystones Road, this pub has had a few famous characters through its portals. Joe and Fred Davis, world champion snooker champions, used to practice here and, slightly more recently, in the sixties and early seventies it has seen the likes of Barbara Dickson, Ralph McTell and Billy Connolly when the pub was well known throughout the folk music world. It is now separated into two distinct areas the front bar area, quiet and more traditional, the other, at the rear, a games room with pool tables, darts, video games etc.
Built in June 1939.

High Greave Inn

206 High Greave, Ecclesfield 5

High Noon

15 Klivington Ave, Sheffield 13

The license for this pub was transferred from the Twelve O'clock which used to stand on Savile Street.

Highland Laddie

Ranmoor, Sheffield

The name probably derives from a popular early 19th century song, Bluebells of Scotland, whose first line is: "Oh where, tell me where, is your Highland Laddie gone?". A song written by a Mrs Grant to mark the departure of the Marquis of Huntly and his regiment, to fight in the Napoleonic Wars.

Highway

Fox Street, Sheffield 3

A fairly modern, estates public house built in around 1963, consisting of two rooms, a tap room and a lounge.

Hillsborough Inn

2 Holme Lane, Sheffield 6

This large stone faced building which bends around the corner of Holme Lane and Middlewood Road, was hit by the full force of the Sheffield flood. It had its floorboard, windows and doors ripped off, but this well built structure remained standing unlike most in the close vicinity.

Its lower floor, the shop front, is now used by a couple of charities.

Hill Top Hotel

65 Attercliffe Common, Sheffield 9
(1850s-1969)

Hind

23 Furnival Gate, Nelson House, Moorhead, Sheffield (aka Nelson, Seamus O'Donnells)

Unfortunately one of the Sheffield public houses in which a murder was committed. In the late 60s, whilst it was still called the Nelson, a young man was stabbed to death during an argument. It subsequently changed names to the Hind and is now known by the name Seamus O'Donnells. The pub itself has an unusual feel to it, a cellar bar and upstairs bar. Discovery Inns now own this public house. The present building replaced the old Nelson in 1963.

Hodgson Arms

47/49 Hodgson Street, Sheffield 3

Hodson Hotel

108/110 Carlisle Road, Sheffield 9

Hogs Head

Delves Road, Sheffield 12

The name is derived from the large cask of various capacities used for wines and beers known as a hogshead.

Hole in Wall

70 Savile Street, Sheffield 3
(aka Wicker Brewery tap)

Towd 'ole in t'wall on't pickle.
Decipher that if you can?
This was probably a fairly common saying at the turn of the century as the Wicker Brewery nicknamed the Hole in the Wall was situated on a stretch of road called the Pickle, now Attercliffe Road.

The Wicker Brewery was turned into the Victoria vinegar brewery (hence pickle), but now all trace of this building is forever gone, submerged under the multi-story office block next door to the old pub.

During the mid 1990s the, then closed, hole in wall was used for a photo shoot for the pop group the Beautiful South, who put up posters and re-did the pub signage to say the words the "Beautiful South" across the frontage of the pub.

Hollin Bush

108 Hollinsend Road, Sheffield 12

Holly Bush Inn

Hollins Lane Stannington, Sheffield 6

Hope and Anchor

52 Pye Bank, Sheffield
also Bridgehouse and Mowbray Street

The name may be from this passage in Hebrews 6:19; "Hope we have as an anchor of the soul". The spare anchor on a ship was often called the hope anchor.

Hope and Anchor

223 Solly Street, Sheffield

Horse & Garter

32 Bridge Street, Sheffield

Horse & Garter

34 Water Lane, Sheffield (opened in 1830)

Horse & Groom

80 London Road, Sheffield (1820s-1916)

Horse & Groom

426 Blackstock Road, Sheffield 14

Horse & Jockey

638 Attercliffe Road, Sheffield 9

Horse & Jockey

14 Sheaf Street, Sheffield

Horse & Jockey

10 Broad Lane, Sheffield

Horse & Jockey

19 Pond Hill, Sheffield
(aka Lyceum Hotel)
(opened in the 18th century)

Horse & Jockey

10 Tenter Street, Sheffield

Horse & Jockey
250 Wadsley Lane, Sheffield 6

Horse & Lion
Norfolk Park Road, Sheffield

Horseshoe Inn
279 Bellhouse Road, Sheffield 5

The horseshoe is a simple visual sign, made all the more significant by the long standing belief that a horseshoe brings luck.

Hospital Tavern
13 Park Hill Lane, Sheffield

Howard Arms
5 Suffolk Road, Sheffield 2

Howard Hotel
57 Howard Street, Sheffield 1

Howard Hotel
94 Howard Road, Sheffield 6

Huntsman
1 Sorby Street, Sheffield

Huntsman
975 Barnsley Road, Sheffield

This particular huntsman takes its name from the trademark of the Tetleys brewery which is depicted by a monacled redcoated foxhunter.

Huntsman Rest
9 Backfields, Sheffield

Hussar
51 Scotland Street, Sheffield

Hussar's were originally a body of light horsemen organised in Hungary in the fifteenth century. The term was later applied to light cavalry regiments formed in other countries. Most pub names using the term hussar's probably refer to the 11th Hussar's (Prince Albert's Own) who were involved in the Famous Charge of the Light Brigade at Balaclava.

Hyde Park Inn
St Johns Road, Park, Sheffield
(aka Cricket Ground Inn)

Imperial Hotel

1 Castle Street, Sheffield 1,
(aka Waverley Hotel)

Imperial Inn

45 Robertshaw Street, Sheffield 3

Imperial Store

45 Robert Street, Sheffield

Industry Inn

34 Broad Street/1 South St, Sheffield 2

The Industry, nicknamed the Dust oyle was mainly used by the market traders in the 50s and 60s. The landlord and landlady for most of this time were a Mr and Mrs Whitham (Anne). Along with the Industry they had kept the Royal, Abbeydale Road, the Albion, London Road, and they were the opening occupants of the Everest in Ballifield Drive.

Industry Inn

9 Washington Road corner of Pearl Street, Sheffield

Industry Inn

206 Dunlop Street, Sheffield 9

Walt Osguthorpe was the landlord, of this beer and porter only pub, in the late1960s.

Industry Inn

89 Main Road, Sheffield 9

Industry Inn

145/147 Young Street, Sheffield 3

Industry

67 Fitzwilliam Street, Sheffield

Industry

Corporation Street, Spring Street, Sheffield

Supposedly given the nickname of the Swarf 'Ole, which slightly contradicts the fact the Corporation Inn on the same road was said to have had the same nickname.

Industry

118 Porter Street, Sheffield (1820s-1920s)

Industry

24 Savile Street east, Sheffield 9
(1850s-1940s)

Industry

2 Mowbray Street, Sheffield

Inkerman Tavern

12 Alma Street, Sheffield 3

Another of Sheffield's many military named pubs, Inkerman was a town in the Crimea, near Sebastapol.
On 5th November 1854 the English and French defeated the Russians here, after the latter made an unexpected attack. A great number of lives were lost on all sides.

Irish Cross

Fargate, Sheffield 1

Unsure if this is not just a nickname for another public house.

Iron Man

Pye Bank, Sheffield 4

A name which was probably based on the steel industry. Exact location not known.

Ivy Cottage

184 Broomspring Lane, Sheffield 10
(aka Springfield Tavern)

Ivy was supposedly dedicated to Bacchus, God of Wine, in the belief that it could cure drunkenness.

Jack in a Box

117 Silkstone Road, Sheffield 12

Opened in 1968 and situated in the middle of a 3,400 dwellings housing estate, at that time the Jack was the only pub so called in the whole of England.

Jervis Lum

Park Grange Drive, Sheffield 2

John Bull

126 Rockingham Street, Sheffield

This pub name is derived from an Essay by John Arbuthnot in 1712. This same writer portrayed the French as Lewis Baboon, the Dutch as Nicholas Frog, and so on throughout the European countries, but it seems only the English John Bull has survived. John Bull himself is perceived as a rather rotund gentleman with a three cornered hat, red waistcoat, leather breeches and carrying an oak cudgel.

John O'Gaunt

151 Blackstock Road, Sheffield 14

A John Smiths public house that gained a dubious reputation during the late eighties and early nineties, during which time it closed and was reopened on more than one occasion. It was chosen to be the pub in which Sean Bean and the cast shot their pub scenes, when making the film Pint O'Beer, I think this title was changed to 'When Saturday Comes'. It was stated in the local newspaper "that if they were looking for a typical Sheffield estate pub filled with proper Sheffielder's then the John O'Gaunt is perfect".

John O'Gaunt (1340-99) himself was son of Edward III and married wisely (three times) to further infiltrate the monarchy of England. From his second marriage, his eldest son was to become Henry IV. One of his wives was Constance daughter of Pedro the Cruel, King of Castile. Wat Tylers insurrection was in 1381 directed at John O'Gaunt and his palace was destroyed. Nevertheless, he was the most powerful man in England for many years. He is mainly referred to in pub names by a reference to his badge the Red Lion.

Jolly Bacchus

19 Holly Lane, Sheffield

Jolly Buffer

144 Ecclesall Road, Sheffield 11

The buffer ladies used to work in the grinding shops of the cutlery trade, buffing or polishing the products.

Jolly Grinders

8 Porter Street, Sheffield

Jordanthorpe

146 Dyches Lane, Sheffield 8

Junction Hotel

354 Brightside Lane, Sheffield 9

Most public houses so named are because of their proximity to a railway line or station.

Junction Hotel

Station Road, Woodhouse

Kelvin Grove Hotel

227-229 Infirmary Road, Sheffield 6

Ted Catling of Sheffield Wednesday fame was, at one time, landlord of the Grove.

Kings Arms

17 Fargate, Sheffield (built in 18th century)

Kings Arms

51 Hollis Croft, Sheffield

The signage varies according to the kings in question. One such sign showed Charles II with his arms around Nell Gwynne, but most just illustrate the King of the day.

Kings Arms

2 Haymarket, Sheffield

Kings Arms

4 Commercial Street, Sheffield

The Kings Arms, which used to stand at the top of Commercial Street, was unique in the Sheffield area, it was the only Sheffield pub to be supplied beer by the Liverpool brewery, Higson. The Kings Arms closed in 1970. One story, was that of a man who had been drinking into the small hours, and then had the misfortune to be allotted a job as one of the demolition gang, who later that same morning, had to knock down the 'Kings'.

Kings Head

95 Dunlop Street, Sheffield 9

Very similar in format to the Kings Arms signage where it is just a matter of landlord or brewery choice. Most, though seemed to plump for Henry VIII. Some signs are of playing cards.

Kings Head
63 Poole Road, Sheffield 9

A traditional no frills public house situated just off Prince of Wales Road. On its sign it shows a man who was Prince of Wales longer than most and was also king for 9 years, Edward VII.

Kings Head
Neepsend, Sheffield

Kings Head
709 Attercliffe Road, Sheffield 9
(aka Champions Rest)

One of the last beer only houses in Sheffield. The Kings Head building was used as a grocers, a earthenwear dealers, a chemist and best of all a beer house. Some of its inhabitants are engrained in Sheffield history: The earthenware shop was run by Robert Jackson, whose son Samuel was born in the building. Young Samuel was co-founder of Spear and Jackson, the world famous tool manufacturers.

George Littlewood, whose athletics career was second to none, was a world champion endurance runner and did his training in Tinsley Park Woods, his trainer being, Thomas Chick. In 1880, September 7th he ran, and won, a race of 406 miles distance. His prize was a gold medal and £50 prize money. Littlewood competed in America, Australia and in Europe. He was landlord of the Kings Head at the turn of the last century.

Another landlord was Billy Calvert, a boxer of some repute who fought for a world championship when he took on Howard Winston in the 1960s.

Kings Head
Manchester Road, Sheffield 10

A Coaching inn dating back to 1829. Until quite recently had a men only room.

Kings Head
13-15 Change Alley, Sheffield 1

This pub was destroyed in World War II during the blitz of December 1940. It was situated just off High Street in Change Alley. It was at one time thought to be the best hotel in Sheffield.

According to some people it was, at the time of its destruction, the oldest public house in Sheffield supposedly dating back to 1572, when in the Burgesses accounts for that year it was stated the landlord, a W. Dickenson owed 4 pence for rent.

It is said that the landlord of 1663 a Robert Broughton issued penny tokens with the Kings Head sign on them, these could be redeemed for beer. These tokens would definitely be a collectors item now!

Leonard Webster was the licensee during the mid 18th century. He was a leading citizen, town trustee and for the year 1748 the Master Cutler, and is said to have been the owner up to 1801. His daughter married a surgeon, John Hawsley, whose practice was on the newly opened Norfolk Street. This appeared for the first time on any Sheffield map in 1771. One of the next landlords was William Wright, a man who is said to have driven the first stagecoach on the newly opened turnpike road from Sheffield to Glossop. Wright owned over 40 acres of land in Attercliffe, and used this open space to breed and train racehorses.

Kings Head
29 Canning Street, Sheffield

Kings Head
105 King Street, Port Mahon, Sheffield

King & Miller
16 or 34 Norfolk Street, Sheffield

Around 1888 Alfred Henry Brown was the licensee for quite a few years before moving on to keep the Paradise Inn on Campo Lane. It is sited at differing addresses in old Sheffield reference books.

King & Miller

1 Chester Street/62 Trafalgar Street, Sheffield

An old ballad kept in the Pepys Collection at Mansfield Public Library, tells of Henry II losing his way in Sherwood Forest where he came upon a miller who offered him hospitality, including a dish of venison, At that time only the King of England could hunt and kill deer, so this could have meant certain death for the miller, but the king was indeed gracious for hospitality received and knighted the miller, there and then, for his services.

King William

5 Holly Street, Sheffield 1

King William

1 Alma Street, and 2 Green Lane, Sheffield (aka William IV)

Son of George III, he was a naval officer who was inclined to disregard orders from his superiors, for this flaw in his character he was never allowed his own ship to command. Later as king he was given to ill considered utterances and was never well liked and given the nickname of Silly Billy. His two children died in infancy and he was succeeded by his niece, Victoria in 1837.

Labour in Vain

62 Princess Street, Sheffield (aka Brewery Tap)

The sign above these public houses implied that anyone looking to better the drink served here would labour in vain. Another had two white women scrubbing a little black child. This original sign was based on an idea from the 15th or 16th century as an example of futility. Others depicting birds eating grain as fast as the farmer could sow it. Also there is one version of a woman trying to hide her newborn child, brought about through extra marital adventures.

Lady's Bridge Hotel

3 Bridge Street, Sheffield 2 (closed in 1993) (aka Brewer on the Bridge, Brewery Tap)

Ladybower

Ladybower Reservoir, Sheffield 2

The sign outside the Ladybower showed a Lancaster Bomber in flight and had the inscription:
"A tribute to 617 squadron". This was the Dam Busters who used this stretch of water for practice with the Barnes Wallis bouncing bomb, before making the now famous, if slightly unsuccessful, raid on the dams of the Ruhr Valley in May 1943.

Lamb

31 Howard Street, Sheff (aka Golden Lamb)

The Lamb is of great Christian significance thanks to the passage in John 1:29 which reads "Behold the Lamb of God, which taketh away the sins of the world". Or maybe it was just named after the landlady, Amy Lamb who ran the pub in the early part of the 19th century.

Lamb
4 Radford Row, Sheffield

The Lambpool
291 Attercliffe Common, Sheffield 9

This public house, The Lambpool, was built in around 1870, and as you can gather from its name it gives some evidence of the once rural aspect that used to be Attercliffe in the late 19th century. The Lambpool was one of about 40 pubs on the main road between Tinsley and Norfolk Bridge mostly built to serve the industrial workers whose houses the steel firm owners built in the vicinity of their works.

The Lambpool was a small two roomed, Whitbreads, public house with a central bar and stood on the corner of Attercliffe Common and Jansen Street, this street being named after Admiral Jansen of World War I fame. It was well frequented up until the slum clearance of Attercliffe Common circa 1958-63 when most people were moved to the estates around Sheffield, Parson Cross, Shiregreen etc. It survived on returning locals and the surrounding, slowly decreasing steel industry for almost 30 years but finally closed in the early 1990s and was demolished in 1993.

Lansdowne Hotel
2 Lansdowne Road, London Road, 11
(closed in 1990s)

Leavygreave Hotel
28 Leavygreave Road, Sheffield 3

Legends
High Street, Sheffield 1 (aka Crazy Daisy)

Legends
Bradfield Road, Hillsborough, Sheffield 6

Leg & Mutton & Trimmings
Smithfield, Sheffield

The leg of mutton was common to many a celebration in the public houses such as that of an apprentice when completing his time. In 1958 the last pub using the name leg of mutton was closed.

Le Metro
Carver Street, Sheffield

Lescar Hotel
303 Sharrow Vale Road, Sheffield 11

Hosts a comedy show called the Last Laugh on Thursday nights.

Levair Hotel
Ecclesall Road, Sheffield 11

Not much is known about this public house, except that a local football side called Lockwood Brothers had its headquarters there. Its main claim to fame is that in the year 1887 this Sheffield based works football team fought their way through to play West Bromwich Albion, the 1886 runners-up, in the fifth round of the FA Cup, then called the English Cup. Lockwood Brothers were the last Sheffield team in the competition that season.

Defeated 1-0 after a brave fight at Bramall Lane in front of a considerable crowd of over 4000, Lockwood put in a complaint. The newspaper of the day the Sheffield Daily Independent wrote "A protest was lodged by the factory club about a goal which they had claimed, alleging that the (Albion) goalkeeper was a considerable distance over the goal-line when he threw the ball out". The FA upheld the complaint and the match was replayed.

So Sheffield United aren't the first to have lost and got a replay, not even the first Sheffield side to do so.

By the way WBA won the replay, which was supposed to be at Bramall Lane but was for some reason transferred to Derby, 2-1, and they went on to finish runners up again this time to Aston Villa.

Licensed Victuallers
408 Brightside Lane, Sheffield 9

Lifeguardsman
262 Moorfields, Sheffield

Lincoln City Arms
114/116 Clarence Street, Sheffield 3

Lincoln Castle
24 or 26 Brocco Street, Sheffield
(aka Old Lincoln Castle)

Lincolnshire Arms
26 Broad Lane, Sheffield

Link Hotel
338 Hague Row, Sheffield 2

The Lion Hotel
2 Nursery Street, Sheffield (aka Black Lion)

This public house situated on the corner of The Wicker and Nursery Street, was closed in the mid 1980s but the building is still there and is now the Grosvenor Guest House. The Lion, The King of Beasts, is well represented in public house names, in fact, the name Lion prefixed by Red, White or Yellow is the most common of all English Pub names in use.

It was a Tetleys public house and unfortunately its last claim to fame (infamy) was that in the early 1980s a man named Arthur Hutchinson met a member of the Leitner family there and later that night he cold bloodedly murdered three members of this well known and respected Sheffield family shortly after a wedding was held in a Marquee in the grounds of their home in Dore.

Lion & Lamb
4 Shude Hill, Sheffield
(aka Cross Keys in 1839)

Possibly owned by a pious person as the symbols that were chosen to represent the pub denotes a slightly religious slant. Lion and Lamb is a Christian symbol of the Resurrection, the lamb of the Redeemer and Cross Keys is a symbol of St Peter.

Lion & Lamb
22 Pea Croft, Sheffield

Little Angel
94 West Bar, Sheffield

Little Atlas
135 Carlisle Street, Sheffield

Little Mesters
Ecclesall, Sheffield (aka Rolling Mills)

Little Mesters is a reference to the men who stamped out blanks for the cutlery industry.

Little Tankard
29 Little Pond Street, Sheffield

Little Tankard
11 West Bar Green, Sheffield

Live and Let Live
36 Hawley Croft, Sheffield

This sign first came to life in the 19th century and was generally seen as a comment by the landlord or owner of the establishment on circumstances which he deemed unfair. The opening of a new pub in the vicinity, or imposing of restriction by way of taxes etc.

Live and Let Live
101 Broad Lane, Sheffield (aka Britannia)

Livery Stables Inn
32 Union Lane, Sheffield

Livery is the food and drink which a horse is given in order that it may survive.

Lloyd's No. 1
Division Street, Sheffield 1

The old Waterworks building, probably holds as much of Sheffield's history as any other premises in the city. The building was owned by Mr J. G. Graves, of Graves Art Gallery and Graves Park fame. A man who probably gave more gifts to this city than anyone else in Sheffield's long history. He started his postal watch selling business in what is now Lloyds No. 1. This business was probably the forerunner of all the catalogue businesses in England today. He went on to make millions, promptly lost it and once again made his millions.

The premises were then sold on to more catalogue traders, then had some time as a Waterworks premises and was, for a few years, Arthur Scargill's headquarters when he was leader of the National Union of Mineworkers.

Local Field Tavern
151 Attercliffe Road, Sheffield (1860s-1932)

Locarno
London Road, Sheffield 2

Locomotive
49 Carlisle Street, Sheffield

Reference to the local railway tracks or station. Later became the Burngreave Liberal Club, situated on the town side of the railway.

Locomotive

42 Fowler Street, Sheffield

Lodge Inn,

47 Spital Hill, Sheffield 4

This inn was only a 6 day license premises, no Sunday opening.
It was later turned into a motor-cycle repair shop.

Lodge Inn

143 Newhall Road, Sheffield 9

London Apprentice

77 Spring Street, Sheffield
(aka Old London 'Prentice)

The name dates from the 15th century.

London Apprentice

81 West Bar Green, Sheffield
(aka London 'Prentice)

London House

110 West Bar, Sheffield

London House

25 Pinstone Street, Sheffield

Lord Nelson

184 Greystock St, Sheffield 4

Horatio Nelson, 1st Viscount Nelson (1758-1805). This great hero has more public houses named after him, directly or indirectly, than any other character. After victories over the Danish, Spanish and French fleets, he was killed, on his ship, the Victory, whilst at Trafalgar. He is also credited with the famous signal of "England expects that every man will do his duty".

Lord Nelson

Norroy Street, Sheffield

Lord Nelson Inn

62 Broad Street, Sheffield 2

Lord Nelson Inn

166/168 Arundel Street, Sheffield 1

In 1940 Fanny Brocklebank kept this pub and to most people to this day the pub is known as Fanny's.

Lord Palmerston

Carlisle Street, Sheffield

Henry John Temple, 3rd Viscount Palmerston (1784-1865) was an English statesman and Prime Minister on two occasions. He was renowned for his gun boat policy when foreign secretary, which to some extent only furthered British prestige at that time.

Lord Raglan
Bridge Street, Sheffield

Fitzroy James Henry Somerset, 1st Baron Raglan, (1788-1855) was a British General who served in the peninsula war and was military secretary to the Duke of Wellington. He was commander in chief of the British troops in the Crimean War.

Lord Ratcliffe
95 Lord Street, Sheffield

Lord Rancliff's Arms
Unsure of location, Sheffield 1833

Low Drop
Attercliffe area (possible a nickname)

Lyceum
153 Langsett Road, Sheffield 6

The Magnet
Southey Green Road, Sheffield 5

A large estate pub, this John Smith house, situated close to the roundabout at Southey Green, was erected about the same time as the Parson Cross estate was being built circa 1936. Of the name, The Magnet, there are two variations given as to its meaning, the first, it was from the logo for the John Smiths brewery and secondly, it was said that it was supposed to pull the passing public into the pub.

On its grounds it has a Stanleys Betting Office which paid rent to the brewery.

For a good many years it was generally a very well frequented public house, whilst such landlords as Ted Catlin of Sheffield Wednesday fame had it, but it always had a chequered history. It was running tossing rings in the late 1940s just after the Second World War and was finally closed down because of general unruliness in the mid 1990s. It tried to reopen a couple of times but to no avail, and was demolished in 1997.

Magpie
88 Low Edges Road, Sheffield 8

At one time in its fairly short existence the Magpie served the local community as a temporary Roman Catholic church for some Sunday masses in 1970.

It is said if one taps at the window at one of these birds it is said to be a death warning. The Magpie is supposed to have refused entry to Noah's Ark, how did it survive?

Mail Coach

149-151 West Street, Sheffield 1
(aka Commercial, Scruffy Murphys)

The name mail coach was first introduced into the English language circa 1784, when postal transport was introduced between Bristol and London, these coaches, were then used to deliver mail throughout the country and stayed in existence for about 65 years until the railway proved its superiority.

One of the many point of call on the now famous West Street Pub Crawl.

Now turned into an Irish themed pub by Allied Domecq's (Tetleys) Irish Venture. No doubt it will soon be back to its original name.

Malin Bridge Inn

194 Holme Lane, Sheffield 6

Ted Elsom was Landlord, and a good one, of the Malin in the 1970s, he also ran the George IV and the Rock, Pitsmoor from where he finally retired.

Malton Hotel

33 Burton Road, Sheffield 3
(closed and demolished in 1970s)

Maltsters Arms

Intake, Handsworth, Sheffield

Manchester Hotel

6 Division Street, Sheffield

Manchester Hotel

108 Nursery Street, Sheff (aka Manchester & Lincolnshire Railway Hotel)

The entire facade of this public house was ripped away during the night of the Sheffield Flood in 1864. Amazing when you think that the Dale Dyke Dam is some 7 or 8 miles away. Supposedly, some bodies that were washed along with the wall of water were eventually found as far afield as Doncaster. One of three pubs still standing called the river pubs, the Harlequin and Brown Cow being the others.

M. S. & L. Railway Hotel or Inn

38 Furnival Road, Sheffield

Manor Castle

239 Manor Lane, Sheffield 2

'Set in the shadow of the Manor Castle on Manor Lane', this is how the pub's location is generally described, unfortunately there has never been a Manor Castle, it is a Lodge a large dwelling house.

The Manor Lodge was built by George, the Fourth Earl of Shrewsbury in 1516, set amongst vast tracts of parkland. The Lodge itself was oblong shaped with two large courtyards and a long narrow gallery containing paintings and tapestries.

The sixth earl's reign saw the imprisonment of Mary Queen of Scots, not as most people believe confined to the turret house but in the lodge itself. She needed the space, after all she had an entourage of over 30 permanent attendents.

The pub is said to be haunted by a white figure, someone once described this figure as wearing a plumed hat and gaiters.

Manor Castle

86 Howard Street,
or New Howard Street, Sheffield

Manor Hotel

Fretson Road, Sheffield 2

Mansfield Hotel

73 Division Street, Sheffield

Market Inn

18 Wortley Road, High Green, Sheffield

Built in circa 1830 and used as a turnpike (a place where a barrier is place for collecting tolls) on the road leading from Wortley to Rotherham at Mortomley.

Marples

High Street, Fitzalan Square, Sheffield 1
(aka London Mart, Wine and Spirit
Commercial Hotel)

In 1876 there was a Wine and Spirit Commercial Hotel that occupied 64 High Street, and was owned by a Mr Astley. The first record of the pub as the Market Street Wine Vaults in 1888 when its owner was a John Marples and the licensee was an Edward Marples, as you can understand it was called locally by the name of "Marples".

On December 12th, 1940 at around midnight the London Mart, pictured below, as it was then known, received a direct hit from a Luftwaffe bomber, that not only destroyed the seven storey building but claimed the lives of 70 people. Of the 77 customers and staff who were there on that fateful night only seven were pulled from the rubble alive, this by local miners especially brought in to help the rescue services operation.

This site was left derelict for some 20 years. Some Sheffield people wanted to have a memorial erected to the dead but instead another public house was erected. It officially took the name Marples in 1959 when it was reopened by John Smiths Magnet brewery.

Marquis of Waterford

2 Russell Street, Sheffield

Marshall Tavern

133 Pitsmoor Road, Sheffield 3
(aka Bacon Box) (closed 1960)

This was one of the smallest public houses in Sheffield and was often referred to by locals as the Bacon Box.

Masons Arms
14 Capel Street, Sheffield 6

A popular name in Sheffield history, with at least 14 public houses so named. The Company of Masons who cut stone into shape for building purposes, were granted a coat of arms in 1473.

Masons Arms
17 Castle Green, Sheffield

Masons Arms
43 Campo Lane, Sheffield

Masons Arms
Attercliffe Road, Sheffield 9
(aka Oddfellows Arms)

The landlord in the 1820s was one John Eyre who was a mason by trade, therefore the Masons Arms. This story is slightly more complex though, for in c1841 whilst Eyre still ran the pub it was called the Oddfellows Arms. We don't know if the locals called it the oddfellows because of Eyres behaviour or it had an Order of Oddfellows Lodge running at that time. In 1849 until about 1860 a Joseph Charlesworth resided over what was still the Oddfellows. After this, the landlord was a Charles H Johnson. Conflicting reports on when this pub was demolished vary, but the general consensus is around the 1860s to make way for a Wesleyan Chapel.

Masons Arms
3 Shude Hill, Sheffield

Masons Arms
85 South Street Park, Sheffield

Masons Arms
Cricket Inn Road, Sheffield

Masons Arms
47/49 Pearl Street, Sheffield 11

Masons Arms
18 Bridge Street, Sheffield

Masons Arms
270 Langsett Road, Sheffield 6

Built in the 1850s the Masons has recently, mid 90s, been refurbished to incorporate a snooker room at the rear of the pub. It used to be made up of three fairly small rooms and a central bar standing area. In the mid 1980s it had one of Sheffield's best darts sides capable of giving any team in England a good run for their money. Dennis Priestley, double World Champion, was one of the players at that time.

Masons Arms
130 Duke Street, Sheffield

Masons Arms
2 Carson Road, Sheffield 10

Masons Arms
Brick Street, Crookes, Sheffield

Matilda Tavern
100 Matilda Street, Sheffield 1

Named after William the Conqueror's wife, the diminutive Matilda who was the daughter of Baldwin, Count of Flanders, the pub was built in 1840 as a coaching house to provide food and drink to weary travellers. Supposedly an archway adjacent to the tavern was the entry to the still existing stable yard for horse drawn carriages.

The Matilda like the Masons on Langsett Road, had a very good darts team, this consisted of a couple of England internationals and several Yorkshire county players. Season after season they swept all before them.

Meadow Inn
81 Main Road, Sheffield 9

Mr William Henry Arnold and his family took up the license of the Meadow in 1925 and can be seen on the Meadow Inn picture, standing amongst the bunting which had been hung to celebrate the 25th year on the throne for King George V, in 1935. Mr Arnold stayed at the Meadow until his untimely death in July 1940.

The Meadow, a Cannon Brewery house was beer only and did not have a license for spirits.

Meadow Street Hotel
110 Meadow Street, Sheffield 3

This one hundred and fifty year old pub takes its name from the road on which it was built.

Mermaid
35 Orchard Street, Sheffield

This Sheffield pub was named after the famous Mermaid Tavern in the capital and was built in around 1821.

The original Mermaid Tavern was in Cheapside London and was frequented by Raleigh, Beaumont, Fletcher, Donne, Ben Jonson and Shakespeare to name but a few. Years later the Poet John Keats wrote:

Souls of poets dead and gone,
What Elysium have ye known
Happy field or mossy cavern
Choicer then the Mermaid Tavern?
Have ye tippled drink more fine
Than mine hosts Canary Wine.

Merrie Monk
60 Manor Park Centre, Sheffield

Merry Heart Hotel
110 Brunswick Street, Sheffield 3

Middlewood Tavern
316 Middlewood Road, Sheffield 6

Midland
18 Turner Street, Sheffield

Midland Hotel
2 Alfred Road, Sheffield

This public house frontage, which looks like a row of council houses, has/had a display of coloured lights that would be switched on 365 nights of the year. Standing near the railway bridge that runs across the top of Newhall Road, it seems to be very isolated, but with custom from returning old locals, dinner time trade or late shift workers it still manages to survive.

Midland Station Hotel
Station Road, Sheffield

Midland Inn
Occupation Road/Grimesthorpe Road, Sheffield

Midland Railway
119 Savile Street, Sheffield

Midland Hotel
26 Burncross Road, Chapeltown

Midland Hotel
2 Spital Hill, Sheffield 4

Milestone
Crystal Peaks Centre, Sheffield 19

Mill Sands
21 Millsands, Sheffield

Mill Stone
12 Cross Burgess Street, Sheffield

The circular stone, one of a pair used for grinding.

Millers Arms
65-67 Carlisle Street, Sheffield (1860-1940s)

Millhouses Hotel
951 Abbeydale Road, Sheffield 7

Used to be known as the Millwright.

Milton Arms

**272 Rockingham Street, Sheffield 1
(closed in the mid 1960s)**

Generally the public houses named after Milton, i.e.
Arms, Head, Hotel, are all named after the poet and prose
writer John Milton (1608-74). He was Latin Secretary to
Oliver Cromwell. Unfortunately he defended the
imprisonment and execution of Charles I and at the
restoration he was fined and driven into retirement. He
was totally blind and dictated his two most famous works,
Paradise Lost and Paradise Regained.

Milton Arms

66 Thomas Street, Sheffield 1 (1820s-1960s)

Milton's Arms

29 Bailey Lane, Sheffield

Milton Arms

81 London Road, Sheffield

Milton Hotel

14 Miltons Street, Sheffield

Miltons Head Inn

29/31 Allen Street, Sheffield 3 (1820s-1958)

Miners Arms

198 Arundel Street, Sheffield

Generally, the pub name miners was in some reference
geographically to a local pit/colliery.

Miners Arms or Rest

7 East Street, Sheffield

Miners Arms

Bradway, Norton, Sheffield

Miners Arms

750 Attercliffe Road, Sheffield

Miners Arms

125 Warren Lane, Chapeltown

Miners Rest

61 Cricket Inn Road, Sheffield

Miners Tavern

Blast Lane, Sheffield

Minerva Tavern

**103 Hillfoot, or 343 - 345 Penistone Road,
Sheffield**

Minerva was the Roman equivalent of Athena, the Greek
goddess of household arts.

Minerva Tavern

**69 Charles Street, Sheffield 1
(aka Yorkshire Grey, Bar Rio)**

Mitre Tavern

**32 Change Alley, Sheffield
(aka Wine and Spirit Merchants)
(closed around 1930)**

The name mitre is the tall cap with a deep cleft in it,
usually associated with a bishop. It is/was also worn by
some abbots on ceremonial occasions. It has been used as
an inn sign for over 500 years.
Most relevant in cathedral towns.

Mitre

27 Orchard Street, Sheffield (1820s-1910s)

Mitre

Fargate, Sheffield
(actual location unknown)

Mojo

**National Centre for Popular Music,
Paternoster Row, Sheffield**

This bar, built in 1999, along the lines of a giant pinball machine has a long bar with offshot cosy booths. Now along with the Leadmill and the Showrooms complex it is bringing more life back into this once dilapidated little area of Sheffield.

Probably named after Pete Stringfellows famous 60s Burngreave club "The Mojo" which featured many of the top stars of the day, Jimmi Hendrix being amongst them.

Montgomery Hotel

1 Montgomery Terrace, Sheffield 4

Of the so named public houses in Sheffield it is not known if any were named after Field Marshal Montgomery of El Alamein.

Montgomery Hotel

225 St Marys Road, Sheffield 2

This hotel's upper floors were demolished and it continued trading for many years as a single storey pub.

Montgomery Tavern

12 Hartshead, Sheffield 2

The 18th century radical Joseph Gales ran a stationery shop and a printing office, the Sheffield Register was printed here. Gales had to flee to America to escape a possible prison sentence because of his (supposedly) seditious literature, publications.

James Montgomery took over the running of the paper, and wisely changed the name of the newspaper to the Iris. When Montgomery retired in about 1862 the building was turned into a tavern that catered for diners and let beds to travellers and carters etc.

The original shop front, which as a matter of interest had the largest display window in Sheffield township in 1787, was painstakingly taken apart and dispatched to America as a souvenir of Gales.

Monument Tavern

25-27 Button Lane, Sheffield

The Sheffield Monument is to the victims of the Cholera outbreak. From the beginning of July until the end of October 1832 the epidemic ravaged Sheffield and 1,347 people contracted the disease and of these 402 died, including the Master Cutler John Blake. As you can see from the following, three public houses were named after the monument which was erected to commemorate the death of the victims. Another outbreak occurred in 1849 and 205 more lives were lost. The actual Cholera Monument was erected in 1834-35 and the local poet and Newspaper Editor, James Montgomery, laid the cornerstone.

Monument Tavern

**61 South Street, Park, Sheffield
(closed 1922)**

Monument Tavern

**190 South Street, Park, Sheffield
(closed around 1920)**

Moon

13 Silver Street, Sheffield (aka Full Moon)

Unusual name not often found, generally prefixed by half, full, silver etc.

Moorfoot Tavern

**Cumberland Street, Sheffield 1
(aka Cumberland, Whetstone)**

Morpeth Arms

108 Allen Street, Sheffield 3 (opened c1800)

Morpeth Arms

Granville Street, Sheffield

Moseley's Arms
81/83 West Bar, Sheffield 3 (aka Rose)

Situated on the corner of West Bar and Paradise Street, the Moseley is now the only pub left on the West Bar stretch, which at one time had around 20 inns and taverns on it.

The Rose, as it was originally known, was situated on the corner of West Bar and Workhouse Croft, but when the legal profession took over Paradise Square, it was thought it would be better to be rid of a name such as Workhouse Croft so it was changed to Paradise Street.

Around 1828 Thomas Moseley took over as the landlord of the Rose and soon afterward we only read of this public house being called the Moseley.

The aforementioned workhouse was closed a year after Moseley took over the Rose, in 1829, it had been open 107 years and was the place feared by all of Sheffield's poorer townspeople who expected to end their days there. The Moseley itself is a three roomed establishment with a large function room upstairs, which used to house a snooker table and has been made larger in the last few years by purchasing the premises next door for extension. Before this refurbishment it had, arguably, the smallest room in the Sheffield licensing industry, it had one table two chairs and a telephone. If both chairs were occupied it was a struggle to use the phone.

Mote Hall
Motehall Road, Sheffield

Moulder's Arms
43 Green Lane, Sheffield
Moulders made the mould for iron castings.

Moulder's Arms
25 Corby Street, Sheffield

Moulder's Arms
Sheaf Island, Sheffield

Moulder's Return
7 High Street, Sheffield (1820-1900s)

Mountain Deer
14 Orchard Lane, Sheffield

Mount Pleasant
291 Derbyshire Lane, Sheffield 8

Mowbray Inn
Mowbray Street, Sheffield

Mowbray Tavern
53 Sussex Street, Sheffield

Mulberry Tavern

2 Mulberry Street, Sheffield 1
(aka Rendez Vous)

The area around which the Mulberry Tavern now stands was proclaimed by James I that it must have Mulberry trees planted on it. This was in order to increase the supply of silk, as our overseas trade had ceased with the normal supplier. Silk worms live on the leaves of Mulberry trees. This tavern is now well over 200 years old, and has its own little unsolved mystery. Many years ago a traveller booked into the tavern but the next morning was found on the pavement outside, he had fallen to his death from his room. His body was searched and no identification was found, although a large sum of money was found on his person. The man was buried in an unmarked grave in the local parish church.

Municipal Inn

175 Burgoyne Road, Sheffield 6

Murrays Arms

58 Queens Street, Sheffield
(opened in the 18th century)

Museum

25 Orchard Street, Sheffield 1
(aka Orchard, Brewing Trough, Hogshead)
(originally opened in 1790s)

This building which now serves good beer and hot meals was once the mortuary for the Medical School which was sited nearby. The old Museum was supposedly haunted.
The Hogs Head is a reincarnation of the Museum, a Whitbread, Tennants pub. It is now a well frequented public house and serves meals and drinks in the open air cafe section in the Orchard Square area to its rear.
At the time of going to print the pub is once again going through some alterations.

Myrtle Inn

33 Alexandra Road, Sheffield 2
(closed in 1970s)

Named after the evergreen plant which has white fragrant glossy leaves, the Myrtleberry.
It also ran one of Sheffield's oldest 'Royal Antideluvian Order of Buffalo' lodges.

Nags Head
325 Shalesmoor, Sheffield 3

A pub that a few years ago had the dubious nickname of the Horses Nut, is now one of the most comfortable public houses in Sheffield. Somewhat tucked away on Shalesmoor, the Nags has had a few refurbishments in its time, the last one gave it a pool room area which was gained from buying out the old army surplus shop next door and knocking through. Originally it had a dram shop that would be deemed crowded with only six standing customers.

A Nag is a small riding horse or pony, and early signs showing a nags head would probably indicate that one could be hired from the inn.

Nags Head
Jehu Lane, Sheffield

The Nags was opened in the late 18th century and in different Sheffield directories is sited at 15 Nags Head Yard, and 1 Jehu Lane, Haymarket, and is called the Nags Head and Billiard Rooms.

Its early landlords were Robert Heaton and John Tasker in 1839.

Nags Head
Stacey Bank, Loxley

Nailmakers Arms
Backmoor Road, Sheffield 8 (built in 1627)

The Nailmakers, has the oldest pub license in Sheffield dating back to 1626, three hundred and seventy three years. The pub itself takes its name from the ancient industry of nailmaking. At one time as with most larger public houses the Nailmakers had its own brewery.

Napier Hotel
95 Napier Street, Sheffield 11
(opened in around 1820)

Named after Sir Charles Napier who is credited with keeping a firm hold on the Chartist movement of the 19th century, mainly, in the North of England. Some would say too firm, especially as of the six reforms the Chartists put forward, four of them were eventually made law.

Napier Hotel
28 Lord Street, Sheffield

Napoleon
34 Green Lane, Sheffield (1820s-1912)

The Napoleon name may well come from the French, self crowned emperor, but it is unlikely that during or even after a war, a public house should be called after your enemy. Its like an inn now being called "Hitler".

Being named after Napoleon Bonaparte himself is probably only likely if there was an inn where men were enrolling in the army or navy of the day and as in some cases on the south coast locals called it Napoleon's House, then it is possible the name would stick. But more likely the name is probably from Napoleon III who came to England in 1871 to begin his exile.

Napoleon
85 Carver Street, Sheffield (1829-1912)

Navigation Inn
9 Castle Street, or Castle Folds, Sheffield

The word Navigation used to mean a 'canal waterway' and therefore the men who excavated the canals were called navigators, shortened, generally, to 'navvies'. The name still exists today, though a 'navvy' nowadays is spelled differently and generally it just means someone who does heavy excavating work. This particular public house would probably have been more for the traders from the Sheffield to Goole canal basin than the navvies who built it.

Neepsend Tavern
144 Neepsend Lane, Sheffield 3
(1830s-1970s)

The tavern is now a sauna suite.

Nelson
78 Trippet Lane, Sheffield 1 (opened 1840s)

Nelson Inn
13 New St, West Bar, Sheffield 1
(opened 1820s)

Neptune
22 New Haymarket, Sheffield
(opened 1830s)

New Ball Inn
18 Osborne Street, Sheffield

New Bridge Inn
Wadsley Bridge, Sheffield 6 (aka New Inn)

This public house is like quite a few in the Sheffield area that have two names on the frontage of the building.

The hanging signage says New Bridge Inn and the carved stone mantle on the frontage, over the main entrance, shows the New Inn!

New Britannia
72 Rockingham Street, Sheffield

New Brunswick
84 Allen Street, Sheffield (1820s-1950s)

Newcastle Arms
35 Newcastle Street, Sheffield
(closed in around 1905)

After its closure in c1905 the Newcastle Arms was converted into a lodging house.

It is said to be named after the Earl of Newcastle who in 1642 took Sheffield castle, for the King, during the English Civil War, supposedly after annihilating any Parliamentary resistance he found in nearby Rotherham and on the way through to the castle itself.

New Crown Inn
343 Handsworth Road, Sheffield 9

Newfield Inn
141 Denmark Road, Sheffield 2

New Gas Tavern
5 Sussex Street, Sheffield

New Hall Gardens
Brightside Lane, Sheffield

New Hall Street Tavern
7 New Hall Street, Sheffield

New Hall Tavern
Sanderson Street, Sheffield

New Inn
211 Carbrook Street, Sheffield 9

New Inn
24-26 Vine Road, or 50 Main Road, Darnall, Sheffield 9

New Inn
2 Effingham Road, Sheffield 9

New Inn
40 Shalesmoor, Sheffield 3

New Inn
2 Penistone Road, Sheffield 6

New Inn
23 Maltravers Street, Sheffield

New Inn
Sheffield Road, Hackenthorpe

New Inn
183 Duke Street, 48 Bernard Street, Sheff

New Inn
378 Brightside Lane, Sheffield 9

The New Inn
108 Ecclesall Road, Sheffield 11

Over the years, Sheffield has had around ten public houses with this name. There are three trains of thought about the name New Inn, the obvious one was that it was recently built, the second was a special inn built to accommodate the large numbers of pilgrims arriving at the tomb of Edward II at Gloucester, and the third was that in the sixteenth century, Queen Elizabeth I complained about the lack of suitable places to stay, therefore a spate of New Inns were built. Unfortunately, which of the three this Tetley house was named from remains a mystery.

A J. Rowbotham, a famous Yorkshire County Cricketer kept this particular New Inn on Ecclesall Road for many years in the early part of the century.

This picture was taken from a passing bus the day before the New Inn was demolished in the mid 1980s.

New Inn
94 Harvest Lane, Sheffield

New Inn
2 Bellefield Lane, Sheffield

New Inn
Hemsworth Road, Sheffield 8

New Inn
282 Hollinsend Road, Sheffield 12

New Inn
10 Montfort Street, Sheffield 3

This public house had to be pulled down after severe damage to its structure in the Sheffield gales of 1962.

New Market Hotel
20 Broad Street/1 Sheaf St, Sheffield 2
(1810s-1960s)

New Market Hotel
13 Exchange Street, Sheffield (1830s-1920s)

Newmarket Inn
28 Furnival Road, Sheffield
(aka Station Inn, Victoria Hotel)

New Music Hall Tavern
116 Barkers Pool, Fargate, Sheffield

New Saddle
88 West Street, Sheffield 1
(aka Saddle Hotel)

The new Saddle was built just a few yards down/up the road from the original Saddle, which can still be seen on the left of this picture.

New Star Hotel & Grand Music Hall
2 Spring St, and 1 Coulston St, Sheffield

New Tankard
41 Sims Croft, Sheffield (1820s-1900s)

New Turks Head

126 Scotland Street, Sheffield

New White Lion

79 Division Street, Sheffield 1

Nimrod

164 Portobello Street, Sheffield

Noahs Ark

140 Tudor Street, Sheffield
(closed around 1910)

The signage of the ark would be instantly recognisable to all. The ark also features in the arms of the Shipwrights Company, who have as a motto "Within the Ark safe for ever". So you can see why an innkeeper would like his sign to give this message.

Noahs Ark

94 Crookes, Sheffield 10

This Crookes pub was refurbished in 1995 to add another room to its small structure. The old pub and bar are intact so it has lost none of its old feel, just a little more spacious.

Noahs Ark

197 Mansfield Road, Sheffield 12

Norfolk

224 South Street, Sheffield 2

Norfolk Arms

Pudding Lane, Sheffield

Norfolk Arms

26 Dixon Lane, Sheffield 1

The pub stands on the corner of Dixon Lane and Shude Hill. Its clientele is mainly made up of the market traders from the nearby markets and the fruit stalls on Dixon Lane itself.

Norfolk Arms

18 Sands Paviours, or Sands Paviers, Sheffield

Norfolk Arms

5 Norfolk Street, Sheffield 4

Norfolk Arms

208 Savile Street East, Sheffield
(aka Slacky's) (opened 1850s)

Norfolk Arms

56 Savile Street East, Sheffield
(closed around 1940)

Norfolk Arms

160 Attercliffe Road, Sheffield 4
(opened 1830)

A Tetleys House pictured standing in the shadow of its main client base, the Tempered Spring Company Limited. It was just one of around 45 public houses adorning the length of Attercliffe Road, from Kirkbridge Road to the Wicker Archers.

The public house itself was a small two roomed establishment, and it obviously catered for the steelworkers and industry in general. Like many other pubs in this area it knew it had a clientele no matter what the state of the premises. After the steel industry diminished in the area around the mid 1970s the Norfolk Arms tried to survive, but it was too much of a struggle and it closed in the 1980s and the building is now being used as a sauna.

Norfolk Arms

85/87 Clarence Street, Sheffield 3
(1830s-1960s)

Norfolk Arms

Manor, Sheffield

In an old 1833 reference book the Norfolk Arms in mentioned but its location is just given as the Manor.

Norfolk Arms

2 Suffolk Road, Sheffield 2

Norfolk Arms

39 Shepherd Street, Sheffield (1830s-1930s)

Norfolk Hotel

64 Mowbray Street, Sheffield

Norfolk Arms

70 Fargate, Sheffield 1
(closed late 19th century)

Norfolk Arms

91 Granville Street, Sheffield

Norfolk Arms

2 Ringinglow Road, Sheffield 11

Nestling on the edge of the Peak District the Norfolk Arms used to have a clay pigeon shoot at the rear. This Bass owned pub is a popular stopping off point for walkers who roam the peaks.

Over 200 years old this pub is reputedly haunted by a ghost called Eric, who roams the premises in cap and rainmac. This apparition reportedly gets upset if a picture of the Laughing Cavalier is removed from the walls.

Norfolk Arms

8 Penistone Road, Sheffield 6

Situated on the corner of Whitely Lane and Halifax Road the Norfolk is a large imposing stone built pub with a beautiful beer garden that overlooks the valley.

Norfolk Arms

29 White Lane, Chapeltown

The Norfolk Arms is set between the intersections 35 and 36 of the M1. Older than all of the motorways the pub was a halfway house between Sheffield and Barnsley during the coaching days of yesteryear. After the pull up Chapeltown Hill the horses and sometimes drivers and passengers needed refreshing.

Norfolk Hotel

1 St Marys Road, Sheffield 1

Norfolk Arms

Rivelin Valley, Hollow Meadows, Sheffield 6
(aka New Norfolk Bar and Brasserie)

Norfolk House

38 Furnival Road, Sheffield

Norfolk Hotel

73 Barkers Place, Sheffield

Norfolk Arms Hotel

225 Handsworth Road, Sheffield 13

Norfolk Arms Hotel

195/199 Carlisle Street, Sheffield 4

Norfolk Vaults

New Haymarket, Sheffield (aka Cowsheds)

Situated underneath the Norfolk Market hall entrance in
Dixon Lane.

Normanton Hotel

123 Grimesthorpe Road, Sheffield 4

Normanton Springs Hotel

65 Normanton Springs Road, Sheffield

North Pole Inn

60/62 Sussex Street, Sheffield 4

In London, public houses were named North Pole years
before the American explorer Robert Edwin Peary, in
1909 reach the pole. It is unknown whether this Sheffield
'North Pole' was named to commemorate Peary's feat or
just a general geographical reference. This particular inn
started its life as a private house known as Riverside
Cottage. The 19th century building is now used as offices.

Norton Hotel

Meadowhead, Norton, Sheffield 8

Nottingham Castle

72 Edward Street, Sheff (opened in 1830s)

The original Nottingham castle was begun by William the Conqueror in 1068.

Nottingham House Hotel

19/23 Watery Street, Sheffield

The reason for public houses being called after other towns has endless possibilities, but most likely is the link of the innkeeper to his home town, to the Royal Navy who had a ship called Nottingham, or it could be that they were named after one of the many earls of Nottingham.

Nottingham House

164 Whitham Road, Sheffield 10

This student haunt public house interior was used for scenes in a film of atomic aftermath based around Sheffield called "Threads".

Nottingham Hotel

13 Bridge Street, Sheffield

Number One

49 Silver Street Head, Sheffield
(closed 1900s)

During the nineteenth century it was easier to obtain a license to brew beer from the Magistrate rather than the excise. In 1869 there were 134,000 licensed brewers in England, today that number is less than 200. In that peak period licenses for beerhouses were issued as numbers and some owners just used the number instead of giving a name to the house, hence No. 1, No. 2, Old No. 12 etc.

Number Two

63 Silver Street Head, Sheffield
(closed 1900s)

Nursery Tavern

8 Johnson Street, Sheffield

Probably so named because of the fields in the near vicinity.

Nursery Tavern

276 Ecclesall Road, Sheffield 11

Ocean View

Wyming Brook Ravine, Sheffield

This beerhouse was situated close by the Redmires dam and it ceased to be a licensed premises in 1885.

Oddfellows Arms

38 Pitt Street, Sheffield (1830s-1890s)

The original reference to this name is from the Independent Order of Oddfellows (Manchester Union), a social and benevolent society with branches throughout the UK and in many other countries. This society has been active since the early 19th century and it is said the name was derived from a remark made about the founding members, The Oddfellows.

Oddfellows Arms

26 Furnace Hill, Sheffield

Oddfellows Arms

25 Silver Street, Sheffield

Oddfellows Inn

200 Duke Street, Sheffield 2

Oddfellows Rest

53 West Street, Sheffield 1

Oddfellows Rest

94 Button Lane, Sheffield 1 (1835-1900s)

Old Albion

103-105 Hill Street, Sheffield

The Old Albion name could derive from the fact that it refers to Old England, a name often used in the licensing industry. Some pubs with this name do have a different reference though and this is to a famous, at the time, 90 gun warship, called Old Albion, built in Plymouth in 1842.

Old Albion

**38 Fowler Street, Sheffield 3
(aka Guards Rest)**

Old Albion

242/244 Hanover Street, Sheffield 3

Old Ball Inn

86 Carver Street, Sheffield 1

Old Blue Ball

**Bradfield Road, Sheffield 6
(aka Blue Dumpling-nickname)**

Recently, 1998, undergoing a renovation costing nearly half a million pound the "Blue Ball" has had the compulsory dining area added and the creation of more space in the lounge.

In times past the Old Blue Ball had its own bowling green. Jimmy Spoors was the landlord after his long and distinguished career with Sheffield Wednesday came to an end.

Also many years ago during the night of the Sheffield Flood the landlord and his wife were luckily upstairs as the wall of water 20 feet high swept by, depositing a tree in the kitchen and totally destroying the stables.

Old Blue Ball

67 Broad Street, Sheffield 2

Old Blue Bell

120 Worksop Road, Sheff 9 (aka Blue Bell)

This building is now a mosque.

Old Bowling Green Hotel
2 Upwell Lane, Sheffield 4

Old Bradley Well
150 Main Road, Darnall, Sheffield 9
(aka Terminus Tavern)

The Old Bradley Well was one of a number of pubs in the Darnall area that served the steel and mining industries, and served them well, but as these once thriving industries receded so did the trade for the pub. The Old Bradley Well survived much longer than most, through to the early 90s recession, when it finally closed. From the ashes sprang the Terminus, with a little help from the Stones brewery, a few years later in June 1994. It is now a free house and serves a large range of beers, hand pulled and electric.

Old Brewery Tap
Snig Hill, Sheffield 1
(aka Merry England Bar, Dive Bar,
Under the Boardwalk)

The place to be seen during Sheffield's emerging swinging 60s scene, just after it was built.

At that time, when the groups were doing their thing upstairs in the Black Swan you would go for a pint in the Merry England Bar or the Dive Bar and wait around till entry to the Swan could be gained.

Now it's a bar that opens infrequently and for a good number of years has just missed out on being a town pub. It is just slightly off the well trodden town circuit.

Old Cart & Horses
2 Wortley Road, High Green

Some say the Old Cart and Horses on Wortley Road, High Green, dates back to the 15th century, and it is definitely shown on a map circa 1720, of the Sheffield area. On the journey between Yorkshire and Lancashire it would have been a resting place or quick stop for shodding or just for that refreshing drink, for travellers, good carrying wagoners or even pack horse travellers. Plus the people who went to and from Wortley Forge and Sheffield. The stables, are still complete with hayracks and generally in good condition.

This Tetley pub, still holds some of that 'olde worlde' charm, with its low beams and old copper and brass ornaments adorning the walls and shelves.

Old Cherry Tree
184-188 Gibraltar Street, Sheffield
(opened in 1820s)

120

Old Cottage

Walkley, Sheffield
(probably Walkley Cottage)

Old Cricket Ground Inn

289 Darnall Road, Sheffield 9

Old Cricket Players

69 Coalpit Lane, Sheffield (opened 1820s)

R. Tracey was licensee in 1839, whilst also trading as a bone dealer.

Old Crown Inn

406 Handsworth Road, Sheffield 13

Old Crown

15 Grindlegate, Sheffield

Old Crown Inn

137 London Road, Sheffield 2

Old Crown Inn

710 Penistone Road, Sheffield 6

Old Crown Inn

33 Scotland Street, Sheffield 3
(aka Crown, R & Bs)(opened late 18th cent)

Old English Gentleman

12 Shude Hill, Sheffield (1780s-1910s)

Old George & Dragon

17 Bank Street, Sheffield (aka Old George)

Old Green Dragon

44 Fargate, Sheffield 1

Old Grindstone Inn

3 Crookes, Sheffield 10

Or Ye Olde Grindstone, as it says over the entrance, is located in Crookes, at the end of a lane which it was said led to several former quarries, the source of the grindstones.

The Grindstone is well over 170 years old and it had a mention in the 1828 chronicle 'The history of Crookes'.

The pub was refitted in 1989, although they had to wait over 3 years for the planning permission for the refurbishment to go through. The size of the public house was increased from 800 to 2200 square feet. The Victorian lounge is a pleasure to sit in and some of the customers say it is without doubt the best pub room in Sheffield. It has an adjoining conservatory with an oak panelled games room to the rear, this is graced with both pool and snooker tables as well as dart boards. A regular student haunt.

It is said that on a clear day you can see Dinnington Church tower which is a good 15 miles away, some view! With its customer base made up of students, lecturer's and even some professors you feel there should be no shortage of quiz league medals here.

Original Old Grindstone Inn
Crookes, Sheffield 10

This public house was situated across from where the existing Old Grindstone Inn now stands. It was set up by the landlady of the Old Original Grindstone Inn after she had an arguement with the brewery.

Old Half Moon Inn
64 Allen Street, Sheffield (1840s-1910s)

Old Harrow Inn
White Lane, Gleadless, Sheffield 12

Old Harrow
34 Harvest Lane, Sheffield (closed in 1950s)

Old Harrow Inn
Grenoside, Sheffield 12

Old Heavygate Inn
114 Matlock Road, Sheffield 6

Supposedly opened in the late 17th century, 1696-7 as a toll house, collecting tolls from travelling tradesman, chapmen, on their way out of Sheffield along Racker Way to Stannington, Bradfield then on to Glossop or Manchester. The original date stone is set into the entrance. It has a wooden two seater alcove called Poachers Corner.

Old Horns Inn
High Bradfield, Sheffield

Run by Tom Cobleigh, The Old Horns Inn is situated in the lovely village of Bradfield. In 1996 it was told by the Peak Park Planning Board to remove some of its signage as it was not in keeping with the traditional feel for its local environment.
A two roomed pub, one of which, the lounge, has excellent views over Low Bradfield, Dungworth and Stannington. Very popular in the summer.

Old House at Home
34 Radford Street, Sheffield
(1820s-1920s)

This beerhouse was probably named after the once popular ballad. It was generally depicted as a 'soldier under fire having thoughts of home'. Transformed into St Philips Road WMC Club.

Old House at Home
33 Water Lane, Sheffield (1790s-1900)

Old Hussar

67 Scotland Street, Sheffield
(aka Travellers Rest) (1816-1920s)

Old King John

35 Attercliffe Road, Sheffield 9
(1850s-1920s)

Old Library

Ecclesall Rd, Sheff (aka Weetwood House)

Tom Cobleigh spent £2.3 million transforming the Ecclesall Library in early 1996 as their flagship pub in the Sheffield area, The Weetwood.

Things change and by late 1998 it was undergoing another refurbishment along with the compulsory name change, this time the emphasis being on a quality restaurant and quality service, supposedly creating 55 new jobs.

The amount spent on this second alteration is unknown but the total cost must have been somewhere in the region of another half million making it probably the most expensive pub in the area.

To be fair the interior is beautiful, the mahogany finish is wonderful to behold and the restaurant is spacious and comfortable; the food, judge that for yourself.

It does have one lovely touch - a large table that has a chess board inlaid into its top and the game pieces, as well as a wide range of other table games stacked up on the shelves behind.

Old Light Horseman

155 Penistone Road, Sheffield 6
(aka Light Horseman)

A Tetleys House, The Old Light Horseman, had a large bar area, which still had the original Victorian bar in 1984 and a small games room. In the early 80s the landlord had a penchant for collecting: walking sticks, brass objects, and beer mats plus many other items and during this period it won Tetleys pub of the year in 1982.

The Old Light Horseman was situated behind the present Hillsborough Barracks. Some earlier barracks (before 1855) were situated on Infirmary Road, where the Kelvin flats used to be. The area was built up around the time of the Crimean war hence the street names, Balaclava Street, Alma Street, Barrack Lane, and the local vicinity public houses had very military names like the Old Light Horseman itself, the Royal Lancer, General Gordon Inn, Barrack Tavern, Alma, Army Stores, Wellington-hero and his horse.

Old Market Inn

Snig Hill, Sheffield 1 (1790s-1890s)

Old Mill Dam

29 Brittain Street, Sheffield (1830s-1940s)

Old Mill Tavern

4 Boston Street, Sheffield

Old Mother Redcap

Prospect Road, Poynton Wood, Bradway,
Sheffield

A pub consisting of a very large open plan lounge and is
well frequented by drinkers of all ages.

Old Mother Redcap was generally the name for an ale
wife. There is a verse that describes the old lady very well:
Old Mother Redcap, according to her tale,
Lived twenty and a hundred years by drinking good ale,
It was her meat, it was her drink and medicine besides,
And if she still had drunk ale, she never would have died.

Old Oak Tree

13 Silver Street, Sheffield
(closed early 1900s)

Old Park Gate

41 Bard Street, Sheffield

Old Queens Head Inn

18 Castle Street, Sheffield 1
(aka Queens Head Inn) (1790s-1920s)

Old Queens Head

40 Pond Hill, Sheffield 1

Supposedly the oldest building in Sheffield, The Queens
Head is riddled with legends of ghosts over the past few
hundred years. Reputedly, there are sightings of an old
man holding jugs of ale, a maid in old fashioned dress and
obviously Mary Queen of Scots, whose ghost is said to
walk the many tunnels underneath the Queens Head.
These tunnels were supposedly linked to Sheffield Castle.
Archivists believe it was initially built as a banqueting and
hunting lodge for the Earl of Shrewsbury, George Talbot,
in c1505. Supposedly known as T'hawle in t'Poandes it
stood just outside the boundaries of the Sheffield Castle,
and had a direct tunnel to the castle, along which Queen
Mary may or may not have walked. I have heard it said
from people who have worked on the Queens Head cellars
and tunnels that a monks well exists in these tunnels, so it
is likely her captors tried to make her walk in the tunnels.
A monks well is where unsuspecting individuals were
taken and thrown to their deaths or even worse to lie
injured until starvation or the rats took their toll.

The Old Queens Head in Pond Street, features in Sheffield
local records as the oldest pub in Sheffield, but this may
not be accurate, as the building itself only became a beer
house in 1841 when James Pilley, a nail and rivet maker
by trade, paid £2 for a license. Fifteen years later Pilley
took out a victualler's license and named the house the
Queens Head Hotel.

Old Raven

61 West Street, Sheffield (closed 1900s)

Old Red House

35 Fargate, Sheffield 1 (1790s-1903)

This public house used to stand where Dorothy Perkins,
on Fargate, is now sited.

Old Red House

15 Smithfields, Sheffield 1

Old Red Lion

210 Main Street, Grenoside, Sheffield

Old Red Lion

18/20 Holly Street, Sheffield 1

A cutting from the Sheffield Daily Independent of November 1915 shows a report of a case in which the then landlord, Edward Platt, father of Gus (Augustus) Platt, the famous old Sheffield boxing champion, was summoned for keeping his premises open during prohibited hours for the sale of intoxicating liquors. The landlord said he was having a little social enjoyment to mark the fact that his son Gus, a member of the Sheffield City Battalion, was being posted to France. Platt stated "this group of brave men were next up to the front, so a few drinks probably would do no harm". The judge, sensibly, thought the same and dismissed the case.

Another boxer Harvey Flood, who was a British lightweight champion, also kept the Old Red Lion.

Nowadays it is a thriving West Street pub which connects through with Edwards, formerly Barkers, which originally was W. Northends Printers premises.

Old Star

26 Gibraltar Street, Sheffield

Old Star

6 Market Street, Sheffield

Old Star Inn

100 Haymarket, Sheffield 1

Situated at the Top of the Old Haymarket. Wine and Spirit Vaults and Bottled ale and porter stores.

Old Tankard Inn

1 Stocks Hill, Ecclesfield, Sheffield

Old Tankard

17 West Bar, Sheffield

Old Turks Head

108 Scotland Street, Sheffield 3
(aka Turks Head) (1800s-1902)

Old Wagon and Horses

2 Kent Road, Heeley 236 Gleadless Road, Sheffield

Old White Heart

7 Waingate & 14 Castle Green, Sheffield
(aka Stag Inn) (1750s-1890s)

Old Windsor Castle

21 Silver Street, Sheffield

Olive Grove Hotel
26 East Road, Sheffield

Omnibus
766 Attercliffe Road, Sheffield 9
This public house, adorned with large cream tiles, was situated on the corner of Attercliffe Road and Worksop Road.

Horsedrawn omnibuses first appeared in the first quarter of the 19th century, followed by the motorised versions. These vehicles inspired many a pub name and sign. The word Omnibus is an excellent name for a public house for in Latin in means "for all".

Orange Branch
28 Hollis Croft, Sheffield
A chapter of Sheffield's public house history started at the Orange Branch when Michael Fagan took his first steps into the licensing trade. Michael went on to keep several pubs in central Sheffield, and stayed in the trade for some 40 years. He was followed by his son, Joe, who spent another 35-40 years as landlord. Unlike his father Joe was only at one pub, the Barrel, since changed by the brewery to "Fagans" in memory of the service put in by Joe.

Orange Branch
56 The Wicker, Sheffield (1770s-1900s)

Orange Tree Tavern
7 Orange Street, Sheffield
The orange tree is said to have been brought to England by Sir Thomas Gresham in the late 16th century.

Original John Bull
6 Division Street, Sheffield

Osborne House
35 Hartshead, Sheffield 1

Possibly named after Queen Victoria's Isle of Wight residence.

Ostrich Inn
39 Mitchell Street, Sheffield

Owl Inn
51 Penistone Road, Sheffield 6

Owl
Norfolk Street, Sheffield 1
(aka Shout 'em Downs) (1770s-1901)
The nickname of this public house is unusual in itself, surely it can only mean it was a very argumentative place or it was frequented by the Paradise Square regulars who would often 'Shout down' the local or Parliamentary politicians.

Oxford
41 Spring Street, Street, Sheffield 3 also
22 Workhouse Lane, Sheffield 3
(aka Blue Pig)

Oxford Hotel
83 South Street, Sheffield 3 (closed 1930s)

Oxford Blue
31 Burgess Street, Sheffield 3 (1810s-1890s)
The annual boat race between two universities. Obviously this pub showed Oxford's colours.

Oxford House
131/133 Moore Street, Sheffield 3

Pack Horse Hotel

2 West Bar, Sheffield 1

The Pack Horse was a large imposing building standing on the grassy area at the side of where the New Law Courts now stand. It was built in the early 19th century and did good business for many years until the coaching and pack horse trade started to diminish, around the 1860s.

Berry Breweries bought the hotel for £9,000 in 1870 and ran it for 30 years before selling it to Sheffield Corporation in 1900 for £25,000. Two years later the Corporation wanted the roadway from Bridge Street into West Bar altered so the Pack Horse was demolished to accommodate this plan. The council, even then, knew how to make a deal that was good for the ratepayer.

At the front of the Hotel there was a balcony from which politicians gave speeches to large crowds which gathered, whilst at the rear was a large room used for boxing matches, invariably on a Saturday night, and promoted by the then landlord, Frank Howson.

Pack Horse

23 Pack Horse Lane, High Green, Sheffield

Named from the horses which carried packs of goods, such as wool, corn, cutlery, etc, before the canal, rail, and the like took these things in bulk. Pack trains, as they were called, travelled in up to 40 horses per run. No wonder some of the Inns needed to be of large proportions to handle the stabling of all these horses.

Painters Arms or Printers Arms

76 Queens Street, Sheffield (1820s-1910s)

Palace Inn

12 Barkers Hill, Sheffield
(open early 19th century)

Palatine Hotel

54 Malinda Street, Sheffield

The word Palatine comes from the latin word palatinus meaning "of or belonging to the palace" The Palatine Hill in Rome had the palaces of the early Roman emperors built on it. Probably this hotel was not quite as luxurious.

Palm Tree Tavern

35 Palm Street, Sheffield 6

In 1865 a man called William Thorpe pulled the first pint at the Palm Tree Tavern and from that day the building has always been a public house.

The Egyptian campaign of 1880s was generally marked by such public house names, but this name origination is a mystery being christened 15 years earlier.

Palmerston Hotel

129 Carlisle Street, Sheffield
(aka Lord Palmerston)

Obviously named after Lord Palmerston, who was the Prime Minister on two occasions, in the mid 19th century. Palmerston died in 1865 one year after this hotel was opened.

Paradise Inn

30 Campo Lane, Sheffield

Probably named from local area names, Paradise Street, Square etc, but could possibly be from Milton's 'Paradise Lost'. In around 1903 it was run by Alfred Brown followed by Mrs Mallinson, Mrs Guest and Edward Lee who were some of the other licensees at this inn which closed around 1905-6 to become the residence of F B Gill, Insurance Brokers.

In the background along Campo Lane the Ball Inn can be seen.

Paradise Street Vaults
Paradise Street, Sheffield

Probably Paradise Inn.

Paragon Hotel
131 Thomas Street, Sheffield

Park Gate
High Street, Park, Sheffield

Park Hotel
Wadsley Lane, Sheffield 6

Park Head Tavern
Park Head, Stannington, Sheffield 6

In a reference book dating circa 1842 there is mention of a public house in Stannington called the Park Head Tavern. No other information can be found to verify this.

Park Inn
51 Cricket Inn Road, Sheffield

Parkside
73 Sussex Street, Sheffield

Parkwood Hotel
16 Douglas Road, Sheffield 3

"Tets" was the local nickname of the Parkwood Hotel, not for any other reason than it sold Tetleys. It was 2 doors away from the Reindeer the 'bottom house'.

Parkway
built into Park Hill flats, Sheffield

Parrot
9 Button Lane, Sheffield (1820s-1908)

In its early days the Parrot was one of the last buildings of the Sheffield township in this direction, before it was engulfed in the city's great expansion.

The Parrot is good for an innkeeper, it provided a bright colourful sign, which is always handy for catching the eye of the passer by, and if, as often was generally the case, a parrot was found inside, its mimicry was always a centre of attraction, whist ale was being purchased.

Parrot
Coalpit Lane, Cambridge Street, Sheffield

Parson Cross Hotel
Deerland Avenue, Sheffield 5

Built in June 1939. Tennents brewery opened The Cross, the Highcliffe Hotel, Greystones, and the Sicey Hotel Shiregreen all in the same month just as the Second World War started. The best of times, the worst of times.

Paul Pry

88 Pea Croft, Sheffield (aka Falcon)
(opened around 1830)

This pub name came from a play, Paul Pry, by John Poole, produced in 1825. The eponymous hero is a man who constantly meddles in other people's affairs because he has nothing better to do. The play was popular and when it toured outside the capital, taverns and beer houses called themselves after the nosey man. Invariably the sign would have a man listening at a door marked private.
From this play came the term 'to pry into other people's business'.

Peacock

198/200 Fitzwilliam Street, Sheffield

Another pub sign which offers the artist great colourful scope.

Peacock

11 Hoyle Street, Sheffield

Peacock Inn

714 Stannington Road, Sheffield 6

Records show that the Peacock was standing in 1828. Twenty three years later, 1851 George March a blacksmith and a farmer was the licencee of the Peacock Inn.
The Peacock is now a Tom Cobleigh pub serving meals throughout the day.

Peacock

Deep Pit, Sheffield

Pear Tree

163 Woodside Lane, Sheffield

This inn name suggests the presence of pear trees in the locale or possibly that perry, a drink like cider, only made from pears was on sale here.

Pear Tree or Palm Tree

Millsands, Sheffield (opened 1774)

Pedestrian Tavern

238 Forncett Street, Sheffield (closed 1920s)

Pegg's

High Street, Sheffield

Penguin

Mason Lathe Road, Sheffield 5

Penny Black

Pond Hill, Sheffield 1

Built into the basement of the Sheffield Post Offices, it is named after the first adhesive stamp ever used. The stamp was the brainchild of Roland Hill and depicted the Queen of the day, Victoria, on its face. It was the reproduction of that stamp which was the sign, outside the entrance for its first few years.

Perseverance

108 Savile Street, Sheffield
(closed around 1930)

A famous stage coach and a troopship around 1850 were named Perseverance or could it have been the landlords sheer doggedness to open all hours that gave this establishment its name.

Peters Hotel

121 Lord Street, Sheffield

J. M. Barrie's forever young hero, Peter Pan or was the landlord called Peter?

Pheasant

436 Attercliffe Common, Sheffield 9
(aka Stumble Inn)

The building on Attercliffe Common you see today was built c1926, the original (pictured below) stood for 3 centuries before that and belonged to the Howden and Fowler families, who like many of the town's landlords kept up their other trade as cutlers, scissor making etc.

Around the turn of the century the Pheasant had behind it a large field where sports meetings and boxing events took place, It is said that large sums of money changed hands on these occasions. This field was used for fairs and circuses etc in the late 40s to mid 50s,

The name Pheasant probably came from the fact that when the original building was erected only fields surrounded it, and the gamebird was quite prevalent.

It also has an historic connection with the Broughton Inn, in the fact that Spence Broughton's wife (name unknown) watched tearfully from the back window of the Pheasant (some say the Arrow) as her husband's remains were placed in a gibbet.

Pheasant Inn

467 Meadow Hall Road, Sheffield 9

Pheasant Inn

30 Trafalgar Road, Sheffield 6

Pheasant Inn

96/98 London Road, Sheffield 2

Pheasant Inn

Barnsley Rd, Sheffield Lane Top, Sheffield 5

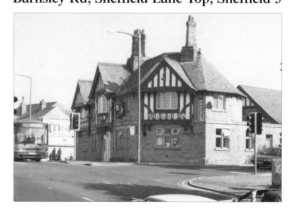

Pheasant

51 Bailey Lane, Sheffield (1820s-1900s)

Pheasant

37 West Street, Sheffield
(closed late 19th century)

Pheasant

10 Broad Street, Sheffield (1790s-1910s)

Pheasant

38 Carver Street, Sheffield 1 (1820s-1900s)

Pheasant

8 Russell Street, Sheffield

Pheasant

Orchard Street, Harvest Lane, Sheffield

Pheasant

170 Worksop Road, Sheffield 9
(opened early 1800s)

This pub at the side of the aqueduct arches used to get flooded at the same time as the aqueduct and you could invariably see young boys diving into the flooded area to inspect the odd submerged car or van. The watermen who navigated this Goole to Sheffield canal must have felt a certain amount of relief, as for their last two miles into Sheffield wharf there were no more locks. The barges around this time were under part sail, part engine or some towed and poled.

Pheasant

48 Green Lane, Sheffield

Pheasant

6 Hoyle Street, Sheffield
(opened around 1820s)

Pheasant

41 Gower Street, Sheffield (opened 1870s)

Pheasant

125 South Street, Moor, Sheffield

Phoenix Inn

High Lane, Ridgeway, Sheffield

Standing on the main road between Gleadless and Ridgeway, it is reputedly an old coaching house dating back to the 17th century.

Pickwick

Pack Horse Lane, High Green, Sheffield

A benevolent old gentleman from a Dickens story, Pickwick Papers.

Pie House

5 Scotland Street, Sheffield

Pig and Whistle

Orchard Lane, Leopold Street, Sheffield

The Oxford dictionary stated in 1861 "to go to pigs and whistle" meant going to ruin. Not a great pub name then!

Pike and Heron

Bawtry Road, Sheffield 9
(built in early 1960s)

Pilot

2 Green Street, Sheffield

Pitsmoor Hotel

448 Pitsmoor Road, Sheffield 3

Players Cafe

Attercliffe Common, Sheffield 9

The players cafe is a £2.5 million transformation of the Old Carbrook School, the infants building, on Attercliffe Common into a sports bar and restaurant backed by Def Leppard stars Joe Elliott and Rick Savage, along with Sheffield Steelers Ice Hockey star Tim Cranston. Film and sports memorabilia hang around the walls, there is a formula one car upside down on the ceiling, items from such films as Braveheart and The Elephant Man as well as many more varied and interesting items. As themed pubs go this one is hard to place, but it does have a nice feel to it, (probably because it was my old school). With its central bar area, Tom Cruise/Cocktail-like barmen, table top playstations and giant TV screens it has something for everyone.

Plough

20 Milner Street, Sheffield
(opened in 1800s)

Plough

28 Broad Street, Sheffield 2

This particular Plough was sited on the corner of Broad Street and Sheaf Lane and was a Duncan Gilmour pub. The plough has been used as a inn sign for well over 500 years. Some of the more enterprising innkeepers have just seven stars on their sign. This is from the night sky, Ursa Major, which is in the shape of a primitive plough, also called the great bear.

Plough

75 Church Street, aka Worksop Road,
Sheffield
(opened in late 18th century)

Plough

288 Sandygate Road, Sheffield 10

The Plough is situated opposite the oldest football ground
in the world. This belongs to the Hallam football club who
are the second oldest club in existence after their local
rivals, and the oldest club, Sheffield F.C.
On Whit Tuesday the noted Hallam Chase takes place, this
is a race from the Plough down through Rivelin valley up
to Stannington church and back to Sandygate Road, with
one final lap around the Hallam Ground before the
winning line.

Plough

New Road, Low Bradfield, Sheffield 6

Beautifully furnished and decorated pub set in the
pleasant village setting of Low Bradfield. A busy place
especially in summer.

Plumpers

42 Greystock Road, 36 Sutherland Rd,
Sheffield 4 (closed around 1990)

A small Tetleys House, The Plumpers was situated on the
corner of Greystock Road and Sutherland Street near the
Norfolk Bridge. It was, like the other public houses in this
area, the Albert and the Norfolk Arms, reliant on local
inhabitants and the large steel firms such as Spear and
Jackson and the Tempered Spring Company for most of
its business. Unfortunately the slum clearance of
Attercliffe and the Steel Industry demise of the mid 70s
condemned these pubs to a long lingering death. The
Plumpers end, demolition, came in the early 90s.
The unusual name The Plumpers, has various possible
meanings i.e. it could mean a vote given to one candidate,
when one or more is put forward, it could mean a
Downright Lie, always a possibility in a well lubricated
pub and the third and likeliest meaning is of men who
were called plumpers, these men stirred up the molten
metal in iron works. Similar to the Puddlers.

Plumpers Inn

49 Duke Street, Sheffield

Plumpers Hotel

Sheffield Rd and 200 Bawtry Rd, Sheffield

Pomona Hotel

213 Ecclesall Road, Sheffield 11
(aka Pomona Gardens)

The Pomona Gardens was set in the Old Broomhall Park and was by all account a wonderful place to behold. In Victorian times the Pomona had extensive gardens attached to it and its patrons could take a pleasant walk or sit and indulge themselves with refreshments.

Pomona was the Roman goddess of fruit and its cultivation. The Latin 'pomum' means fruit or apple.

Originally built in 1800.

Only Home brewery pub in Sheffield.

Unfortunately, in its recent past the Pomona had an attempted murder when a Sheffield man armed with a combat knife decided to attack a group of students, one was nearly disembowelled and two others were scarred for life. Fortunately for everyone, no lives were lost.

Poplar Tree Tavern

180/182 Broomhall Street, Sheffield 3

A Poplar is a tree noted for its slender tallness.

Portland Arms

39 Portland Street, Sheffield 6

The name Portland could possibly be from the location in Dorset where the lighthouse is situated on Portland Bill, or more likely as with a large number of public house names, it could be named after a member of the aristocracy. In this case the Duke of Portland who once owned a huge stately mansion in Clumber Park. Once being the operative word in this case, as earlier this century the Duke argued with the Government of the day about the taxes he owed for the house and he had it pulled down. (that showed 'em!)

The 3rd Duke of Portland, William Bentinck was Prime Minister of England in 1807-1809.

Portland Arms

184 Rockingham Street, Sheffield

Porter Cottage

66 Porter Street, Sheffield

Named after one of the five rivers that run through Sheffield, the River Porter.

Porter Cottage

286 Sharrow Vale Road, Sheffield 11
(aka Porter Tavern)

Original name Porter Tavern built in 1856 or slightly earlier. Another public house named after the River Porter which runs very close by.

Porter Brook

Ecclesall Road, Sheffield 11

Portobello

248 Portobello, Sheffield

Most likely this inn was called after the 1739 feat of Admiral Vernon who captured Porto Bello in Panama from the Spanish, a feat he accomplished with just 6 ships.

Pot Makers Arms

30 Cross Bedford Street, Sheffield 6

This is a beer house that, to my knowledge, has not been mentioned before in any reference about Sheffield.

In the early part of 20th century a Samuel Worrall was licensee of this beerhouse. It is unknown if this name, Pot Makers Arms, is the correct inn title or just a nickname given by the local steelmen. The potmakers were the crucible steel men who made the pots from material that contained no impurities.

Potters Arms

20 Paradise Street, Sheffield
(aka Paradise Street Vaults)

Pressers Arms

20 Burgess Street, Sheffield

Built in the mid to late 18th century the Pressers Arms survived for about a hundred and 50 years before demolition in 1927.

Prince Hotel

100/102 Pomona Street, 12 Plumpton Street, Sheffield 11

Prince Leopold

37 St Philips Road, Sheffield

Leopold was the 4th youngest son of Queen Victoria and in 1881 he was created Duke of Albany and Earl of Clarence.

Prince of Wales

150 Derbyshire Lane, Sheffield 8

Prince of Wales

95 Ecclesall Road South, Sheffield 11
(aka Woodstock Diner, Woodstock, Macaw)

After sixteen years of name changing, sometime amid much furore the Prince of Wales has now reverted back to its original name.

Allied Domecq Inns had been given the pub from its sister company Allied Domecq Leisure, after a cheap refurbishment, a £60.000 "doing down" of the pub, the Brewery's words.

But when it did revert, the price of beer did drop by up to 20 pence a pint, so a very nice transformation.

Prince of Wales

20/22 Adsetts Street, Sheffield 4

Most references to the Prince of Wales, and there are many, are credited to Edward VII, Queen Victoria's oldest son. At one time or another there has been about 15 inns in Sheffield and there were well over 100 Prince of Wales pubs in the capital, London.

Prince of Wales

12 Bardwell Road, Sheffield

Prince of Wales

Carbrook Street, Sheffield 9

Prince of Wales

103 Sussex Street, Sheffield

Situated almost next door to the Wilson Brothers Brewery from which it took its supplies, this Prince of Wales closed in 1902. Wilson Brothers sold 'Entire Beer', a stout that was amazingly popular in the late part of the last century. The brewery closed, two years before the public house, in 1900.

Prince of Wales

38 Sycamore Street, Sheffield (1820s-1890s)

Prince of Wales

25 Fawcett Street, Sheffield

Prince of Wales

271 Shalesmoor, Sheffield

Prince of Wales

301 Langsett Road, Sheffield (1820s-1920s)

Prince of Wales

19 Charlotte Street, Sheffield

Prince of Wales

67 Meadow Street, Sheffield

Prince of Wales

116 South Street, Sheffield

Prince of Wales

240 Savile Street, Sheffield

After service as an inn for many years the Prince was transformed into a Billiard Saloon until its demise in 1920.

Prince of Wales

49 Egerton Street, Sheffield (1830s-1910s)

Prince of Wales

127 St Philips Road, Sheffield 3

Prince of Wales

143 Gilbert Street, Sheffield (1820s-1900s)

Prince of Wales Feathers

46 Bard Street, Sheffield

Prince of Wales Inn

80 Burncross Road, Chapeltown

Princess Hotel

199/201 Fitzwilliam Street, 38 Prince Street, Sheffield 1

Princess Royal

28 Langsett Road, Sheffield 6

Princess Royal

137 Trafalgar Street, Sheffield

Princess Royal Hotel

43 Slinn Street, Sheffield

Princess Royal Hotel

680 Retford Road, Woodhouse, Sheffield

Princess Hotel

Bright Street, Sheffield

Prospect View Hotel

500 Gleadless Road, Sheffield 2

The Prospect View was sited near to the Upper Heeley Club and was nicknamed by its locals as the 'Cuckoo'. This name is reputedly derived from the landlord giving short measures.

Puddlers Arms

73 Earsham St, Clun St, Sheffield 4

A puddler is a worker who worked on the Puddling Furnace producing wrought iron during the early days of steel and iron manufacture.

Pump Tavern

79 South Street, 77 The Moor, Sheffield

Until only a few years ago one of the bars was restricted to gentlemen only.

Punch Bowl

12 Coulsdon Street, Sheffield

Coulston Street, Coulsdon Street, Coulson Street, Spring Street, this particular Punch Bowl has been on all these thoroughfares according to the street reference books of old Sheffield. It was, according to all accounts, a rather notorious place, not in a good way, plus it was kept at one time by Alfred 'Spotty' Milner. Let's hope he didn't make the sarnies.

Punch Bowl

66 Bridge Street, Sheffield

Punch as a drink was established in England in the 1630s and seems originally to have been a seaman's drink.

Punch Bowl

140 South Street, Moor, Sheffield (1820s-1938)

Punch Bowl

50 Silver Street Head, Sheffield (1800s-1900s)

Punch Bowl

56 The Wicker, Sheffield

Punch Bowl

95 Hurlfield Road, Sheffield 12

Punch Bowl

236 Crookes, Sheffield 10

This public house used to have a bowling green adjacent to it, unfortunately progress takes its toll, it is now a car park.

Punters Bar

111 Arundel Street, Sheffield 1

Q in the corner

17-19 Paradise Square, Sheffield
(aka Shrewsbury Hotel)

The Q in the Corner opened around the turn of the 18th century and was noted as a meeting place for Sheffield's thespians. It was the first place to run a Buffalo Lodge in Sheffield. The landlord in those early days was one Samuel Goodlad who used to play the fiddle to entertain his customers and the noted blind fiddlers also frequented the 'Q'.

It later changed names to the Shrewsbury Hotel around 1860 and the building now houses the legal & professional businesses who occupy Paradise Square today.

Queen Adelaide

32 Bramall Lane, and
1 Hermitage Street, Sheffield

The wife of William IV, whose full title was Queen Adelaide of Saxe Meiningen, was on the English throne for seven years between 1830 and 1837.

Queen Adelaide

Mowbray Street, Sheffield

Queen Bays

16 Joiner Street, Sheffield

Queen Hotel

37 Dun Street, Sheffield

One of three public houses situated on Dun Street, the other being the Gardeners, and Bulls Head.
This street was less than 100 yards long.

Queen

1 Whitehouse Lane, Sheffield

Queens

88 Savile Street, Sheffield

Queens

20 Attercliffe Road, Sheffield

Queens Ground Hotel

401 Langsett Road, Sheffield 6
(aka Queens Hotel)

Built in 1851 and originally known as the Queens Hotel, but the brewery always referred to it as the Queens Ground because of the cricket field at the rear. This cricket field was later turned into a running track. At one time it had a sign outside that had an athlete breasting the winning line tape. This was probably the only evidence left of a history of athletic events that took place behind the Queens Ground. This running track attracted runners from all over the world to events that paid excellent prize money and developed attendances of up to 20,000. These event were generally sponsored by the incumbent landlord. One man who attended these meetings was Harry Hutchens "the fastest man on two legs". It is said that Hutchens won the first prize of £80 in 1890 when he ran 131.25 yards in 12.4 seconds, if this is to be believed it puts him on par with most of today's athletes.

It is said that the military used this running track to keep the resident soldiers of the Hillsborough Barracks, which is directly opposite, in good physical shape.

The Barracks themselves were commissioned in 1848 and they were finally completed in 1854 as a replacement for some older barracks, built in 1794, which were situated between Wood Street and Barrack Lane.

The older barracks being sold for the princely sum of £2,850 at auction in 1848.

The new fortifications set on 23 acres, were erected at a cost of around £124,000 and included parade ground, riding school, a hospital, rifle range, mortuary and chapel. All this expense by the government of the day was to quell any more disturbances like the 1791 uprising against a local magistrate, Vicar Wilkinson, who had allowed land to be taken from the church yard for the road widening of Church Lane.

The Third Dragoon Guards were first to use the barracks in 1849, the Northumbrian Fusileers followed in 1914 and the Green Howards returned from France to occupy the barracks in 1918, followed respectively by the Leicesters, the Chesters, and the King's Light Infantry. The last regiment to occupy Hillsborough Barracks were the 29th Battery of the 19th Field Brigade, Royal Artillery, who finally left in 1932.

Queens Head

20 Sheaf Street, Sheffield

Queens Head

4 Campo Lane, Sheffield
(opened in 18th century)

Most inn signs of this name were of Queen Elizabeth I. But these early signs, mostly painted by the innkeeper or a local were not to Elizabeth's liking. The Queen had them all removed and actually made a proclamation that unless signs met certain standards they could not be hung. Now British public houses are legally bound not to depict the monarch of the day.

Queens Head

660 Attercliffe Road, Sheffield 9

Queens Head

12 Main Road, Ridgeway, Sheffield

Queens Head

12 Wortley Road, High Green

Queens Head

Woodhouse, Sheffield

Built by French prisoners around 1815. A plaque in the wall at the rear inscribed 'Palais Royale' so obviously it was called the Palace by the locals.

Queens Head Hotel

Adelphi Street, Port Mahon, Sheffield

Queens Hotel

85 Scotland Street, Sheffield 3

The Queens closed a couple of years ago, the shell of the building still remains, boarded up.

A pub that in its last few years survived on the dinner time trade and at night on ex locals who travelled from far and wide to have a good sing along to the organ music that was on offer 3 or 4 nights per week. It stood just over the hill from the Scotland Street Debtors Gaol.

This 19th century pub was one of a number of Sheffield public houses who had a three-quarter size snooker table and played in the Sheffield 3 Quarter Snooker League.

One of its landlords was Vernon Hookway, who worked over 30 years in the licensing trade, about 20 of them serving at the Queens, he kept the Original Grindstone, Crookes before taking over this Scotland Street premises.

Queens Hotel

Stannington, Sheffield
(closed in 1913) (aka Cricketers)

The old Queens Hotel building is still standing at the corner of Nook Lane and Stannington Road, and was for a period of time around 1920s-1960s, a police station. In fact the wording stating this can still to be seen above the bricked up doorway.

The last landlord was Mr Jack Milner who was there when the Queens finally closed.

The building was used, at one time, for keeping dead bodies awaiting burial.

Queens Hotel

River Lane, Sheffield

Queens St. Hotel

57 New Queens Street, Sheffield

Rabys Inn

16 West Bar, Sheffield

A strange name for an inn, one can only assume it was the landlord's surname, although it could have been named after a place in Cheshire, meaning settlement near a boundary mark. Or even possibly named after Raby Castle in Durham.

Raglan Arms

Meadow Street, Sheffield

Named after the commander in chief of the Crimea War campaign, Lord Raglan (1788-1855).

Raglan Inn

Arundel Street, Sheffield

Railway Hotel

299 Hollywell Road, Sheffield 9

The coming of the Railway in the 19th century had a huge impact on everyday life in England and this is obviously reflected in the amount of public houses with the title railway or similar attribution.

Railway Inn

70 Nursery Street, Sheffield 1

Railway Hotel

37 The Wicker, Sheffield 1

Railway Hotel

97 Broughton Lane, Sheffield 9
(aka Stadium, Noose and Gibbet,)

The legend of the Sheffield highwayman Spence Broughton was never really used by the Broughton public house which was a hundred yards down the road, so it is perhaps no surprise that the more enterprising 90s have brought this villain back to the forefront for the Noose and Gibbet.

The inept highwayman was caught, in 1791. He was tried, found guilty and hung in York and gibbeted in this area, where his body hung for 27 years till it fell away. Supposedly the hand on show in the pub is from the original Spence Broughton, also the body chain which supposedly held Broughton in his Gibbet was lent by the Kelham Island Museum.

The Noose must exhibit the most unusual pub sign in Britain, that of Broughton himself in his Gibbet.

It was the fourth pub on the Lane, The Broughton, The Bird in Hand and the Enfield being the others. The Railway consisted of 2 rooms and had very basic fare. The pub was alive in the 40s 50s and 60s due to the plethora of steelworks situated about it, but started to fade in the mid 70s when the Attercliffe slums were starting to be cleared and also with the demise of the Sheffield steel industry. It survived on less trade for a few years then closed in the early 80s. It re-opened as the Stadium, unfortunately wrongly named as it is situated 50 yards from the Arena not the Stadium which is two thirds of a mile away. The Landlord or owner bought the shell of the Railway and in 16 days and nights of continuous work had it fitted out for the opening ceremony of the 1991 World Student Games (which to this day still divides the good people of Sheffield as to whether we could afford it) and for that 3 week period he sold out of his stock nightly. Unfortunately 3 weeks solid trade and full houses on concert nights at the Arena, ie Elton John, Prince, Pavorotti could not sustain the pub again. The owner sold back to the brewery in October 1993. The pub ticked along on poor custom for two years until it was re-named the Noose & Gibbet. Supposedly a quarter of a million pounds was spent refurbishing the pub, an amount probably a thousand times more than poor old Spence Broughton actually stole.

Railway Hotel or Rail Hotel

Blackburn Road, Kimberworth

Railway Hotel

184 Bramall Lane, Sheffield 2

Railway Hotel

19 Penistone Road, North, Sheffield 6

Railway Inn

64/66 Princess Street, Sheffield 4
(1860s-1912)

Railway Tavern

46 Carlisle Street East, Sheffield

Ram

82 Pea Croft aka Solly St, Sheffield,
(opened early 19th century)

The male of the sheep family which appears in the arms of the Worshipful Company of Clockmakers and some livery companies associated with the wool trade. It has been a pub sign for over 600 years.

Ram

272 Rockingham Street, Sheffield

Ram Hotel

100 Ecclesall Road, Sheffield

Ram Inn

15 Kenninghall Street, Sheffield
(1860s-1914)

Ram Inn

272 Rockingham Street, Sheffield

Rancliffe Arms

10 Anson Street, Sheffield

Randell Hotel

29 Randell Street, Sheffield

Ranmoor Inn

330 Fulwood Road, Sheffield 10

Sitting in the shadow of the imposing St Johns Church, the Ranmoor Inn is situated in the heart of the hall of residences for Sheffield University. The clientele varies from students aplenty, solicitors, doctors, etc.

Rat & Parrot
West Street, Sheffield 1

Another New Cafe Bar based around the City Hall in the centre of Sheffield!
Two floored establishment which is now situated where Andrews Graphics plied their trade for many a year keeping artists, and local schools well supplied

Ratteners Rest
Globe Buildings, Penistone Road, Sheffield

The name Ratteners, comes from the Stirrings era in Sheffield's history. Ratteners were like the Luddites and damaged new machinery in order to safeguard their jobs. The present day Ratteners Rest is a traditional stone flagged public house situated in the historic Globe building. The Ratteners Rest was a beautifully conceived idea, almost a museum in itself, with cutlery and other examples of manufacturing steel trades placed around the walls and displayed in cabinets. It had large dining tables and comfortable chairs, several sofas for the customer to relax in, and had a lovely relaxed feel to it. Unfortunately it was a short lived idea for it lasted only about 2 years. Customers did not come from far and wide as it was thought they would and with no local housing nearby it was a grand idea doomed to failure. Sadly missed.

Raven Hotel
12/14 Fitzwilliam Street, Sheffield 1
(aka Hornblower, O'Hagans Bakery & Lounge)

George Harvey Flood, built and ran a small boxing gymnasium behind this public house when he was landlord. Many a Sheffield young man learned the ropes there.
The Hornblower, named after Horatio Hornblower, the fictional character created by C S Forester for a series of books from 1937 onwards. Hornblower starts his naval career as a midshipman and goes through the ranks to become Admiral. In the 17th century a raven on an inn sign intimated Jacobean sympathies.

Rawsons Arms
161 Attercliffe Road, Sheffield 9

Rawsons Arms
85 Tenter Street, Sheffield 1

Red Deer Inn
18 Pitt Street, Sheffield 1

The Red Deer, a Tetley's house, Victorian building on Pitt Street, is a very well frequented pub. It could easily be missed by anyone, when visiting the supertram route pubs on West Street. It's just off Mappin Street, near the university library and used to consist of quite a few rooms, but after refurbishment the Red Deer is now a one room public house. It does have an open fire, which in the winter is so much warmer (it seem that way, anyhow) than the central heating most pubs offer. The Deer, runs some of the hardest quizzes to be found in Sheffield.

Redford Arms
88 Harvest Lane, Sheffield

Red Hill Tavern
33 Red Hill, Sheffield 3 (1780s - 1940s)

Red House
168 Solly Street, Sheffield 1

This public house was for many years known as the Irish Embassy. Some years ago, in the mid 70s an Irish woman wrote in the pub's "visitors book" that the pub was great for homesick exiles. The Red House is near to the St Vincent's Catholic club and possible this is why, along with the Dog and Partridge on Trippet lane and The Barrel (Fagans) on Broad Lane, it is, or was frequented by a host of Irish people. The Red House was built in about 1820 and was supposedly named after the sandstone rock which was to be found in the vicinity. It is a well frequented Wards public house that serves good beer.

Red House
Lee Croft, Sheffield

Red Lion
145 Duke Street, Sheffield 2

Red Lion
262 Shalesmoor, Sheffield

Red Lion
15 Smithfields, Sheffield

Red Lion
32 Hartshead, Sheffield 1 (1750s-1890s)

There was an old house up Hartshead Passage at the end of the 18th century at the back of Haslehurst's bank which was supposedly this long lost Red Lion. We can say with certainty that Christopher Bennett was the landlord in 1755 and certain references place the Red Lion on High Street near to Market Place.

Red Lion
109 Charles Street, Sheffield 1

Well over a hundred years old, the Red Lion was in times past used as an old Palace of Varieties and had many a Victorian audience crowding its concert room which adjoined the bar. Supposedly, many an impromptu performance was given by some of the entertainers who after their stint at the Empire Theatre would come into the Red Lion, and as with most theatricals could not resist playing to the audience. The interior at present boasts an original Can Can dress and many a picture of the old Empire Theatre.

A mystery that remains unsolved about the Red Lion is that of a small piece of stone that was found well hidden under a flagstone in the cellar. On this stone is engraved a quotation in Arabic with wording from the Koran, the sacred book of Islam.

The Red Lion was the original Wards Company Catering House.

Red Lion
Forncett Street, Sheffield

Red Lion
622 Penistone Road, Sheffield 6

Red Lion
52 Coalpit Lane, or Cambridge St, Sheffield (aka Nells Bar) (opened 1790s)

The Red Lion or Nells Bar as it was also known was unique in Sheffield at one time for holding a supper license, this allowed it to stay open into the early hours. Sometime later another four or five public houses in the same locale gained this license and it was the place to be seen at one time on the Sheffield scene.

Red Lion
103 Eyre Street, Sheffield

Red Lion
51 Lambert Street, Sheffield (open in 1830s)

Red Lion

18 Johnson Street, Sheffield (early 1820s)

Red Lion

89 Trippet Lane, Sheffield (1820s-1930s)

Red Lion

653 London Road, Sheffield

This was the tram terminus in 1902

Red Lion

95 Penistone Road, Grenoside

Red Lion Hotel

972 Gleadless Road, Sheffield 12

Red Place Tavern

91 Garden Street, Solly St, Sheffield
(1820-1910s)

Reform Tavern

76 Coalpit Lane, Sheffield (opened 1780s)

Thomas Barket kept the Reform, but also kept his trade as a silversmith going to enhance his income.

Reform Tavern

41 Smithfields, Sheffield (1820s-1920s)

Reformers

39 Duke Street, Sheffield

Refreshment Rooms

Victoria Station, Sheffield

Reindeer

Hawley Lane, Sheffield

Reindeer

Cattlefoulds, Sheffield (aka Royal)

The Reindeer was opened in 1779, and had several name changes before becoming the Royal Hotel in 1841, it remained so named for another 72 years before demolition in 1913.

Reindeer Hotel

139 - 141 Devonshire Street,
30 Eldon Street, Sheffield

The term 'reindeer' comes from the reins used when the deer draws a sledge.

Reindeer Inn

39 South Street, Park, Sheffield

Reindeer Inn

20 Douglas Road, Sheffield 3

The "Bottom House" is what the Reindeer Inn was called locally, as it was at the bottom of Douglas Road hill.

Retreat

The Oasis, Meadowhall Centre, Sheffield

This privately owned pub was built to give the husbands of Sheffield a "Retreat" when their wives were shopping in the 270 plus shops that adorn Meadowhall shopping complex.
The pub, on the outside, is Mediterranean looking to suit the Oasis decor, but inside a quite traditional pub. Its customer base is obviously the husbands, but also a mixture of general shoppers, filmgoers waiting for their chosen film to start and staff coming in after their days work.

Reubens Head

50 Burgess Street, Sheffield
(closed late 19th century)

Reubens Head

63 Campo Lane, Sheffield (1820s-1900s)

Reubens Head

16 Shepherd Street, Sheffield
(opened 1820s)

Reubens Head

117 South Street, Park, Sheffield
(1820s-1900s)

Richmond Hotel

443 Richmond Road, Sheffield

Built in the 1930s and is a typical piece of this era's public house architecture. In the 70s it was the largest public house the Wards Brewery owned.

Rifle Corps Hotel

137 Carlisle Street East, Sheffield
(1850s-1958)

Rifleman's Canteen

16 Charles Street, Sheffield
(aka Empire Canteen, Music Hall)

Rifle Tavern

15 Bower Street, Sheffield

Ring Of Bells

8 Pea Croft, Sheffield (aka Ball)

As the name indicates it was probably used by the local bell ringers, campanologists.

Rising Sun

11 Pear Street/72 Pomona St, Sheffield 11

The Rising Sun was a very common heraldic symbol, relating to Edward III.

Rising Sun

45 South Street, Park, Sheffield
(closed 1900s)

Rising Sun

146 West Street, Sheffield (closed 1903)

Rising Sun

127 Corby Street, Sheffield 4 (1870s-1940s)

Rising Sun

Abbey Lane, Sheffield 11

This popular 18th century public house had a £500,000 refurbishment in the late 90s and Bass, its owners, were looking to establish it as the premier house in the west side of Sheffield. The alterations retain many original features such as wooden beams and real fires alongside all that is best in modern technology in a bid to attract "nice people - courteous and respectable" - the brewery's words. Supposedly the Rising Sun had both bear and bull baiting as entertainment for its customers, many years ago.

Rising Sun Inn

49 Jenkin Road, Sheffield 9

Rising Sun

88 Sorby Street, Sheffield

Rising Sun

38 Matthews Street, Sheffield

Rising Sun

67 Hermitage Street, Sheffield

Rising Sun Hotel
471 Fulwood Road, Sheffield 10

Around the 1760s the landlord of the Rising Sun was Sampson Brookshaw who combined his trade, that of a common pocket and pen knives maker with his running of the hotel. These dates show that this hotel has been serving the Sheffield public for over 230 years.

Rivelin Hotel
Tofts Lane, Rivelin Valley, Sheffield 6
(aka Rivelin Tavern)

This gritstone building was constructed in c1850 as a mill cottage and was transformed into a public house a few years later. It has stunning views over the Rivelin Valley and is just a short walk from Stannington Village. On the walk from Stannington you can see quite clearly the "Man's Head Rock" that overlooks the Rivelin.

It has a lounge that is or was nicknamed the "surgery". It apparently got its name years ago when the regulars, who must have been hypochondriacs, used to meet and discuss their ailments and illnesses over a pint. That's the way to see the doctor!

The interior has a lovely feel to it, brasses, olde worlde artefacts and pictures of local scenes and a large black iron fireplace. Comfortable.

Rivelin View H
204 Bole Hill Road, Sheffield 6

River Don Inn
712 Brightside Lane, Sheffield 9

Situated on the corner of Brightside Lane and Hawke Street (the bottom end of Janson Street) the River Don Inn was built around 1850 and survived in this mainly industrial area for about a century. After its closure it remained derelict for many years until it was demolished to make way for the roundabout and the junction of Upwell Street, Brightside Lane and Hawke Street. The name the River Don Inn is from the Yorkshire river which at one point forms the boundary between Lincolnshire and Yorkshire, it also runs through the length of Sheffield.

Robin Hood
548 Attercliffe Road, Sheffield 9
(aka Mr Smiths Funbar)

One of literally thousands of public houses in England so called. The majority opened in the 19th century, probably more from the Ancient Order of Foresters opening new lodges, than the English's love of old Robin Hood.

Robin Hood Hotel
46/48 Ellesmere Road, Sheffield 4

Robin Hood and Little John
Greaves Lane, Little Matlock, Stannington, Sheffield 6 (aka Robin Hood)

This building, commissioned by Reverend Thomas Halliday in around 1794 was built in the hope of attracting the people of Sheffield to visit this place of interest. He hoped they would stop for refreshment and stay to be entertained. Halliday carved paths through the wooded slopes surrounding this part of Stannington and even gave the area a new name, Little Matlock, to attract custom. Matlock in Derbyshire at that time being a very popular resort. It was said that the walkers, visitors, sightseers of those days were easily pleased with unsophisticated pleasures.

Robin Hood
86 Duke Street, Sheffield (1810s-1950s)
The Robin Hood public house was pulled down to make way for the Park Hill Flats complex.

Robin Hood Hotel
Millhouses Lane, Sheffield 7

Rock Cottage
Crookes, Sheffield
The name Rock is often so called because of the British association with the Rock of Gibraltar.

Rock
51 Carlisle Street East, Sheffield (1850s-1930s)

Rock House
168/172 Rock Street, Sheffield 3

Small two roomed local set in the heart of Pitsmoor, it had a couple of refurbishments in the 70s and 80s and ended up with the two small rooms being made into one open plan room and part of the living quarters being transformed into a lower level pool room. In the 1970-80s it had one of the best darts teams in Sheffield

Rock House
13 Stour Lane, Wadsley, Sheffield

Rock Inn
40/42 Pye Bank or 42 Pitsmoor Road, Sheffield 3 (closed in 1958)

Rock Tavern
20 Dixon Lane, Sheffield 1 (1780s-1970s)

The Rock was the building that is showing the for sale sign.

Rocket Inn
106 St Philips Road, Sheffield
This inn was opened in 1830 and fits in nicely with the historic launching of George Stephenson's Rocket in 1829. Stephenson designed the Rocket to win a contest that had been set. It ran on the Manchester and Liverpool railway from 1830.

Rockingham Arms

194 Rockingham Street, Sheffield 1
(opened in 1820s)

Rodley Inn or Rodney Inn

97 Leadmill Road, Sheffield 1

Rodney Arms

46 Leadmill Road, Sheffield 1

Named after Admiral Rodney, who led the British to victory over the Spanish and French in the Atlantic in 1780s.

Rodney Arms

35 Fargate, Sheffield 1

Roebuck

21 Porter Street, Sheffield

Possibly named after the male of the roe deer, a small species of spotted deer.

Roebuck Tavern

72 Charles Street, Sheffield 1 (aka Newt & Chambers, Emporium)

The Roebuck, a Wards pub, which opened in late 18th century, disappeared in the late 1990s, £300,000 and fourteen weeks of refurbishment later, the Newt and Chambers arose. The change of name is said to come from the old Sheffield firm of Newton Chambers (those people who made the Izal toilet paper) which had offices nearby and whose staff would use the Roebuck after work. Does this really warrant a reason to change a pub name? Especially one which could be associated with a man who was probably one of the best orators Sheffield ever had, John Arthur Roebuck. In 1849 Roebuck was an MP for the Sheffield area and possibly one of a select band of speakers who tamed, and even gained applause from, the dreaded Paradise Square crowd, which as you will read elsewhere in this book was noted for its sometimes violent hostility towards the men who dared to address them.
(Around May '99 it has changed name again to the Emporium).

Rollers Tavern

70 Princess Street, Sheffield
(closed in 1920s)

Roman Ridge

Roman Ridge Road, Sheffield

This name serves to remind us that for half a millennium we were occupied by the Roman Empire. They had fortresses here at Wincobank and one at Templeborough. They finally left, 500 years after first conquering the British, in around the 5th century AD, when the Western Roman Empire's ruler Romulus Augustulus resigned or abdicated and the Empire simply ceased to exist.

Rosco Arms

65 Hoyle Street, Sheffield (1800s-1910s)

In close proximity to the Roscoe, a cinema which survived much longer than the pub even though it had to resort to bingo on a nightly basis.

Rosco Tavern

27 Henry Street, Sheffield

Rose & Crown

65 Queens Street, Sheffield 1
(opened 1780s-1890s)

The name Rose and Crown on an inn or tavern sign generally indicates loyalty to the monarch of the day and also to England itself.

Rose & Crown

31 West Bar, Sheffield 1
(opened 1790s-1900s)

Rose & Crown

Silver Street Head, Sheffield 1

Rose & Crown

27 Holly Street, Sheffield 1

Rose & Crown

21 Paternoster Row, Sheffield 2

Rose & Crown

12 Waingate, Sheffield 1
(aka Britannia) (1760s-1926)

Rose & Crown

Market Place, Sheffield 1 (1690s-1770s)

The reference about this Rose and Crown along with the one mentioned in the next entry are both gleaned from electoral registers and other local reference books and is probably a little speculative.

The first mentioned landlord was Nevil Simmon who ran the Rose & Crown in 1692, he was there for nearly thirty years until 1720. Various other people ran the inn, including the well known Watson family, the last landlord before closure was Samuel Leech or Peech, who left to run the Angel in 1776. This, unfortunately, does not totally gell with the fact that in 1791 it was mentioned, along with two other Rose and Crowns on High Street, and all three standing within 200 yards of each other.

Supposedly after it closed, whenever that really was, it was used as Bardell's auction rooms and shops. It was probably situated between Hartshead Passage and the Bankers Draft.

Rose & Crown

37 High Street, Sheffield 1
(1670s-1812) (aka Peggs)

First mentioned in 1675 when the landlord was James Goodie. In 1681 Thomas Pegg was licensee, succeeded by his son, Christopher who was survived by his widow, Jane, she carried on the family business until 1723. For some of this 42 year period it is known that the pub was locally called by the name 'Peggs'. From this period onward it came under the ever widening business empire that was the Watson family. William Watson took charge of the Rose from 1723 onwards. Watson himself is no less a Sheffield monument, having been a town trustee for 43 years, he had interests in the confectionery business (hence his nickname Frecky) and he built the George public house also on High Street/Watson Walk. He had 23 children and lived till he was 97 dying at Hag House, Cannon Hall, Fir Vale in 1791.

A Thomas Watson was running the Rose and Crown in 1812 when it ceased to trade and was converted into shops, and a workshop.

Rose & Crown

52 Sarah Street or 52 Brightmore Street, corner of Mitchell Street, Sheffield

Rose & Crown

245 Main Street, Darnall, Sheffield 9
(aka Connelly's)

In 1996 the Rose and Crown became another Irish themed pub, Connelly's. This two roomed pub has a sizeable lounge and a large pool room. Many a band has rehearsed in the function room.

Rose & Crown

Bankfield Lane, Stannington, Sheffield 6

Nicknamed Minnies by the local of Stannington Village.

Rose Cottage

70/72 Cricket Inn Road, Sheffield 2

Rose House

316 South Road, Sheffield 6

Rose Inn

627 Penistone Road, Sheffield 6

The Rose Inn was demolished in 1997 after a battle by the Historic Society of Bradfield, the Sheffield Flood Group and a couple of local councillors who tried to point out that this was probably one of the finest example of a Garrison pub anywhere in Yorkshire, or England for that matter. It was also used as a makeshift mortuary in the Great Sheffield Flood, therefore, surely contributing to the city's heritage. But the site is still derelict waiting no doubt to be made into a car park for a fast food restaurant nearby.

The Sheffield Flood claimed over 200 lives and a number of public houses - The Rowell Bridge Inn at Loxley, The Cleakhum Inn and the Stag at Malin Bridge, the last two both totally washed away. The Landlord of the Mason Arms at Hillsborough Corner along with his wife were drowned and quite a few miles further on it still ripped out the facade of the Manchester Hotel, on Nursery Street. Around this era it was customary for inquests to be held in public houses. This practice came to an end in 1867, when it was made illegal.

Rose Inn

41 Workhouse Lane, Sheffield (1780s-1840s)

Rose & Crown Inn

21 Stour Lane, Wadsley, Sheffield 6

A Tetley pub, tucked away in a pleasant cul-de-sac in Wadsley Common and overlooks the Loxley Valley. Nicknamed the Top House by locals, it is made up of a small row of cottages and consists of three rooms. The straightforward tap room has a couple of steps leading up to the well decorated lounge. Ted Catlin the ex Wednesday player was landlord at one time.

Rotherham House

27 Exchange St, Sheffield 1
(opened late 18th century)
(aka The Sun, Old Number 12,
Double 6, Market Tavern, The Garden,
Bernies Restaurant)

Obviously, a pub that has seen a few name changes, the Rotherham House or Market as it is now called, can boast more name changes than any other Sheffield public house. It is reputed to have a ghost named Charlie inhabiting its interior. In 1971 (when it was called the Old Number 12) a situation arose that whilst the landlady and landlord were sleeping, their phone was tinkling as though someone on the downstairs bar line was lifting and replacing the receiver, also this was followed by banging and thumping. Being frightened (rightly so) they phoned the police who within minutes surrounded the premises. Upon entering they found nothing, except someone saw Charlies' trademark black cloud floating through the bar. At one time in the sixties you could walk through from the pub into the fast food premises next door.

Roundabout Bar

Leopold Street, Sheffield 1

Rowell Bridge Inn

Loxley, Sheffield

Swept away in Sheffield's Great Flood the Rowell was the first pub to be caught by the giant wave that swept down Loxley Valley from Dale Dyke Dam. The landlord, John Walters and his family escaped by clambering through the attached cornmill and out on to the hillside behind the mill, watching in the moonlight as the torrents rushed towards Sheffield. The Rowell Bridge was totally swept away.

Royal

233 Langsett Road, Sheffield 6
(1830s-1920s)

Royal

2 Arthur Street, Sheffield

Royal

86 West Street, Sheffield 1

Royal Hotel

Main Street, Dungworth,
Stannington, Sheffield 6

For the last few decades the Royal Hotel has gone up for
sale quite a few times, but in 1854 it was purchased for
just 200 guineas, the asking price is slightly more today.
Locals swear there is a ghost within the walls of the
Royal, most say the presence is mainly in the toilets.

Royal Exchange

283 Langsett Road, Sheffield 6

Generally this sign is depicted with Richard III on bended
knee trying to give up his crown to a yokel in exchange
for his nag. (A horse, a horse, my kingdom for a horse).
Another one shows half a sign with Charles I and the other
half with Oliver Cromwell.

Royal Exchange

64 Garden Street, Sheffield

Royal George

60 Carver Street, Wellington Street, Sheffield 1 (1820s-1970s)

Samuel Plimsoll spoke at a trade union meeting at the
Royal George, whose landlord at the time was one William
Broadhead. The Royal was used as the headquarters/
meeting place for the Sawgrinders Union whose secretary
just so happened to be Broadhead himself.
Industrial unrest was rife in around 1840 when the
Rattening Outrages took place and it is believed that
Broadhead, a radical agitator, was one of the main
instigators of this sometimes violent movement.

Royal George

94 Cricket Inn Road, Sheffield 2

Royal George

60 West Bar, Sheffield

Royal George

167 Greystock Street, Sheffield

Royal George

498 Brightside Lane, Sheffield 9

Royal Hotel

65 Earl Street, Sheffield 1

Royal Hotel

106 Eyre Lane, Sheffield

Royal Hotel

2 Bradfield Road, Sheffield 6

A Whitbreads Brewery House, The Royal Hotel was a
large imposing building situated on the corner of
Bradfield Road and Penistone Road, across from the
Owlerton Greyhound Stadium. It was a thriving pub when
the dogs and the speedway were taking place at the
stadium and the Sheffield Wednesday matches also
created a large customer base for the Royal.
It was demolished in the 80s to make way for one of the
many road widening developments that took place in
Sheffield around this time.
It is unknown whether the name The Royal Hotel was
derived from some local loyalty to the Royal Family, in
the early part of this century, or it was named, more
probably, after the Royal Dragoon Guards who were
stationed at the Hillsborough Barracks.

Royal Hotel

2 Finlay Street, Sheffield (aka Royal Albion)

The original pub with no name! This beer house on the
corner of Finlay Street and Hammond Street for many
years went unnamed.

Royal Hotel Tap

6 Waingate, Sheffield 6 (aka Reindeer)

Built as the Reindeer in 1797 by Godfrey Fox, a man who later became gaoler and liberty bailiff of the King Street gaol, supposedly given this position by the Duke of Norfolk himself.

Fox later became landlord of the Royal Oak, Pudding Lane, now King Street.

Royal Hotel

10 Market Sq, Woodhouse, Sheffield

Royal Hotel

617 Attercliffe Common, Sheffield 9

From an illustration by M. R. Liversidge.

Royal Hotel

114 Walkley Street/Cundy St, Sheffield 6

Royal Hotel

1 Abbeydale Road, Sheffield 7

Royal Hotel

36 West Bar Green, Sheffield

Royal Lancers

66/68 Penistone Road, Sheffield 6

Royal Mail

131 West Street, Sheffield

Royal Oak

484-486 Attercliffe Road, Sheffield 9

This sign is second in popularity only to the Red Lion as a British pub name. It is from the fact that on 29th May 1651, Charles II and his aid Colonel Carless hid in the Bascobel Oak, after defeat at the Battle of Worcester. After the Restoration this day was annually called Royal Oak Day.

Obviously the sign did not appear until after the Restoration

Royal Oak

29 King Street, Sheffield (1170s-1940s)

The landlord, of this Royal Oak, Thomas Smith was constable in 1818. The King Street Debtors Gaol was next door to the Royal Oak and Smith was the head gaoler. The gaol was moved to Scotland Street, taking over the Edinburgh Castle, a warehouse building at the top of Snow Lane.

Royal Oak

138 Pond Street, Sheffield

Royal Oak

Blackburn Road, Sheffield

This building used to be a farmhouse dating from the early 18th century and converted into a public house in around 1880.

Royal Oak

11 Hollis Croft, Sheffield 1

The Royal Oak is a public house that for many a year survived on its dinner time business, the Midland Bank (national headquarters), Footprint Tools and other office and local industry workers. At night it does rather less trade. Walking past the Broad Lane roundabout you could be excused for missing the pub, as it is just a door with not much signage.

Royal Oak

12 Lancaster Street, Neepsend Lane, Sheff 3

Royal Oak

136 Lansdowne Road, Sheffield 11

Royal Oak

354 Mansfield Road, Intake, Sheffield

Royal Oak

250 Savile Street, Sheffield 4

Royal Oak

92 Savile Street, Sheffield 4

Royal Oak

91 Upper Allen Street, Sheffield

Royal Oak

44 West Bar Green, Sheffield 3

Royal Oak

16 Allen Street, Sheffield (1810s-1930s)

Royal Oak

107 Corby Street, Sheffield

Royal Oak

73 Milton Street, Sheffield

Royal Oak

12 Pear Street, Sheffield

Royal Oak

23 Walkley Road, Sheffield 6

Royal Oak Hotel

17 Cemetery Road, Sheffield 2
(aka Beer engine)

Royal Oak Hotel

60/62 Earsham Street, Sheffield 4

Royal Oak Hotel

10 Station Road, Chapeltown

Royal Rifle Corps

137 Carlisle Street east, Sheffield 4

Royal Standard

36-38 West Bar Green, Sheffield 3

This is the name given to the Royal Flag or Standard which changed with the passing of the centuries and many different monarch, i.e. Edward III had a Fleur de Lys on his standard, James I had Scottish Lion and Irish Harp adorning his.

Royal Standard

156/158 St Marys Road, Sheffield 2

Opened in 1845 and called the 'Flag' by its then regulars. This three roomed pub had a compulsory purchase order hanging over it for a about 20 years, due to road widening in the area. This claimed the Truro Tavern which was situated directly across St Marys Road.

The Standard, was one of the calling points along with the Montgomery and the Truro Tavern for blades fan making their way to Bramall Lane football ground on Saturday afternoons, sadly only the Royal Standard remains.

Recently, 1998, undergone a massive refurbishment.

Royds Inn

213 Attercliffe Road, Sheffield 9

Rubens Head

117 South Street, Park, Sheffield

Rutland Arms

80 Neepsend Lane, or 3 Rutland Road, Sheffield

Possibly named after England's smallest county which disappeared, from an administrative point of view, in 1974.

Rutland Arms

86 Brown Street, Sheffield 1

This imposing Grade II listed building was built by the brewer Duncan Gilmour. The yellow and brown tiled exterior still has the name Gilmour emblazoned upon it. The Rutland is situated in what is now called the cultural industries quarter, an area that has definitely thrived with the moneys supplied for the Popular Music Museum, the Showrooms, The Science Park, and the Red Tape studios. Possibly the name comes from the Dukes of Rutland who owned a shooting lodge on the outskirts and vast tracts of land around Sheffield

RSVP

Corner of Cambridge St and Division St, Sheffield 1

Built on the old Albert Hotel sight at the corner of Cambridge Street and Division Street in Barkers Pool. Most of the new Cafe/Bars in Sheffield, of which there are plenty, have made a virtue of the fact they have used old, sometimes listed, buildings, firestation, waterworks, bank etc. which have been inherited.

The RSVP is a purpose built tower like structure overlooking the War Memorial.

The window tables on the upper floor of the Tower part of the RSVP afford you a rewarding view of the busy surrounding area.

The RSVP is the seventh such pub in a national chain operated by Whitbreads.

Saddle Inn

94 West Street, Sheffield

The Saddle was closed in around 1992 after 190 years of trading and moved about 60 yards further down West Street and opened up as the Saddle in 1993 leaving the old pub derelict!!

St George's Tavern

93 Broad Lane, Sheffield

The Patron Saint of England represented by a red cross on a white flag or in pubic house signage, red cross on white square or otherwise a mounted knight killing, generally with a lance or pikestaff, a dragon.

St Legers Tavern

Pinstone Street, Sheffield

Named after the locally run horserace. The St Leger is a race for three year olds run in September at Doncaster and was named after Colonel Anthony St. Leger. It started in 1776 and it is the last classic flat race of the season.

St Philips Tavern

92 St Philips Road, Sheffield

It was nicknamed the 'Monday Morning Knocking Shop', possibly because people missed work and went for a drink on Monday dinner time at the St Philips Tavern.

St Stephens Tavern

St Stephens Road, Sheffield

Salutation Inn

85 Upper St Philips Road, Sheffield 3

Salutation Inn

85 West Street, Sheffield

Salutation Inn

126 Attercliffe Common, Sheffield 9

This large cream tiled public house stood on the corner of Coleridge Road and Attercliffe Common and was two doors away from the Pavilion Picture Palace. With those two doors being taken up by a bookmakers and a tobacconist/newsagents, most men didn't want to move far from this little oasis in Attercliffe.

The Salutation had one of the largest concert rooms in Attercliffe, which accommodated many of the early 50s and 60s popular music stars.

Salutation Inn

170 Wortley Road, High Green

This is a popular public house name with religious connotations, it is the old English word for Annunciation and represents the Archangel Gabriel saluting the blessed virgin with the words: Ava Maria.

A public house that has seen a fatal shooting. In the early 90s the landlady shot and mortally wounded her partner.

Samuel Plimsoll

Hyde Park, Sheffield

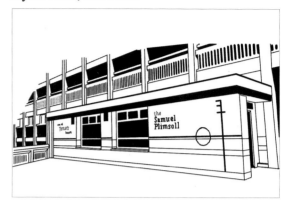

Named after Samuel Plimsoll, (1824-1894) who was the Member of Parliament for Derby from 1864-1880. From his Parliamentary position he endeavoured to pass a Bill to prevent the use of overladen and unseaworthy ships. In Parliament, upon hearing of Mr Disraeli's intention to drop this bill, Plimsoll created a scene in the House, that to this day remains unparalleled. He completely lost control and described the ship owning members as murderers and villains and shook his fist in the speaker's face. The furore that this outburst created did Plimsoll's case no harm at all with the British public.

The Merchant Shipping Act of 1878 was passed and made compulsory a maximum load line, a Plimsoll Mark, which will have helped save many seamen's lives over the years since its inception.

Plimsoll was born in Bristol and spent some of his early years studying in Sheffield, where for a time he lived at Whiteley Wood Hall.

The pub itself, which was built into the Hyde Park Flats complex showed a Plimsoll line on its frontage.

Sawmakers Arms

1 Neepsend Lane, Sheffield 3

Sawmakers Arms

40 Burnt Tree Lane, Sheffield

Sawmakers Arms

63 Russell Street, Sheffield

Scarboro Arms

104 -106 Milton Street, Sheffield 3

Scarboro Arms

79 Fargate, Sheffield 6

Scarborough Arms

13 Rockingham Street, Sheffield 6

Scarborough Arms

34 Addy Street, Sheffield 6

The Scarborough is a public house well over 120 years old. Over the years has had a succession of nicknames including Chapel of Rest and the Zoo

Scissorsmiths Arms

114 Harvest Lane, Sheffield

Scottish Queen

South Street, Park Hill Flats, Sheffield 2

Mary Queen of Scots was imprisoned for a time in the Manor Castle (Manor Lodge) which is within sight of this pub.

Seven Stars

36 Trippet Lane, Sheffield

Seven Stars were worn in the celestial crown supposedly worn by the Virgin Mary. Seven Stars are in the Pleiades, a cluster of stars in the constellation of Taurus. Also in Greek mythology the Seven Stars represented the seven daughters of Atlas and Pleione.

Around 1785 Thomas Beet was the landlord of this inn and was the only knifemaker in Sheffield to stamp his own trademark on to his wares. These were known as spotted knives.

Shades Vaults

Various number on Watsons Walk, Sheffield (1790s-1940)

Found in local street reference books as being at 19, 20 & 22 in the late 19th century and 22 Watsons Walk, in 1940. Samuel Turner (known as Gin Sam) kept the Shades in 1805 when it was known locally as the 'hole in wall'.

Around this period, early 19th century, the Archbishop of York was having his evening meal at the Shades, after a day of giving confirmations at the Parish Church, when a man, Thomas Dunn brought his son to the Archbishop's table, explained that his workload had made him late and could he have his son confirmed. This the Archbishop promptly did and then resumed eating his meal.

Shakespeare Hotel

146/148 Gibraltar Street, Sheffield 3

An old coaching house, whose cobbled passageway leading to the courtyard still remains to this day, so too do the old hayloft and stables. It used to afford bed and breakfast lodging to weary travellers at one time but the top floor has been derelict for many a year.

The Shakespeare Hotel is supposed to have a ghost that wanders the cellars.

A succession of landlords have tried to keep the, slightly off the beaten track, Shakespeare going over the years. It has defeated most, some quicker that others but the present landlady Marg Phillips seems to be making a good fist of it.

Shakespeare Tavern

16 Sycamore Street, Sheffield
(aka Crown & Shakespeare, 1839,
or Shakespeare & Crown, 1841)

Shakespeare Inn
196 Bradfield Road, Sheffield 6

Sheaf
1 Victoria Quay's, Wharf Street, Sheffield 1

This large structure left derelict for many years in the Canal Wharf has been transformed into a beautiful modernised building, which is used for conferences and seminars as well as a restaurant and public house.

Sheaf Tavern
2 New Cattle Market, Sheffield

Sheaf
Fraser Road, Woodseats, Sheffield

Sheaf House Hotel
329 Bramall Lane, Sheffield 2

Unbelievably it was Sheffield Wednesday, not United who used to play on the sports arena attached to the Sheaf House Hotel in the late 1870s.

Sheaf Inn/Tavern
11 Effingham Street, Sheffield 4

Sheaf Tavern
Sheaf Street, Sheffield 4 (1820s-1900s)

Sheaf View Hotel
25 Gleadless Road, Sheffield 2

Now, sadly, standing derelict.

Sheffield Arms

107 Upwell Street, Sheffield 4

Sheffield Arms

42 Meadow Street, Sheffield (1810s-1940s)

Sheffield Moor

114 South Street, Moor, Sheffield

Sheffield Utd Social Club

Bramall Lane, Sheffield 2

Sheldon

27-29 Hill Street, Sheffield 2

Sheldon Inn

10 Edmund Street, Sheffield

Shepherd Inn

118 Duke Street, Sheffield

Shepley Spitfire

Mickley Lane, Sheffield

This pub, which opened in 1979, is named after a young Sheffield flyer, Douglas Shepley, killed in the first few day of the Battle of Britain, on August 12th 1940. Only 21 years of age he died heroically in a dogfight over the English Channel, taking on three German enemy aircraft. His wife of only six weeks and his mother started a campaign to raise cash to replace the plane. The nationwide appeal was successful and the plane was known as the "Shepley Spitfire". This aircraft was also shot down but fortunately this pilot survived.

The public house was named in memory of young Shepley.

Sherwood

Birley Moor Road, Sheffield

Shiny Sheff

Crimicar Lane, Lodge Moor, Sheffield

This Whitbread owned pub is really well worth a visit, opened in 1969 it has naval memorabilia spread around the Plymouth and Portsmouth bars, and it is a treasure especially if you are at all interested in naval history.

The "Shiny Sheff" takes its name from the nickname of the HMS Sheffield, one of three so named ships: The first, a cruiser took part in the chasing of the Bismark in 1941 and was later broken up, in 1957, whereupon its bell, badge and ensign were placed in safe keeping in the Sheffield Cathedral. The second, a guided missile destroyer received a direct hit by an Exocet missile in the Falkland's War, on May 4th 1982. Around 20 seamen were killed and many injured.

The third, which is now in service, is a frigate.

Ship Inn

312 Shalesmoor, Sheffield 3
(opened in early 19th century)

Charlie, a spectre who haunts the cellars and tunnels, is reputedly the ghost of one of two men who are said to have drowned when the Sheffield Flood, 11th March 1864, caught the staff and overnight guests asleep. No bodies were ever recovered.

There is a plaque outside this public house giving details of this terrible disaster.

Ship Inn

31 Water Lane, Sheffield

Shiregreen Hotel

416 Sicey Avenue, Sheffield 5

Built in 1939 and opened in June of the same year.
It is a large estates public house and well frequented.

Shoulder of Mutton

Top Road, Worrall, Oughtibridge

In some villages a name such as this showed that the landlord was also the butcher.

An old converted farmhouse set in the village of Worrall, it has outer walls three feet thick. On a clear day Barnsley and Rotherham can be viewed from the pub.

Shop on the Ground Floor

near Corn Exchange, Sheffield

Shrewsbury Tavern

26 South Road, Park, Sheffield
(1820s-1920s)

Shrewsbury Arms

109 South Road, Park, Sheffield
(1820s-1930s)

Shrewsbury Arms

74 Broad Street, Sheffield

Shrewsbury Tavern

102 South Street, Park, Sheffield

Sicey Hotel

Sicey Avenue, Sheffield 5

Built in June 1939.

Sidney's Hotel

23 Haymarket, Sheffield

Sign Post

31 Andover Street, Sheffield 3

This Stones house along with the Rock House, Furnival, Bowling Green and Catherine Arms made up a lively quintet of pubs in the Pitsmoor area. The Landlord and Landlady in the 70s were, Harry and Dorothy Benson, who kept a lovely pub, with good beer and totally trouble free environment. They used to be in charge at the Staffordshire just down the road.

The lounge, a sizeable room, had a large mirror running along one wall and seating for about 100 people.

Also there was the customary piano in the lounge, which about 9pm every night someone got up and started to play. That was generally the cue for some customers to move into the other room, or take themselves back to the Rock, Furnival etc. for the last hour.

The public bar was also quite large and always had someone playing darts, dominoes or crib almost all the time, dinner and night.

Sir Admiral Lyons

174 Eyre Street, Sheffield (1810s-1900s)

Sir Francis Burdett

8 Pond Hill, Sheffield (1820s-1910s)

A Member of Parliament for Westminster for 30 years. After publishing a speech which denied the right of the House of Commons to imprison delinquents, his own arrest was ordered. He barricaded himself in his house and resisted arrest for four days.

The residents of Sheffield, at that time, would have thought anyone who was against the government's policies was probably worth naming a public house after.

Sir John Falstaffe

48 The Wicker, Sheffield

Sir Robert Peel

159 Carlisle Street, Sheffield
(opened 1860s-1917)

Named after British Prime Minister Robert Peel, who died in a horseriding accident in 1850. Peel was twice elected as Prime Minister but is probably remembered more for his creation of the modern police force.

Slug and Fiddle

261-267 Ecclesall Road, Sheffield 11

Herbie Armstrong, guitarist for Van Morrison, owns a third partnership in this trendy bar on Ecclesall Road. Situated nicely within easy walking distance of the Pomona, Nursery Tavern and Champs Bar.

Smithy Door Tavern

26 Hawley Croft, Sheffield (1800s-1890s)

Smithfield Hotel

29 Furnival Road, Sheffield

Smithfield Hotel

29 Blonk Street, Sheffield

Snow Lane Tap

Snow Lane, Crofts, Sheffield

Snow Lane and the Crofts were set in the heart of what would be the equivalent of today's red light areas of Sheffield. It is known that in the mid 19th century the landlord was John Poole, who was arrested and fined £5, a princely sum, for running his establishment as a brothel. It is said that when raided by police, all four bedrooms were occupied by prostitutes and their clients.

Social Tavern

38 Bailey Street, Sheffield (closed 1900s)

Solferino

130 Cemetery Road, Sheffield

Soldiers Return

42 Water Lane, Sheffield (1780s-1890s)

South Sea

3 Spooner Road, Sheffield 10

South Street Hotel

71 South Street, Sheffield

Sovereign

70 Rockingham Street, Sheffield

This is named after the British Standard gold coin which, existed from 1817, for one hundred years, until 1917, with a value of 20 shillings. Henry VII gold sovereign coins were worth 22/6d.

Spirit Vaults

30 Castle Street, Sheffield

This name is normally a reference to the fact that the premises previously used as a wine merchants, especially one who sold gin.

Spital Inn

24 Spital Street, Sheffield

Generally the word Spital is derived from the word hospital, especially one dealing in contagious diseases. Possibly a hospital dealing with these medical problems would be sited nearby.

Spitalfields

57 Stanley Street, Sheffield

Sportsman

41 West Bar, Sheffield

The Sportsman, years ago, was generally so named to commemorate someone, normally the innkeeper, landlord or a famous regular, who was a well known sportsman. In Sheffield, we've had footballers, from both city clubs, boxers, athletes and cricketers, all of whom have kept sportsman public houses. As you will see from the following list of like named public houses the Sportsman is the most popular pub name in Sheffield, outstripping the national forerunner the Red Lion nearly 2 to 1.

Sportsman

20 South Street, Moor, Sheffield

Sportsman

14 Bridgehouses, Sheffield

Sportsman

504 Attercliffe Road, Sheffield
(aka Hope and Anchor, Bar Indigo)

The present building occupying the Sportsman was built in the 50s to replace the original Sportsman that was bombed and destroyed in the German blitz on Sheffield in 1940. The old Sportsman was mentioned in Sheffield literature as long ago as 1888, then called the Hope and Anchor.

Sportsman
71 Harvey Clough Road, Sheffield 8

This public house used to have a bowling green at the side of it. It was a well known venue for pigeon, poultry and rabbit showing.

Sportsman
100 Walkley Bank Road, Sheffield 6

Sportsman
33 Bridge Street, Sheffield

Sportsman
133 Infirmary Road, Sheffield 6

Sportsman
7 Cornish Street, Sheffield

Sportsman Cottage
74 Button Lane, Sheffield

The Sportsman's Group
851 Penistone Road, Sheffield 6

The origin of the name the Sportsman's Group is unknown, the best offering that can be made is probably that groups of people used to gather on land adjacent to the pub to watch bare knuckle fights, potty rise and other sporting events take place.

Like the Royal Hotel just a couple of hundred yards along Penistone Road, The Sportsman's Group used to do good business when the Greyhounds, Speedway and football were taking place. Also, like the Royal, it was demolished for road widening purposes.

Sportsman Group
5 Fargate, Sheffield 1

Sportsman Inn
Barnsley Road, Sheffield 4

Jimmy Hendrix, 'All around the Watchtower' fame, once had a pint of Tennants in this public house along with Trevor Bloom, who at that time was the Mojo Club disc jockey. The Mojo was Pete Stringfellow's first foray into the nightclub business.

Mr Bloom reliably informed the author this incident happened before Hendrix did his gig at the now defunct Burngreave club.

Sportsman Inn
13 Maltravers Street, Sheffield 4

Sportsman Inn
4 Paternoster Row, Sheffield

Sportsman Inn
140 Arundel Street, Sheffield

Sportsman Inn
1 Hardy Street, Sheffield

Sportsman Inn
Blackburn Road, Sheffield

Sportsman Inn
123 High Street, Ecclesfield, Sheffield

Sportsman Inn
Main Street, Hackenthorpe, Sheffield

Sportsman Inn
155 Marcus Street, Sheffield 3

Sportsman Inn
21 Marcus Street, Sheffield 3

Sportsman Inn
2 Oldfield Road, Sheffield 6

The building that now houses the Sportsman was once used as an old farmhouse and stands on the gateway to Stannington village at the fork of Oldfield Road and Stannington Road.

Sportsman Inn
45 Park Hill Lane, Sheffield 2

Sportsman Inn
569 Redmires Road, Sheffield 10

The land behind the Sportsman carries some points of history for the city of Sheffield. During World War I it was called Redmires camp mainly because it housed the Sheffield City Battalion, a fighting group of men who suffered appalling losses in their first engagement in France.

The camp lay unused for about twenty years until once again Europe ignited into a Second World War. From this theatre of war, prisoners, mainly Italian were interred here at Redmires when the land was turned into a P.O.W camp.

Sportsman Inn
84 Sheldon Street, Sheffield 2

Sportsman Inn

83 Well Road, Sheffield 8
(aka T'Boilers, Boilers Rest)

The Sportsman may be Sheffield's most common pub name, but this sportsman used to be known more commonly by its nickname, The Boilers Rest. This name came about when in 1896 a large boiler was being towed up the very steep hill, that is Well Road, and came loose and rolled backwards into the Sportsman, causing great damage, but thankfully no serious injuries.

After rebuilding the pub, it was for its remaining days always known as the Boilers Rest or T'boilers. It is said that the walls of the refurbished pub were awash with pictures of the incident. Where are they now?

Sportsman Inn

183 Worrall Road, Sheffield 6

Sportsman Inn

125 Thomas Street, Sheffield 1

Sportsman Inn

23 Oak Street, Sheffield

Sportsman Inn

24 Cambridge Street, Sheffield 1

Sportsman Inn

57 Benty Lane, Sheffield 10

One of Sheffield Wednesday's most famous players, Ernest Blenkinsop was the landlord of this Sportsman, in the forties/fifties. This player played in Wednesday's golden era, two championships 1930s and an FA cup victory 1935. To this day the Owls have never repeated these glorious halcyon times. Blenkinsop is also one of a select band who have played for Wednesday to have gained more than 20 England caps. Truly a great player.

Sportsman Inn

156/158 Darnall Road, Sheffield 9

Sportsman Inn

10 Denby Street, Sheffield 2

Graham Shaw, the ex-England and Sheffield United full back, was, for a period of time, the landlord of this public house, situated just of Bramall Lane.

Sportsman Inn

33 Otley Street, Sheffield 6

Spotted Cow

70 Russell Street, Sheffield

Spread Eagle

19 High Street, Sheffield 1 (closed in 1890)

This entry and the following one could be one and the same public house. The Spread Eagle was situated amongst the buildings at the top of Chapel Walk in the late 18th century, when its landlord was James Richardson who also owned the Grey Horse which was lower down High Street.

Spread Eagle

9 Fargate, or 2 Chapel Walk, Sheffield 1

At the top of Chapel Walk where Richards Shop used to be sited, it is said that the Spread Eagle once stood here and was one of a number of thriving licensed beer selling establishments in the late 19th century.

Spread Eagle

37 Addy Street, Sheffield 6
(closed around 1960)

This name is originally derived from the Roman Empire national emblem which was the Spread Eagle. Austria, Germany, Russia, Spain and France are all heraldically associated with the Spread Eagle.

Spread Eagle

39 West Bar Green, Sheffield 1
(aka Eagle Tavern)

Spread Eagle

49 Burlington Street, Sheffield 6

Springfield Tavern

182-184 Broomsping Lane, Sheffield 10
(aka Ivy Cottage)

Spring Tavern

74 New George Street, 2 Boston Street, Sheffield

Springvale Hotel

1 Commonside, Crookesmoor, Sheffield 10
(aka Beer Engine)

The Springvale Beer Engine as it is now known consists of a long narrow room which opens out at one end. It was formerly two rooms before its alteration. This Whitbreads pub is one of an explosion of public houses across not only Sheffield but the whole of England to be turned into a "spit and sawdust boozer". The Springvale hasn't suffered too much from the alterations, it does have the wooden floorboards and old look to it (luckily no spit) but it has come out of the refurbishment well.

It is said that the night he was caught by two Sheffield policemen, PC Hydes and Sgt Ring, Peter Sutcliffe (the Yorkshire Ripper) had been drinking in the Springvale Hotel.

Springwood Inn

67 Freedom Street, Hampden View, Walkley Sheffield 6

Springwood Hotel

Hastilar Road South, Sheffield 13

Stafford Arms

30 Stafford Street, Sheffield

Staffordshire Arms

38-40 Sorby Street, Sheffield 4

The Staffordshire Arms, Sorby Street, Burngreave, a Stones pub, just off Spital Hill, was for many years, until 1986, a beer only licensed pub. In January of that year the Staffordshire Arms was renovated and a Spirit license was granted, leaving only the Kings Arms, Attercliffe Road, with a beer only license, in the Sheffield area.

In the sixties the then landlord was blasted to death by his wife, allegedly because of his unfaithfulness. Whatever happened to the old fashioned get out clause, divorce?

It is said his head was blown completely off when he was shotgunned whilst asleep. If rumour is to be believed the room where it happened is still locked and unused.

Some years after the dreadful happening took place a woman customer came hurriedly out of the upstairs toilets very distressed and shaken, whereupon her partner, to prove nothing was amiss took her back up to the loo. Upon entering he was pushed by some unknown force into the bath itself.

Stag Inn

15 Psalter Lane, Sheffield 11
(aka Stags Head)

Old coach house on road to London via Bakewell built in circa 1805. Reverend Alexander McKenzie had this building erected in the late 18th century.

Stag Inn

Market Square, Woodhouse

Stag Inn

170 Harvest Lane, 2 Wilson St, Sheffield 3

Stag Inn or Stagg Inn

14 or 45 Carver Street, Sheffield

The spelling of the word Stagg with two Gs is an indication of great age as is Swann with two Ns.

Stag Inn

28 Pea Croft, Sheffield

Stag Inn

Pond Street, Sheffield

Stag Inn

Malin Bridge, Sheffield 6

Destroyed by the Sheffield Flood in 1864.

Standard Hotel

38 West Bar Green, Sheffield

The English defeated the Scots at the Battle of the Standard in 1138. The Battle earned it title from the fact that the standards of St Peter-York, St Cuthbert-Durham, St John-Beverley and St Winifred-Ripon were raised and placed at the centre of the fighting Englishmen. Supposedly when the St Cuthberts standard was raised it lifted the English forces to new heights of ferocity and the battle swung their way. Because of this event the name Standard was used for many an inn sign.

Staniforth Arms

261 Staniforth Road, Sheffield 9

The Staniforth Arms, is sited just over Broad Oaks Bridge, between Attercliffe Road and Darnall.

The pub consists of three rooms, one a large concert room at the rear, was also used for wedding receptions etc., the other two rooms were smaller but still sizeable, one being a dram shop cum games room with a large juke box, pool table, dartboard and a threequarter size snooker table. The third room seemed totally out of place, it was like an oasis in the desert. It was a place where you could take a girlfriend or wife and sit in total tranquillity in plush surroundings. All the upholstery was in red velvet and all the tables were brass topped, and brass light fittings and sedate lighting made this room really pleasant to be in.

So whilst fights were going on (and these were plentiful) in the other rooms, you could sit oblivious in the 'best room'.

Stanley Street Tavern

24 Stanley Street, Sheffield

Star

15 Orange Street, Sheffield

Originally a religious symbol, referring either to the Star of Bethlehem or the sign of the Virgin Mary.

Another option is that since 1634 a 16 pointed star had appeared in the Worshipful Company of Innholders.

Star

16 Silver Street, Sheffield
(opened around 1750)

Star

8 White Croft, Sheffield

Star

26 Haymarket, Sheffield

Star

39 Cemetery Road, Sheffield

Star & Garter

82/84 Winter Street, Sheffield 3

Referring to the Most Noble Order of the Garter, the highest order of knighthood in Britain. Instituted by Edward III in 1348. Supposedly the Order is limited to the Sovereign, members of the Royal Family and 25 knights.

Star Hotel

45 High Street, Sheffield (1790s-1900s)

Star Inn

11 Meadow Street, Sheffield

Star Inn

83 Pea Croft, Sheffield (aka Old Star Inn)

Star Inn

49 Danville Street, Sheffield 4 (1870-1960s)

Star Inn (Old)

181 Gibraltar Street, Sheffield

Star Inn

65 Rural Lane, Sheffield 6

Star of Brunswick

85/87 Cemetery Road, Sheffield

Possibly named in deference to the Duke of Brunswick who died whilst fighting with the Duke of Wellington at Waterloo in 1815.

Star of Lemont

27-29 Hermitage Street, Sheffield

Station Inn

Naseby Street, Sheffield

Station Inn/Hotel

732 Attercliffe Road, Sheffield 9

The Station was built in 1833. Situated on Attercliffe Road it was a Wards public house. The Station itself is long and narrow and is supposed to have been three cottages transformed into one long structure.

It is, was, well known around the Attercliffe area that the Station has/had a ghost, supposedly an occupier of one of the above mentioned cottages was savagely knifed to death. The ghost now (according to the regulars) tips glasses upside down, spills drinks and heavy footfalls can be heard coming from the upper floor. The public house itself is made up of two rooms, one, very small having about four tables with a small serving bar area and the door leading directly on to Attercliffe Road. The other room is quite long and it was in this room that turns or acts would perform on a Friday and Saturday night in the 60s and 70 whilst Attercliffe was still a thriving area. The pub once had a pub sign saying Station Inn and Station Hotel as its main wall painted name, very strange.

This beer house was licensed before Victoria came to the throne, in 1833, but it took it another 140 years to get its spirit license.

Station Inn

Brightside Lane, Sheffield 9

Station Hotel

165/167 Granville Street, Sheffield 2

Station Hotel/Inn

95 The Wicker, Sheffield 3

Station Inn

2 Harmer Lane, Sheffield

Steam Clock

352 Brightside Lane, Sheffield 9
(closed 1917)

Steelmakers Tav

109 Carver Street, Sheffield (closed 1890s)

Steel Inn

135 Harborough Avenue, Sheffield 2

Steers Hotel

20 Old Haymarket - 2 Dixon Lane, Sheffield

Jason Steer was landlord in 1862, presumably this is where the hotel name derived from.

Stocks
Ecclesfield, Sheffield

A well known item of punishment, in which an offender would be placed and held secure by 2 planks with small holes for the ankles or wrists to fit into. Depending on the offence that had been perpetrated, sometimes the townspeople would be allowed to throw missiles at the victim. This means of punishment was still in extensive use well into the 19th century.

Stone House
Mulberry Street, Sheffield 1

On the lower side of Mulberry Street was the old Stone House for many generation known as the wine and spirit vaults. The Greaves's of Page Hall owned this hostelry, and then it was sold to the Watsons, then on to the Howards family and finally on to the Prest family who ran it till it was to fall victim to Sheffield's perennial problem street improvements.

Stone House
21 Church Street, Sheffield 1

Situated next to the Cutlers Hall there has been a public house on this site for more than 200 years.
The present house is pleasant and welcoming, but the lovely pub of the sixties, early seventies was a masterpiece. When it was refurbished it had a courtyard with artificial shop frontages all around, benches to sit and drink at. Carts and olde worlde figures were also dotted around to give it a turn of the century feel.

Strad Hotel
101 Stradbrook Drive, Sheffield 13

Strines
Bradfield, Sheffield

Strongarms
1 West Bar, Sheffield

Outside this public house used to be two bronzed arms protruding and each holding a lamp.

Suffolk Hotel
24 Turner Street, Sheffield

Summer Tavern
Summer Street, Sheffield

Summerfield Hotel
21/23 Soho Street, 26 Summerfield St, Sheffield 11

Sun Inn
134 West Bar, Sheffield 3 (opened in 1820s)

The Sun Inn sited on the corner of Gibraltar Street and Bower Springs is now a painting and decorating wholesale warehouse.

Sun Inn

110 Lansdowne Road, Sheffield 2

Sun Inn

76/78 South Street, Sheffield 2

Variations on the theme of the name are: it was the landlords place in the Sun or more likely a round yellow illustration was easy to portray on the public house sign.

Sun Inn

12 Walker Street, Sheff (opened in 1830s)

Sun Tavern

27 Old Haymarket, Sheffield
(aka Old Number 12) (1780s-1950s)

Situated across from the top of Exchange Street, the building is now an amusement arcade.

At one time in the early 19th century it was a place where you could get the news before most of the populace. Murdo Young used to place his newssheets in the window of the Sun. When Thomas Wiley took over the license of the Sun he kept the practice going, and in 1832 he travelled back from London by stage coach. after hearing the Reform Bill Riots, in a trip that took only twelve hours and it was posted in his Sun Tavern window less than 13 hours after being passed.

Speedier news than today's Sun Newspaper!!!

Sunny Bank Hotel

74 Powell Street, Sheffield 3

Sunnyside Hotel

26-28 William Street, Sheffield 10

Surrey

Masonic Hall, Surrey Street, Sheffield 1

Surrey Arms

176 Granville Street, Sheffield 1

Surrey Vaults/Theatre

86 West Bar, Sheffield

Built in 1851 it actually only lasted 14 years before it burned down, and was left derelict for 15 more years before a vestry hall was built on the site.

The Surrey Theatre was the biggest of the public houses that sprang up in the mid 19th century built almost entirely for light entertainment, dancing and singing. It gave the ordinary man and woman a chance to forget their workload, as opposed to the hard drinking spit and sawdust inns of that era that just dealt with the steelworkers and other related industries in bare essential type hostelries.

Swan

29 Snig Hill, Sheffield 1

Swan Inn

Main Road, Ridgeway

Swan Tavern

74 Duke Street, Sheffield

Swan with Two Necks

28 Furnival Street, Sheffield

Possibly from a corruption of its correct title which should read A Swan with Two Nicks.

At one time swans had nicks cut into their beaks to indicate who owned them, i.e. 2 nicks The Dyers Company; 1 Nick The Vintners Company; No nicks means it was wild and belonged to the reigning monarch. It was mentioned in listings until the mid 1930s then it was either demolished or just ceased to be a public house.

Sycamore Tree

24 Sycamore Street, Sheffield (1820s-1910s)

Talbot Arms

50 Cricket Inn Road, Sheffield

The name could either be derived from the Talbot family who were well known in the Sheffield area or from the hunting hound of the same name, of which two can be found on John Talbot, Earl of Shrewsbury coat of arms.

Talbot Arms

**39 Water Lane, Sheffield 2
(aka Spotted Dog)**

The Talbot or as it was more commonly known the Spotted Dog stood on the corner of Alma Street and Spring Street.

Talbot

Blast Lane, Sheffield

Talbot Inn

**40 Hoyle Street, Sheffield 3
(aka Good Doctor, Ye Old Toad)**

Originally the Talbot, this pub was situated near to the Sheffield Royal Infirmary, now also defunct. On the pub sign pictured was a doctor with his stethoscope.

Talbot Inn

19/21 Talbot Road, Sheffield 2

Talbot Hotel

57-59 Boston Street, Sheffield 2

Talbot Hotel

Blackburn Road, Kimberworth

Tankard
29 Little Pond Street, Sheffield

The drinking vessel, the tankard was originally made of wooden hoops, something akin to a miniature wooden tub. Usually, today's tankards are made of pewter or silver.

Tankard
91 West Bar, Sheffield

Tankard & Punchbowl
94 Broad Street, Sheffield

Target Arms
12 Langsett Road, Sheffield 6

Target Arms
75 St Johns Road, Sheffield 2

This Wards public house at one stage had 1,300 dwellings right next door. It was situated in the shadow of the Hyde Park Flats tower block complex. Now that is a customer base.

Tea Gardens Hotel
88-90 Grimesthorpe Rd, aka Occupation Rd, Sheffield 4
(aka Tea Garden Cottage Hotel, Public Gardens, Gardeners Arms, Saracen's Head)

The Tea Garden was a coaching stop on the Barnsley to Sheffield route where the horses were changed, and food and rest could be had. Around this era most of the hotels trade would have come from the Occupation and Pitsmoor Collieries, both long since closed.

Temple
296 Sheffield Road, Templeborough, Sheff

The Temple was mainly kept alive by its customers from the steel industry, as were most public houses built into the infrastructure of this area. From the 1930s, to the 1960s, the Temple was packed to capacity with shift workers quenching their thirst after every shift. But nowadays the customer base in no longer there, only a handful of men now work in this area that used to employ more than 20,000 people.

In early '99 the landlord Peter Youle was reported in the Sheffield Star as "not having seen a woman customer for over a year and not even opening on a Saturday night", the publicans best night supposedly. Hopefully when the area is converted to the Magna Centre, which is a futuristic Iron and Steel heritage centre, and is expected to attract up to 500,000 visitors a year, the future could look brighter for the Temple!

Thatched House Tavern
2 High Street, Sheffield 1
(closed early 20th century)

This pub, at the top of High Street, backed on to Crooked Billet Yard, a place that found a modicum of notoriety in the 17th century when it was reported that one Thomas Wild cutler/knifemaker had made the knife with which a man named Fenton stabbed the Duke of Buckingham at Portsmouth in 1628, a pretty tenuous link to a major event, but that's history.

Theatre Tavern
49 Arundel Street, Sheffield

Generally taverns with similar names are built in the vicinity of the local theatrical area.

One of the many Sheffield Friendly Societies started in the Theatre Tavern in the late 18th century. It was called the Rawson Society and was named after the Rawson family of Wardsend, who made a generous donation when it started.

Probably, along with the landlord, the society moved lock stock and barrel to the Victoria on High Street in 1828.

Thorncliffe Arms
135 Warren Lane, Chapeltown

At one time in its history, the Thorncliffe built a room especially to accommodate the Irish navvies who worked on the nearby railway tunnel. In later years this room was turned into the snooker room and in the 1970s it had a table in the room that was over 70 years old.

Three Cranes
74 Queen Street, Sheffield 1

Only remaining public house on Queen Street. Well over 200 years old, modernised in 1966.

Three Feathers
Bowden Wood, Prince of Wales Rd, Sheff 9

Opened in 1957 as a Wards public house, it is the only beerhouse on Prince of Wales Road, even though, to be fair it does stand slightly off the main road.

In 1987 it had a £130,000 refurbishment, which added a self contained games room with its own bar, and the door into this room had a lovely etched Prince of Wales three feathered crest on it. Also scattered around are sepia pictures of the Princes of Wales, Edward VII and Edward VIII.

Three Horseshoes
Jehu Lane, or 12 Commercial Lane, Sheffield
Bombed and destroyed in the blitz, 1940.

Three Horseshoes Hotel
92 Norfolk Street, Sheffield
Another public house destroyed by German bombers in 1940. As well as being a hotel it was also an Oyster Bar.

Three Legs
30 Union Street, Sheffield
Possibly a reference to a Manx man or the three legged milking stool.

Three Magpies
Bonet Lane, Brinsworth

Three Merry Lads
610 Redmires Road, Sheffield 10

Richard Marsden first opened this licensed house in 1861 with a tap room made up in his cow shed and originally named after his three sons, one of whom, Frederick, was still landlord in the 1920s. Both the Three Merry Lads and the Sportsman were opened to cater for the trade that was coming into the area by the building of the Redmires Dams. It is said the three dams were built in 1836, 1839 and 1854.

Three Merry Smiths
55 Holly Street, Sheffield

Three Pigeons
20 Button Lane, Sheffield
This was formally a common London sign, used by various tradespeople and not just innkeepers. Unusual as the sport of pigeon racing is more of a North of England pastime.

Three Pigeons
117 Carver Street, Sheffield

Three Stags

Carver Street, Sheffield (opened 1810s)

Three Stags Heads

24 Pinstone Street, Sheffield (1810s-1890s)

Three Travellers Inn

82 Snig Hill, Sheffield (opened 1820s)

Three Tuns

55 Leopold Street, Sheffield 1
(aka Old Three Tuns) (1810s-1987)

The John Smiths one roomed public house pictured was a well frequented establishment that along with the Buccaneer bar which was situated across Leopold Street used to be the place to start your Friday or Saturday night on the town. From this vantage point you could either wander around the city centre pubs or the more robust drinkers would venture up into the West Street drinking establishments.

This widespread public house name probably originated from the fact that a tun was equal to 2 Pipes, 4 hogsheads or 252 old wine gallons. Tuns were used for wholesale distribution for retailing purposes the measures were gallons, pottles (half gallons,) quarts and pints. The Three Tuns appears in the arms of the Worshipful Company of Vintners in 1437 and the Worshipful Company of Brewers also in 1437, this obviously leading to the plentiful use of this name and sign.

Closed in 1987 for the Orchard Square development.

Three Tuns

39 Silver Street Head, Sheffield 1

This building set deep in legal and professional office territory is a Grade II listed building and it is believed to have been a pub since around the 15th century. Other stories abound that the place was a washhouse for St Vincent's Convent in the 1700s.

A particularly ghostly story circulates that the noise of a woman's sobbing comes from a bricked up tunnel in the cellar, this has been heard on many occasions.

During 1996 the Tetleys owned "Tuns" was earmarked to be turned into an Irish themed pub, like the Wig and Pen just up the road and the Mail Coach on West Street. Regulars fought against the plan (a signed petition of over 1000 names) insisting that the building being listed could not be expanded and could not be greatly altered outside so why bother in the first place. A highly distinctive, unusually shaped public house, when viewed from outside it seems to rise like the prow of a ship. A lovely, Tetleys, public house and long may it remain so.

Three Tuns

110 Bridge Street Head, Sheffield 1

Three Whitesmith

1 Bridge Street, Sheffield 1

Tinsmiths were called whitesmiths.

Timbertop
Shirecliffe Road, Sheffield 5

Built in the 1960s and for quite a few years, along with the Horse and Lion-Norfolk Park, Sheaf-Fraser Road, Woodseats, they were pubs to be seen in which were outside the normal city centre pub walk.

Tinsley Hotel
2 Sheffield Road, Sheffield 9

Tollgate
408 Pitsmoor Road, Sheffield 3
(aka Hallam Gate Inn)

Generally a reference to a place where a toll was paid as a fee for the use of a bridge, stretch of road, etc.

Tontine
22 Haymarket, Sheffield 1
(aka Tontine Tap) (built in 1785)

The Tontine was probably the largest public house in Sheffield at the time with a 12.000 square foot banqueting hall on the second floor and many more sizeable rooms to boot. It had stabling for over 60 horses and its own brewery and cottages for the footmen were built behind the Hotel. It was also one of the three main coach departure centres for designated routes all over England, the others being the Angel, Snig Hill and the Kings Head, Change Alley.

The word Tontine is derived from Neapolitan origins, Lorenzo Tonti, an Italian banker, living in France initiated this collective form of raising money whereby subscribers actually gambled on how long they lived.

In Sheffield's case, 50 of the towns prominent dignitaries subscribed £100 each to a 'Tontine', a device out of which the hotel was to be built and equipped. Then from profits made, dividends were paid equally to the fifty participants. Throughout the forthcoming years shareholders died and dividends were shared in less numbers and the last shareholder surviving became the lock, stock and barrel holder of the Tontine.

People of great British historical importance stayed at the Tontine, Lord Palmerston, William Wilberforce, the Duke of Wellington to mention just a few. In fact, whilst at the Tontine the Iron Duke presented a Waterloo medal to one William Proctor of Trinity Street, West Bar who had served valiantly at the famous 1815 battle, and who was a cutler by trade.

Unfortunately there is in Sheffield's past a worrying chapter of unrest around the early 19th century and on 14th December 1832, following the passing of the Government's Reform Act it was declared that of the 90,000-100,000 people in Sheffield boundary only 3,500 were allowed to vote. This in itself caused uproar, but when the first elected candidate was named, John Parker, the crowd went wild. Trouble flared and general riotous behaviour soon started. This behaviour carried on all day and into the evening. The 18th Irish Foot, under Captain Graves were called in from Rotherham to quell the disturbance. At 10pm that night, in the Foreyard of the Tontine, a confrontation took place and Graves ordered musket fire to be laid down above the heads of the unruly crowd. When the smoke cleared five people lay dead and scores were injured, one of whom died soon after in the infirmary. Justifiable homicide was the outcome of this terrible incident in Sheffield's history.

Surely though, when the 18th Irish Foot went back to Rotherham they should have ordered target practice, or at the very least learned how to obey orders.

The Old Tontine was demolished in 1851 to make way for what was then a remarkable structure for Sheffield, the Old Norfolk Market Hall, built at a cost of more than £40,000.

Town Arms
166 Duke Street, Sheffield

Tramcar Inn

851 Attercliffe Road, Sheffield 9
(closed late 1970s)

Situated on the corner of Clay Street and Attercliffe Road.

Tramway Hotel

126 London Road, Sheffield 2

Tramway Hotel

16 West Bar, Sheffield

A tramway was originally blocks of stone or wood sunk into the ground in parallel lines so wagons/trams had a firm surface to run on.

T P Woods

Leopold Street, Sheffield 1 (opened 1998)

A new, comfy feel, cafe bar situated where the Grand Hotel used to stand.

Travellers Inn

784 Attercliffe Road, Sheffield 9

From about 1780 unit c1892 the Travellers was run by the Miller family who kept their trade of pocket and pen knife makers running in parallel with the licensed premises.

In the 1960s Peter Swan was the landlord, and a good one too, for a number of years. Peter played for Sheffield Wednesday and England and is probably the best post war centre half the Owls have had.

Unfortunately Peter Swan will probably be remembered more for the sad case that arose in 1963, when a bribes scandal took place and three Wednesday players were implicated. Swan, Tony Kay (then Everton) and David Layne, all England international class, were subsequently banned for life.

Travellers Inn

82 Snig Hill, Sheffield (opened 1770s)

Travellers Inn

82 Newhall Road, Sheffield

Travellers Inn

72 Penistone Road North, Sheffield 6

Part of the present bar, which used to be the kitchen area has a large granite fireplace with the initials G.C. carved into it along with the date 1697.

Travellers Inn
286 The Common, Ecclesfield

Travellers Rest
426 Langsett Road, Sheffield (closed 1920s)

Now used as a shop selling window frames.

Travellers Rest
106 Broad Street, Sheffield

Travellers Rest
525 City Road, Sheffield 2

Travellers Rest
93 Langsett Road South, Oughtibridge

Travellers Rest
141-143 The Moor, Sheffield 1
(aka Billy Lees)

Nicknamed Billy Lees after one of its landlords, the Travellers Rest was a popular house for entertainment and during the Second World War it was regularly packed with many allied servicemen as well as the Sheffield locals.

Travellers Rest
Southey Green, Sheffield
(demolished in 1929)

Along with the Southey Hall, this public house, the Travellers Rest was pulled down to make way for the new Southey and Parson Cross estates. It was taken over by the Sheffield Corporation in 1923 from the Ecclesfield hamlet of Southey Green. After 2000 dwellings were built the council for some reason pulled the Travellers down and caused instant uproar amongst the newly placed tenants who now had no public house at all. The Magnet and the Parson Cross Hotel were erected in 1930s to placate the residents.

Around this area there were outlying farms called Moonshine, Doe Royd, Deerlands and Toad Hall.

True Briton
61 Brown Street, Sheffield

The name of an East Indiaman, a sailing ship of large tonnage engaged in the East India trade, which disappeared with all hands.

Truro Tavern
189 St Mary Road, Sheffield 2

Demolished to make way for the road widening of St Mary's Gate.

Tudor Tavern
5 Arundel Street, Sheffield

Henry VII became first Tudor King, 1485. Elizabeth was the last Tudor monarch in 1603.

Tunnel
89 Pye Bank, Sheffield

Turf Tavern
65 West Bar, Sheffield

Turf Tavern
17 Arundel Street, Sheffield

Turf Tavern
336 Handsworth Road, Sheffield

Possibly some connection to horse racing.

Turks Head (New)
120 Scotland Street, Sheffield

These names Turks Head, Old Turks Head, Saracen's Head are generally derived from the Crusades. Occasional in their religious fervour the knights would sever the head of their mortal enemy and would actually carry it back from the Holyland. This Scotland Street Turks would, hopefully, just have had a Turks or Saracen's head on the pub sign.

Turners Arms
Brown Street, Sheffield

Possibly named after landlord i.e. surname or his trade or after the Worshipful Company of Turners (1604) which was a guild for wood turners.

Turners Arms
Burgess Street, Sheffield

Tuscan Tavern
17 St Thomas Street, Sheffield
(aka the Noted Club House)

Twelve O'Clock
1 or 127 Attercliffe Road, Sheffield 9

A large clock face was the sign of this public house which had the hands indicating, as you would expect, at 12 O'Clock. It stood at the point where Savile Street and Attercliffe Road meet just before the Wicker Arches. This site was also known as the Twelve O'Clock toll bar up until 1866. The site were it stood is today commemorated by a large clock on a pedestal.

One unfortunate story from the old Twelve O Clock is that of a visitor who was not familiar with the pub getting up and going to the toilet. He chose the wrong door and fell to his death down the cellar steps. To make matters worse, he was not found for a few days until the landlord went to tend his ale in the cellar.

Umpire

9 New George Street, Boston St, Sheffield

Cricket umpire? Possibly, being as it is situated in the Bramall Lane cricket ground area.

The Umpire used to let rooms throughout its time as a beerhouse and even when it closed as a beer selling establishment it still kept its occupants.

Union

61 Silver Street Head, Sheffield (1820s-1900s)

Generally named from the Acts of Union, 1707 England and Scotland should be one kingdom and one parliament. England and Ireland another Union in 1801.

Union

1 Division Street, Sheffield

Union

Cherry tree Hill, Sheffield

Union

18 Fargate, Sheffield 1 (closed in 1910)

Union

26 Furnace Hill, Sheffield

Union

12 Bridgehouses, Sheffield (opened 1820s)

Nicknamed the Hand in Hand or Old Hands Shakes.

Union

22 Scotland Street, Sheffield (opened 1780s)

Union

16 Lambert Street, Sheffield

Union

50 Hawley Croft, Sheffield

Union Hotel

1 Union Road, Sheffield 11

Union Inn

651 Attercliffe Common, Sheffield 9 (Closed in 1960s)

Situated across from Tinsley Wire Industries and the Tinsley Hotel and just a few doors away from the Royal Hotel, the Union was one of the first pubs to fall to the lack of trade from the failing steel industry and slum clearance that affected the lower Attercliffe Common area slightly earlier than the upper part of the 'Cliffe.

Union Tavern

14 Newcastle Street, Sheffield

Union Tavern

Cotton Mill, Sheffield

Upperthorpe Hotel

159 Upperthorpe Road, Sheffield 6

Upwell Inn

132 Upwell Street, Sheffield

Viaduct
108 Corby Street, Sheffield

Viaduct
79 The Wicker, Sheffield

So called because of its close proximity to a viaduct, which in this case is the Wicker Arches.

Victoria
56 Jericho Street, Sheffield 3

Victoria Hotel or Gardens
248 Neepsend Lane, Sheffield

This small Wards house, nicknamed the Monkey by its regulars, made into offices of the Le Pla works in 1992, stands on the corner of Neepsend Lane and Parkwood Road. This area used to be the industrial heart of Sheffield Steel perched along the River Don, and the "Monkey" was a thriving house for many years whilst, as in most cases, the steel industry survived. When the local employers made redundancies, moved location or closed firms it was just a matter of time how long the pub could survive. It made it into the mid 90s. The Victoria Hotel was standing during the Great Sheffield flood of 1864, the wall of water that passed by in the middle of that fateful night had receded from the 50 foot high wave that started out from the Dale Dyke Dam in Bradfield but was still well over seven feet high and did severe damage not only to the Victoria but to the Farfield, The Army Stores and further into the city centre ripped off the front of the Manchester Hotel on Nursery Street.

Victoria Hotel
38 High Street, Sheffield 1

One of the oldest savings clubs in Sheffield 'The Beardshaw Funding Society' came to the Victoria Hotel when Jonathan Beardshaw, grandson of the Original fund instigator, John Beardshaw moved it from the Cock Inn, Hollis Croft into this High Street premises. He then proceeded to change its name to the Victoria Club Funding Society.

A large amount of money was saved this way, with more people trusting their local landlord than the bank.

Victoria Hotel
28 Furnival Road, Sheffield

Named after England's longest reigning monarch, Queen Victoria, 64 years on the throne.

Victoria Hotel
923 Penistone Road, Sheffield 6

Demolished for road widening purposes on Penistone Road, just before Hillsborough Park. The pub was demolished but its not clear if the road was ever widened.

Victoria Hotel
621 Attercliffe Road, Sleaford Road, Sheff 9

Most people who still remember the Victoria, which is a memorable feat in itself, say it was across Attercliffe Road from John Banners, a large general store that stood out like a beacon.

The Victoria had large swing doors at the entrance.

Victoria Hotel
170 Gibraltar Street, Sheffield

Victoria Hotel
327 Langsett Road, Sheffield 6

This hotel closed in the early seventies and was situated next to the toll gate house, which is still standing. Another public house that was demolished for road widening purposes but yet the plot of land it used to occupy is still lying unused.

Victoria Hotel

1 St Philips Road, Sheffield

Victoria Hotel

80-82 Addy Street, Sheffield

Victoria Hotel

146 Carlisle Road, Sheffield 4

Victoria Hotel

203 Gleadless Road, Sheffield 2

Known to all and sundry as the "Round House" obviously from its unusual circular frontage.

The Signage would never have had the Queen's head on it until 1901 at the earliest as Queen Victoria would not let her head be depicted on the sign whilst she was alive. This rule still applied today to all members of the royal family, whilst still alive. A pub called the Princess Diana had to make do with a train of that name instead of a portrait of Diana, in the early 90s.

Victoria Hotel

22 Thomas Street, Sheffield

Victoria Hotel

136 Savile Street East, Sheffield 4

Victoria Hotel

Station Approach, Old Station, Sheffield
(aka Royal Victoria Stn, Victory Station Rd)

The Victoria Hotel was built in 1862 and opened in 1863. It was erected with monies found by a number of shareholders, similar to the format of the Old Tontine. In fact it was built soon after the demise of the Tontine.

It was erected, as you can still see today, near to the Victoria Railway Station and its five storey structure still stands proudly on view as you look from the city centre towards the Wicker. The building itself contains large public rooms and over 50 bedrooms.

Victoria Inn

22 Grammar Street, Sheffield 6

Victoria

40 Mulberry Street, Sheffield 1
(aka Queen Victoria) (1780s-1900s)

Victoria Park Hotel

Clarkehouse Road, Sheffield 11

Situated opposite the Botanical Gardens. Whilst not a public house in the true sense it did serve alcohol and had a bar for locals. Also it had a bowling green and an American Bowling Alley?

Vine Tavern

4 Hartshead, Sheffield 1
(aka Barrel, Jolly Tar, Chequers Inn)
(closed 1893)

In 1807 this pawnbrokers shop was turned into a beerhouse and was called the Barrel Inn and was owned by Samuel Hall. It was then called the Jolly Tar, when under the landlordship of George Mass. Next came Francis Liley, in 1816 and along came its third name change, this time to the Chequers Inn. Eleven years later in 1827 it was run by Richard Alexander and undertook its final name change when it became the Vine Tavern, it stayed so named for the next 70 years till its closure. For a few years before the turn of the century it was used as a policeman's institute.

Vine Hotel

**81 Brunswick Road, Sheffield 3
(closed 1961)**

The Vine can be representative of the Worshipful Company of Distillers (1638), whose arms show a vine bearing grapes. But some much older inns and taverns have used the name Vine from 250 years earlier, from around 1380s just because the vine was growing in abundance in England.

Vine Hotel

35 Addy Street, Sheffield

Vine Inn

160-162 Cemetery Road, Sheffield 11

Vine Tavern

49-51 Newhall Road, Sheffield 9

Vine Tavern

7 Hodgson Street, Sheffield 3

Vine Tavern

17 Furnace Hill, Sheffield

Vine Tavern

38 Broad Street, Sheffield

Virginia Vaults

64/66 Queen Street, Sheffield

Vulcan

51 Hawley Croft, Sheffield

Roman God of natural fire. Using this natural fire he forged thunderbolts for Jove/Jupiter. Vulcan's name is therefore synonymous with blast furnaces and forges.
Also Vulcan can be seen in all his majesty atop the Sheffield Town Hall.

Vulcan

22 Northern Avenue, Sheffield

Another of Sheffield's Estates public houses. It has an excellent view over Sheffield.

Vulcan Inn or Tavern

58 Sussex Street, Sheffield 4

Named supposedly from its proximity to the Old Park Blast Furnace. The volcanic flare, which is said to have glowed brightly all night, afforded a useful light to the many night travellers bringing their wares to the early morning Sheffield markets.

Wadsley Jack
Rural Lane, Wadsley, Sheffield 6

Reuben Hallam was born in 1818 and when he was about 38 he was commissioned by Sir William Leng who was the then owner of the Telegraph to develop a character to gain the public interest. "Wadsley Jack" was the eponymous hero who was developed, and he pushed his 'barrah' from village to village and invariably had some humorous adventure in each of these places. It served its purpose. The papers started to sell in the outlying places where people would read of their village as and if it appeared in Jack's travels.

Reuben Hallam was the landlord at one time of the Shoulder of Mutton in Bradwell and he passed away in 1908 aged 90.

Waggon & Horses
Abbeydale Road, Sheffield 7

It was first recorded in 1725 when a Richard Bagshawe was the owner of the Waggon and Horses.

Waggons and horses were a familiar sight before the advent of the railways.

It has been said that Dick Turpin used to stay here and that his horse, Black Bess's hoof beats are still to be heard in the yard.

To be teetotal was to be on the water wagon, shortened to 'on the wagon'.

Waggon & Horses
2 Kent Road, 236 Gleadless Road, Sheffield
(aka Old Waggon and Horses)

Waggon & Horses
Market Place, Chapeltown

Waggon & Horses
13 Arundel Street, Sheffield

Walkley Cottage
46 Bole Hill Road, Sheffield 6

Wapentake Bar

Cambridge Street, Wellington Street,
Sheffield 1 (aka Casbah)

The pub to be seen in if you were a rocker in the 60s, 70s
and into the 80s. Now with a new name, the Casbah,
which technically means either a fortress or the native
section of a city. In the 40s the phrase "come into the
casbah" was used as an invitation to sample exotic
delights.
Owned by The Wapentake Co. Ltd.

Warm Hearth Stone

1 or 7 Town Head Street, Sheffield

A name which those in the steel industry would interpret
slightly differently from the norm. They may think of it in
the sense of the open-hearth steel making process. Others
may just think of it in the domestic comfort sense.

Washford Arms

380 Attercliffe Road, Sheffield 9
(1850s-1970s)

After it closed in the mid seventies it became a chip shop.

Washington

79 Fitzwilliam St, Wellington St, Sheffield 1

Washington Arms Hotel

23 Washington Road, Sheffield 11
(aka The Cripples)

Watermans Rest

3 Sussex Street, Sheffield 4

A waterman is one who makes his living working on or
with boats or barges. Worshipful Company of Watermen
and Lightermen 1827.

Waterloo Tavern

3 Andrews Street, Sheffield

Named after the most famous battle in British history,
outshining even the 1066 Battle of Hastings - well we did
lose that one.
It took place in 1815 in a small town in Brabant, 12 miles
south of Brussels in Belgium.
Along with Blücher's Prussian forces, and some Dutch
and Belgium troops, Wellington battered Napoleon into
submission. Four days later the self crowned emperor of
France abdicated and was sent into exile.

Waterloo Tavern

18 Pinstone Street, Sheffield 1

Waterloo Tavern

26 Watsons Walk, Sheffield
(aka Waterloo Turf Tavern, Turf Tavern)

Weigh House Inn

168 Duke Street, Sheffield (1830s-1902)

This was a platform scale, flush with the road, for
weighing vehicles cattle etc.

Weir Head Hotel

Penistone Road, Sheffield 6

Closed in 1936 and became Hillfoot Workingmen's Club.

Weir Head Hotel

1 Sutherland Street, Sheffield
(closed around 1925)

Weir Head Inn

287 Attercliffe Road, Sheffield

Wellington Inn

122-124 Carlisle Road, Sheffield 4

Arthur Wellesley (1769-1852). English soldier and politician born in Dublin who entered the army when just eighteen in 1787. In 1796 he went to India where he was the victor in the Mahratta War of 1803. In 1808 he was sent to the Peninsula and won the Battle of Vimiero. Given full command after the Battle of Corunna he drove the French from Oporto and in July 1809 won a victory at Talavera. In 1815 he won his and probably Britain's most famous victory, Waterloo. He became Prime Minister in 1828.

Wellington Inn

720 Brightside Lane, Sheffield 9

This pub was humourously nicknamed the Rubber Boot by the steel workers who frequented it.

Wellington Tavern

11 Coalpit Lane, Cambridge Street, Sheffield

Elias Shirt was the licensee in 1839 and also kept up his trade as a saw handle maker

Wellington Inn

56-58 Langsett Road, Sheffield 6
(aka Hero and his Horse, Hillsborough Htl)

When this Burtonwood public house was coming to the end of the road as the Wellington Inn it tried to survive with relief staff but dwindling custom and a parting shot from an old landlord to remove the snooker table, which upset the regulars, meant its fate was sealed.

It has since been refurbished and opened (Spring '99) as the Hillsborough Hotel.

Wellington Inn

222 Main Road, Sheffield 9

The Wellington has a ghost called Big Jim, this is supposedly James Elliott a former landlord of the pub.

Wellington

653 Attercliffe Road, Sheffield 9

Wellington

78 Macro Street, Sheffield

Wellington Arms

90 Wellington Street, Sheffield

Wellington Tavern

21 Coalpit Lane, Sheffield

Well Run Dimple

112 Fargate, Sheffield 1

It is supposedly from an exclamation of commendation said to a horse which was running, and winning, at Crookesmoor Racecourse. One assumes the landlord who supposedly bought this pub from the proceeds put his money on a horse called Dimple.

The inn stood on the original site of Barker's Pool and was first mentioned in 1567 although it is thought to be much older.

Welsh Harp

St Philips Road, Sheffield

A harp with three rows of strings and used on inn signboards for its distinct shape and also generally to indicate the innkeepers connection to Wales.

Wentworth House Hotel

26 Milford Street, Attercliffe, Sheffield 9

Set in the heart of the east end of Sheffield, The Wentworth stood in the shadow of the now defunct English Steel works. The pub was a beer only house until 1979 when it had a costly and timely refurbishment. The back-to-back houses disappeared in about 1970 around this area, the general smaller steel industry keep the Wentworth going and with the new urban regeneration it is a pub that does seem to be a survivor. Viewed late at night, when illuminated, it is the most dramatic of public houses in Sheffield.

Wentworth House

262 Rockingham Street, Sheffield

Wentworth House

78 Button Lane, Sheffield

Wentworth House

18 Wentworth Street, Sheffield 6

West End Hotel

412 Glossop Road, Sheffield 10

The name West End usually conjures up visions of the London Theatre area. Well, the Sheffield Drama studio is next door, so some slight compensation. The tall imposing building, standing on the corner of Glossop Road and Upper Hanover Street, deep in the heart of the student residential community. The Tetleys, public house itself is split into two levels, the lower is comfortable and fairly standard whilst the upper area is more modern and caters for the younger end, pool tables etc.

Weston Park Hotel

96 Weston Street, Sheffield 3

West Street Hotel

128 West Street, Sheffield 1
(aka Bull and Bush)

West Street Vaults

112 West Street, Sheffield 1

We Three Loggerheads Inn

30 Hawley Croft, Sheffield

The name has Shakespearian connections and at some pubs it would have on its sign two wooden heads, the visitor was supposed to fall for the joke by asking where the third one was, whereupon he immediately became the third one himself.

Wharncliffe Arms

**42-44 West Street, Sheffield 1
(aka William Macready, Manchester)**

Around 1840, when the Wharncliffe Arms was called the Manchester, the landlord was one William Abednego Thompson, or the The Great Bendigo, (a corruption of Abednego, the name of a biblical character) a heavyweight bare-knuckle fighter of great repute. Believed to be the first boxer to adopt the southpaw stance, he became All-English champion in 1832, at the age of just 21. Such was his acclaim that a memorial was set up to him in his native city of Nottingham and (supposedly) a Town in Australia was named after him. He fought many fights, but three of them against one man named Benjamin Caunt, nicknamed Big Ben, and this was before the London bell of that name ever sounded, averaged 66 rounds per fight. Winning the decider to make it 2 to 1 in his favour, Thompson fought Caunt for 197 rounds in all, and don't forget all bare knuckled. Some say the third fight was a draw!

Wharncliffe Hotel

127 Beavercotes Road, Sheffield 5

Wharncliffe Hotel

13 Kings Street, Sheffield

Opened after 1818 on the site of the old debtors gaol.

Wharncliffe Arms

365 Burncross Road, Chapeltown

The date stone over the door is marked 1874.

Wharncliffe Arms

72 Main Street, Wharncliffe

Situated on the A616 Manchester to Sheffield road at Wharncliffe Side this 200+ year old pub was originally used for spindle making. It was in circa 1840 that it became a licensed premises.

Wheatsheaf

Parkhead, Sheffield

This is a 15th century sign of the Worshipful Company of Bakers (1486) also on Brewers coat of arms.
The Wheatsheaf has a cricket pitch attached and a game against Yorkshire County Cricket Club takes place annually.

Wheatsheaf

78 Bailey Lane, Sheffield

Wheatsheaf

149 Harvest Lane, Sheffield

Wheatsheaf

81 Eyre Street, Sheffield

Wheatsheaf
18 Penistone Road, Sheffield 6

Wheatsheaf
21 Button Lane, Sheffield

Wheatsheaf Hotel
Ecclesall Road South, Sheffield 11

Wheatsheaf Hotel
13 Bridge Street, Sheffield 1

The Wheatsheaf in Bridge Street had a 4 foot high gravestone in the dram shop, and its inscription read "Deer Foot, killed March 22nd 1887". As with most stories from many years ago, no one really knows the full story behind them, but here are some of the variations: The stone is thought to commemorate a man named Tommy Lightfoot, who was killed when ran over by a dray and horses. Another story has him unlawfully killed in a drunken brawl outside the Wheatsheaf. The real mystery is why Old Tommy didn't have his stone atop his grave, unless he was a pauper, of course, as paupers then were not allowed headstones. Others have it that his friends bought his headstone and decided as none of them would visit the local cemetery to pay their regular respects it would be more practical to place it in the dram shop. The stone stayed in that room for some 80 years until demolition in the early 1970s. Unfortunately, its whereabouts is now unknown.

Wheatsheaf Inn
2 Platt Street, Sheffield 3

Wig and Pen
44-46 Campo Lane, Sheffield 1
(aka Shenanigans)

This Mansfield brewery-owned public house took the plunge to turn what was a very nice place into another Irish themed pub. It still attracts the office workers and the legal professionals who work around this area at lunchtime. The place livens up during the evening when the younger generation start their tour of the city centre. One of the landlords of the Wig and Pen traced the history of the building back to the 1830s, when at that time, he says it was known as the Old Cock.

Whirlow Bridge Inn
Ecclesall, Bierlow

Whitby Hotel
106 Addy Street, Sheffield 6

Whitby Hotel
1 Arthur Street, Sheffield 6

White Bear Inn

Stocks Hill, Ecclesfield

The White Bear is often found in heraldic reference to Earls of Kent or to a famous galleon built in 1563, it formed part of Drake's fleet when he attacked Cadiz in 1587. The Royal Navy sold the ship in 1629.

White Bear Inn

8 High Street, Sheffield (1750-1811)

This part of High Street is now at the top of Chapel Walk. Set in a passage called White Bear yard was the White Bear public house and in 1811 Fosters the clothiers took over the frontage of the 'Bear' for their new shop

White Hart

27 Greenhill Main Road, Sheffield 8

White Hart

62 Russell Street Sheffield 3
(aka Kelham Island Tavern)

At the start of Richard II reign, was the first time this sign was seen. The White Hart was Richard's heraldic symbol. Richard made all his followers wear this symbol, not to do so was seen as an insult to the king, so it was probably prudent for the tavern keepers to display their allegiance by naming their inns and taverns the White Hart.

This particular tavern changed its name fairly recently to the Kelham Island Tavern possibly to gain some custom from the museum nearby or just to fall into line with most of the remaining public houses in Sheffield by changing its name at some time in its history.

White Hart
101 Wortley Road, High Green

White Hart Inn
18 Langsett Road North, Oughtibridge

White Hart Inn
184 St Philips Road, Sheffield 3

White Hart
64 Doncaster Street, Sheffield

White Hart Inn
119 Worksop Road, Sheffield 9

White Horse
19 Grammar Street, Sheffield 6

A galloping white horse refers to the House of Hanover and dates from the accession of George I in 1714 to the English throne.

Some later white horse inns are named after the animal who seemed to be controlling the crowd at Wembley stadium in 1923, when the Bolton and West Ham fans spilled on to the pitch. Some say the sight of the policeman on the white horse, made people feel safe and averted a major disaster.

White Horse
57 Malinda Street, Sheffield 3

This public house was being renovated when part of it suddenly collapsed on to the workmen who were carrying out their job. The brewery called it a day and demolished the remainder of the building.

White Horse (Old)
22 Copper Street, Sheffield

White Horse
104 Halifax Road, Sheffield 5

White Horse
87 Creswick Street, Sheffield

White Horse
275 Solly Street, Sheffield

White Horse
18 Effingham Street, Sheffield

White Horse
Matilda Street, Sheffield

White Lion
92 College Road, Sheffield

White Lion
61 Division Street, Sheffield

White Lion
131 Dunlop Street, Sheffield

White Lion
615 London Road, Sheffield 2

Tetley owned pub set in Heeley Bottom, which was once a bowling club. Kept for a time by Billy Marsden, one of the famous Sheffield Wednesday half back line: Strange, Marsden, Leach.

White Lion
3 The Wicker, Sheffield 1
(aka Old White Lion,)

White Lion
23 The Wicker, Sheffield 1
(aka New White Lion)

The last two mentioned public houses were also stated as being at Nos. 2 and 12 in a 1833 reference book.
The way in which the numbering was done many years ago was highest number nearer the city centre. It is now obsolete and the lower numbers are nearer the city centre. This particular New White Lion premises is now a fishing tackle wholesalers.

White Lion

12 West Bar Green, Sheffield (1780s-1900s)

White Lion

25 Holly Street, Sheffield
(opened late 18th century)

White Lion

86 New Queen Street, Sheffield 1

White Lion

37 Queen Street, Sheffield 1

White Lion

112 Fargate, Barkers Pool, Sheffield 1
(1790s-1920s)

This White Lion was demolished to make way for the War Memorial that now stands in the centre of Barkers Pool and was unveiled in 1925 two years after the closure of this popular public house.

This area was named after a Mr Barker, and the pool reference is to his reservoir which he constructed in 1434. Water was released periodically to run through the streets and clean the causeways and swill away rubbish, excrement etc.

White Lion

30 Bailey Street, Sheffield

White Lion

54 Woodside Lane, Sheffield 1

White Rails

Upperthorpe, Sheffield

White Rose

Handsworth, Sheffield 13

Duke of York Badge 1411-1460 War of the Roses.

White Swan

57 Greenhill Main Road, Sheffield 8

This village pub made up of five rooms, is owned by Whitbread. This bird appears in Vintners, Poulters and Musicians Company coat of arms, and the earls of Essex and Edward III.

White Swan

36 Charlotte Street, Sheffield

White Swan

57 West Bar, Sheffield 3

White Swan Hotel

105 Meadow Hall Road, Sheffield 9
(aka Old White Swan)

Who Can Tell

33 Botham Street, Sheffield 4

Why Not Inn

27 Clun Street, Sheffield 4

John Turley called this inn after his grand national winner
"Why Not" in 1889 or 1894, it won twice. Its as simple as
that, but what it was called before is slightly harder to find
out.

Widows Hut

21 Meadow Street, Sheffield 1

This hut was kept by James Wood in 1833, when it had no
name above the door. By 1920 it was known locally as the
Widows Hut, supposedly a meeting place for local
women.

Willow Tree

147 Portobello Street, Sheffield 1

Wincobank Hotel

72 Newman Road, Sheffield 9

Windsor Hotel

35-39 Southend Road, Sheffield 2

George V who by Royal Proclamation in 1917 changed
the name of the Royal House to Windsor, it was
previously Saxe Coburg and Gotha.
Probably a good idea being as we were at war with the
Germans.

Windsor Castle

50 School Croft, Sheffield (1780s-1900s)

Windsor Castle

129 Princess Street, Sheffield

Wine and Spirit Vaults

2 Market Street, Sheffield

Used to store wine and other liquers.

Wine Vaults

30 Castle Street, Sheffield

Wine Vaults

59-63 Scotland Street, Sheffield

Wisewood Inn

539 Loxley Road, Sheffield 6

Woodbourn Hotel

2 Worthing Rd, 2 Lovetot Rd, Sheffield 9

Woodman

137 Edward Street, Sheffield

Woodman

321 Langsett Road, Sheffield (1830s-1921)

Woodman

137 New Edward Street, Sheffield

Tree fellers also known as woodmen was a regular occupation in the 17th and 18th century around England with well over 500 inns, taverns being so called.

Woodman

166 South Street, Sheffield
(aka Ye Woodman)

Woodman Hut

46 Garden Street, Sheffield

Woodman Inn

87 Carlisle Street East, Sheffield

Woodman Inn

158 Woodside Lane, Sheffield 3

Woodseats Hotel

743 Chesterfield Road, Sheffield 8
(aka Floozey and Firkin)

Woodside Tavern

126 Woodside Lane, Sheffield

Became a working man's club and eventually closed in the early 1940s.

Woodthorpe Arms

102 Mansfield Road, Intake

Woolpack

2 Percy Street, Sheffield

Woolsack

277 Allen Street, Sheffield

Law Lords traditionally sit on woolsacks at the official opening of Parliament. Supposedly these seats were there to remind the Houses of Parliament how much the national wealth of the country depended on the wool industry.

Wordsworth Tavern

Wordsworth Avenue Sheffield 5

Named after the English poet who lived in the Lake District, close to Lake Windermere.

He was Poet Laureate in 1843. Not a particularly successful poet whilst alive. It is said he used the language of the common man. He was a poet who had many critics. Wordsworth, Coleridge, Southey and Byron were all romantic poets whose names are still used in the Sheffield area, with schools, streets as well as public houses being named after them.

Wrekin

143 Carlisle Street East, Sheffield

The name of an isolated hill or hillside.

Wybourn Hotel

204 Cricket Inn Road, Sheffield 2

Wyvern Hotel

379 Leighton Road, Sheffield 14

Imaginary animal is a winged dragon which has feet of an eagle and the tail of a serpent.

Yates Wine Lodge
Division Street, Sheffield 1

Situated on the corner of Division Street and Carver Street it was built in 1993.

Ye Old English Samson
1 Duke Street, Sheffield 2

Ye Olde Harrow
80 Broad Street, Sheffield 2

Ye Old Shakespeare Inn
106 Well Road, Sheffield 8

An old mosaic tiled floor in the entrance shows the full and correct name of the public house.

Ye Olde Tankard
1 Stocks Hill, Ecclesfield

Yellow Lion
18 Haymarket, Sheffield 1

The Yellow Lion was situated on the Haymarket where British Home Stores is now to be found. It was supposedly well frequented, mainly, it is said, by farmers. The hotel was pulled down in 1927 to build a new Woolworth's, which was also demolished, to make way for its present occupant, BHS.

Yellow Lion
1 Coalpit Lane, & 123 Barkers Pool, Sheff 1

Yellow Lion
12 Coalpit Lane, Sheffield 1

A Mr Jno. Renwick in the 1839 listings was stated to be licensee and also trading as a Pen and Pocket Knife maker. Christian name, Jonathan?

Yellow Lion
59 Clifton Street, Sheffield

Yeomany (Yeomanry) Hotel
34 Norfolk Street, Sheffield

Young man, country man, villager, less than a squire more than a knave. Groups of these men who served their king, queen and country would keep their collective name; Yeomanry.

Yew Tree Inn
147 Hollinsend Road, Sheffield 12

Yew Tree

Loxley New Road, Malin Bridge, Sheffield 6

York Hotel

247 Fulwood Road, Sheffield 10
(aka O'Neils)

Named after Frederick, Duke of York and Albany, 1783-1827 who was the second son of King George III. He was also commander in chief of the British Army for many years and unfortunately never reached the pinnacle of the throne of England. He died of dropsy.

Stones transformed and extended the York Hotel at Broomhall which is set in the heartland of the Sheffield student base and turned it into an Irish themed pub. Another one!

Yorkshire Clown

24 Paradise Square, Sheffield 1

It was a booksellers by 1940 owned by a Mr. Warde.

Yorkshire Cricketers

79 Pea Croft, Sheffield (1820s-1890s)

Yorkshireman Arms

31 Burgess Street, Sheffield
(opened around 1790s)

There has been a public house on this site for well over 200 years.

Yorkshire Stingo

54 Division Street, Sheffield 1

This name is at least 200 years old and is derived from a very strong barley wine type Yorkshire ale.

Young Street Tavern

162 Young Street, Sheffield

Index of public houses

found in the listings only as - also known as (aka)

public house	page	public house	page	public house	page
Army Stores	13	Garden	150	Paradise Street Vaults	134
Assembly Rooms	36	Gardeners Rest	55	Peggs	149
		Golden Ball	15	Phoenix	9
Bacon Box	103	Golden Ball	16	Prince of Wales	72
Ball	145	Golden Ball	16	Prospect House	72
Ball and Whitesmith	15	Good Doctor	172	Providence Inn	64
Ballith'tree	17	Great Gun	25		
Bar Indigo	162	Greenland	66	Queen Victoria	21
Barrel	45	Grey Horse	26		
Bar Rio	107	Grove	83	R & Bs	121
Barrow House	64			R & Rs	88
Bath Cottage	20	Harveys Bar	88	Red Lion	15
Bay Horse	21	Havelock Inn	87	Rendezvous	110
Beer Engine	154	Hero and his Horse	186	Reindeer	152
Bijou	78	Hillsborough Hotel	186	Reservoir Inn	87
Blackamore Head	80	Hope and Anchor	162	Ring O Bells	14
Black Lion	98	Hornblower	142	Rockwells	22
Blue Boar	85	Horse and Cat	21	Rolling Mills	99
Blue Dumpling	119			Rose	109
Blue Pig	126	John Thomas	24	Round House	182
Boardwalk	27	Jolly Tar	182	Rovers Rest	79
Bodega	75			Rovers Return	79
Boilers Rest	165	Kelham Island Tavern	190		
Bold Dragoon	30			Sam Hills Parlour	36
Boot and Slipper	30	London Mart	103	Saracens Head	173
Brewer on the Bridge	96	Lyceum Hotel	90	Shout em Downs	126
Bridge	36			Shrewsbury Hotel	138
Britannia	99	Mad House	31	Slackys	115
Britannia	149	Macaw	135	Spotted Dog	172
		Manchester	188	Springfield Tavern	92
Cannon	64	Market Tavern	55	Squints	78
Canterbury Inn	37	Market Tavern	150	Stadium	140
Casbah	185	Masons Arms	25	Stag Inn	125
Cavells	29	Maunche Hotel	65	Star Music Hall	78
Champions Rest	95	Merry England Bar	120	Stumble Inn	130
City Arms	24	Miners Arms	31	Sun	150
Clarence House	29	Mr Smiths Fun Bar	146	Swarf Ole	48
Clifton	13	Mucky Duck	27		
Crazy Daisy	97			Terminus	120
Cricketers	139	New Barrack Tavern	18	Three Fluer de Lys	68
Cricket Ground Inn	91	Nelson	89	Towd Shake Hands	84
Cripples	185	New Haymarket	77	Travellers Rest	123
Cross Keys	98	New Inn	68	Turf Tavern	185
Cross Keys	30	New Inn	77	Turnpike	77
Crown and Anchor	11	Newt and Chambers	148		
Crown and Cushion	36	Noose and Gibbet	140	Union	7
Cock and Bottle	61	Norfolk Arms	29	Under the Boardwalk	120
Commercial	102				
Compleat Angler	27	Oddfellows Arms	104	Venue	44
Cornmill Inn	44	Office	64	Victoria Arches	49
Cow Sheds	117	Old Albion	81		
		Old Ball	15	Waverley Hotel	92
Dallas Bar	64	Old Ball Inn	15	Walkley Cottage	121
Derby	30	Old Barrel	19	Weetwood House	123
Dive Bar	120	Old Bird in Hand	25	Well Green House	85
Double Six	150	Old Black Boy	26	Wellington	41
		Old Black Lion	27	Westminster	21
Eagle	26	Old Blue Bell	29	Whetstone	108
Empire Canteen	145	Old Cow	43	Wicker Brewery	89
Emporium	148	Old Monk	71	William Macready	188
		Old No 12	150	Woodstock Diner	135
Fagans	31	Old No 12	171		
Falcon	129	O'Neils	198	Yellow Lion	39
Ferret and Trouserleg	76	Orchard	110	Ye Old Toad	172
Filesmiths Arms	51	Owl	65	Yorick	69
Foundry and Firkin	22	Oxford	30	Yorkshire Grey	107
				Yorkshireman	72